The Making of Chinese Criminal Law

By examining the reasons behind the preventive criminalization of Chinese criminal law, this book argues that the shift of criminal law generates popular expectations of legislative participation, and meets the punitive demands of the public, but the expansion of criminal law lacks effective constraints, which will keep restricting people's freedom in the future.

The book is inspired by the eighth amendment of Chinese criminal law in 2011, which amended several penalties related to road, drug and environmental safety. It is on the eighth amendment that subsequent amendments have been based. The amendment stemmed from a series of nationally known incidents that triggered widespread public dissatisfaction with the Chinese criminal justice system. Based on John Kingdon's theory of the multiple streams, the book explains the origins of the legislative process and its outcomes by examining the role of public opinion, policy experts and political actors in the making of Chinese criminal law. It argues that in authoritarian China, the prominence of risk control through criminal justice methods is a state response to uncertainties generated through reforms under the CCP's leadership. The process of criminal lawmaking has become more responsive and inclusive than ever before, even though it remains a consultation with the elites within the framework set by the Chinese Communist Party (CCP), including representatives of the Lianghui, government ministries, academics and others. The process enhances the CCP's legitimacy by not only generating popular expectations of legislative participation, but also by meeting the punitive demands of the public.

The book will be of interest to academics and researchers in the areas of Chinese criminal law and comparative law.

Ying Ji is Assistant Professor at the Law School of the University of International Business and Economics, Beijing, China.

The Rule of Law in China and Comparative Perspectives

Series Editors:
Yuwen Li, Erasmus University Rotterdam, The Netherlands and Fu Hualing, University of Hong Kong, Hong Kong

There is no doctrine more effective than the rule of law in portraying the complex transformation of Chinese society from the rule of men towards the rule of law—a process inaugurated in post-Mao China which is continuing to advance legal reforms to the present day. In other parts of the world, striving for the rule of law is also evident: countries in transition face a similar mission, while the developed democratic countries are forced to tackle new challenges in retaining the high benchmark of the rule of law that has been established.

Research on the legal system in China and in comparison with other countries in the framework of the rule of law covers broad topics of public and private law, substantive law and procedural law, citizens' rights and law enforcement by courts. Based on this broad understanding of the rule of law, the series presents international scholarly work on modern Chinese law including comparative perspectives, interdisciplinary and empirical studies.

Other titles in this series:

The Power Of The Supreme People's Court
Reconceptualizing Judicial Power In Contemporary China
Ding Qi

China, the EU and International Investment Law
Reforming Investor-State Dispute Settlement
Edited by Yuwen Li, Tong Qi, and Cheng Bian

Hong Kong Constitutionalism
The British Legacy and the Chinese Future
Richard Cullen

National Security Review of Foreign Investment
A Comparative Legal Analysis of China, the United States and the European Union
Cheng Bian

Law and Social Solidarity in Contemporary China
A Durkheimian Analysis
Han Peng

The Making of Chinese Criminal Law
The Preventive Shift in the Context of the Eighth Amendment
Ying Ji

The Making of Chinese Criminal Law

The Preventive Shift in the Context of the Eighth Amendment

Ying Ji

Routledge
Taylor & Francis Group
LONDON AND NEW YORK

First published 2021
by Routledge
2 Park Square, Milton Park, Abingdon, Oxon OX14 4RN

and by Routledge
52 Vanderbilt Avenue, New York, NY 10017

Routledge is an imprint of the Taylor & Francis Group, an informa business

British Library Cataloguing-in-Publication Data
A catalogue record for this book is available from the British Library

Library of Congress Cataloging-in-Publication Data
Names: Ji, Ying, author.
Title: The making of Chinese criminal law: the preventive shift in the context of the Eighth Amendment / Ying Ji.
Description: Milton Park, Abingdon, Oxon ; New York, NY : Routledge, 2021. | Series: The rule of law in China and comparative perspectives | Includes bibliographical references and index.
Identifiers: LCCN 2020042571 (print) | LCCN 2020042572 (ebook) | ISBN 9780367674670 (hardback) | ISBN 9781003131441 (ebook)
Subjects: LCSH: Criminal justice, Administration of--China. | Criminal law--China. | Criminal procedure--China. | Legislation--China.
Classification: LCC KNQ3800 .J59 2021 (print) | LCC KNQ3800 (ebook) | DDC 345.51--dc23
LC record available at https://lccn.loc.gov/2020042571
LC ebook record available at https://lccn.loc.gov/2020042572

ISBN: 978-0-367-67467-0 (hbk)
ISBN: 978-1-003-13144-1 (ebk)

Typeset in Galliard
by Deanta Global Publishing Services, Chennai, India

Contents

List of figures viii
List of tables ix
List of abbreviations x
Preface xi
Acknowledgments xiii

1 Introduction 1

1.1 The Chinese landscape 1
1.2 Literature review 4
1.2.1 Chinese scholarship 5
1.2.2 Western scholarship 8
1.3 Methodology 11
1.4 Book structure 15
Notes 17

2 Reforms in Chinese criminal law and their implications 24

2.1 Conceptualization of "crime prevention" 24
2.1.1 Crime prevention in the Chinese context 24
2.1.2 Crime prevention in the Western context 26
2.2 Three case studies: Based on the 2011 eighth amendment of criminal law 28
2.2.1 Three offences in Chinese criminal law 28
2.2.1.1 Crime of drunk driving 28
2.2.1.2 Crime of manufacturing and selling fake medications 30
2.2.1.3 Crime of environmental pollution 31
2.2.2 Similarities among the changes 32
2.2.3 Weak constraints of the law 35
2.3 Analytical framework of risk society and its limitations 36
Notes 40

3 The history of lawmaking and the multiple streams approach 46

3.1 Legislative initiative, bill passing and final amendments 46
3.1.1 Amendment on the crime of drunk driving 47
3.1.2 Amendment on the crime of manufacturing and selling fake medications 48
3.1.3 Amendment on the crime of environmental pollution 49
3.2 Applying John Kingdon's theory in the Chinese context 50
Notes 55

4 Problem stream for Chinese criminal lawmaking 59

4.1 Studies of nationally known cases as focusing events 60
4.1.1 Three case studies 60
4.1.2 The public, the media and the government 62
4.2 Opinions of netizens on focusing events and Chinese criminal law 64
4.2.1 Rapid growth of the Chinese internet: Social background 64
4.2.2 Netizen opinions on focusing events 65
4.3 Public sense of security in the surveys 67
4.3.1 Public sense of security: Based on survey results 67
4.3.2 Reasons for public satisfaction and divergence from internet sentiment 70
4.4 Conclusion 73
Notes 75

5 Policy stream for Chinese criminal lawmaking 79

5.1 Roles of the specialists in the policy stream 80
5.1.1 Proposal drafting specialists: The policy entrepreneurs 81
5.1.2 Adaption and refinement of Kingdon's model 83
5.2 Legal concerns of the proposals 85
Notes 88

6 Political stream for Chinese criminal lawmaking: Role of the CCP and the bureaucracy 91

6.1 The role of the CCP in Chinese criminal lawmaking 92
6.2 The role of other participants in the legislative process 95
6.2.1 The NPC 95

6.2.2 The judicial system 97
6.2.3 The administration 100
6.2.4 The media 103
6.2.5 The legal experts 106
6.3 Conclusion 109
Notes 112

7 The role of the state in the criminal justice system: Through a comparative perspective 119

7.1 Risk control in the Western criminal justice system 119
7.1.1 Conceptualizing risk in the Western criminal justice system 119
7.1.2 State's role of risk control in the Western social context 121
7.2 Risk control in the Chinese criminal justice system 123
7.2.1 The "it works" belief in criminal justice in China 123
7.2.2 The Chinese mixed problem-solving approach 128
7.3 Conclusion 129
Notes 130

8 Policy window of Chinese criminal lawmaking and conclusion 134

8.1 Legal renewal: Easily opened windows for law reforms 135
8.1.1 Frequent coupling of the streams 135
8.1.2 Two important streams for legal renewals 136
8.1.2.1 Public influences: Public mood and public participation 137
8.1.2.2 Political influences: Focusing on social stability and public security 139
8.2 Reflections on Chinese criminal justice 141
8.2.1 Will an authoritarian regime necessarily lead to harsh penalties? 141
8.2.2 Is China an exclusive or inclusive society? 143
8.3 Conclusion 144
8.4 Changes after the eighth amendment 145
Notes 147

Bibliography 151
Index 167

Figures

3.1	Multiple streams framework (MSF)	52
4.1	Categories of police-filed cases from 1995 to 2010 per 100,000	71
6.1	Roles of the participants in Chinese lawmaking	110

Tables

3.1 Number of nationwide cases tackled by the Food and Drug Administration Bureau from 2008 to 2012 49
4.1 Comparisons of survey results regarding public sense of security 69
4.2 Six models of agenda building 74

Abbreviations

ACEF	All-China Environment Federation
ASBO	Anti-Social Behaviour Orders
CCP	Chinese Communist Party
CNNIC	Chinese Internet Network Information Center
CPPCC	People's Political Consultative Conference
LAC	Legislative Affairs Committee
MSA	Multiple streams approach
NPC	National People's Congress
PRC	People's Republic of China
UK	United Kingdom
US	United States
USA	United States of America

Preface

My interest in the current topic originated from a study I did years ago as a postgraduate back at Nanjing University in China. In the early 2010s, Chinese scholars of criminal law started to examine the new role of criminal law as an essential tool of risk control. Professor Lao Dongyan of Tsinghua University raised this topic first in her article "Public Policy and Criminal Law in the Risk Society" in *Social Sciences* in China. Lao suggests that in China criminal law turns into a proactive tool of the government whose function has now been completely changed to risk management. That criminal law is increasingly subordinate to public policy pursuits brought about significant transformations to the current social control techniques. After that, studies of so-called "criminal law and risk control" dominated the legal ideas of Chinese criminal law in a short time. Faced with a series of nationwide scandals of road, food and environmental safety at that time, it was easy for scholars to accept the idea that the Chinese society had entered into the so-called "risk society."

Inspired by this, my dissertation for my master's degree was related to the topic of preventive justice in China, with a focus on endangerment crimes with the mental state of negligence. However, in my studies, I realized that a global perspective was necessary for the study of Chinese criminal law since the preventive shift is not limited to China. To gain a better understanding about the features of the Chinese legal system, a researcher needs to conduct comparative studies among institutions and policies of different countries around the world. While most Chinese scholars of criminal law learn from theories of other civil law countries, like Germany and Japan, studies on criminal laws and policies of common-law countries are missing. What are the similarities in legislation between China and the West, such as the UK and the US? What are the particular state and social structures that make Chinese lawmaking distinct from that of other countries?

With those questions in mind, I decided to pursue further study in the School of Law at the University of British Columbia, in Canada. Under the supervision of Professor Ben Goold, I compared the development of Chinese criminal law (mainly the eighth amendment) with laws of the US and the UK. What was happening in those two countries had been the focus of academia. I also paid special attention to the trends and features of their criminal policies, especially after the

1970s. Multiple seminal works had great influence upon my work, including *The Culture of Control* by Professor David Garland, *Governing through Crime* by Professor Jonathan Simon, *Understanding Crime Preventive* by Professor Gordon Hughes, etc. I also noticed the series of crucial studies on the UK's preventive justice and security governance by Professor Lucia Zedner and Professor Andrew Ashworth at Oxford University. Unlike many existing Chinese literatures, an international perspective has been integrated in this study.

I chose three revisions of offences in the eighth amendment to the Chinese Criminal Law as my case study to examine the influence of public opinions, of the shaping power from the policy groups and of the censorship from the Chinese Communist Party. On the one hand, the thesis informs the Chinese academy that we may have witnessed a similar preventive move in other countries in the past decades. It fills the gap in current studies in China that are mainly focused on the laws of China and of the other civil law countries. On the other hand, my thesis would help scholars from China to gain an updated understanding of recent developments of Chinese criminal justice and Chinese society, bearing in mind that related literature is limited.

In my research, I argue that public opinion is vital for the development of Chinese criminal law. One of the major factors explaining the several revisions to the criminal law is that they were a response from the Chinese legislature to the voices of the public, especially those on the internet. The party-state tolerates some social pluralism on non-political problems, as long as it maintains ultimate control over agendas and outcomes. It is also consistent with the "mass line" principle adopted in both lawmaking and implementation after the founding of the country. However, we also have to keep in mind that, first of all, public opinions are always subject to manipulation and censorship, not only in China but also in other parts of the world. Second, not all Chinese criminal legislations are the results of fluctuations in public opinion. Public opinion is one of the shaping powers, and what I depicted in the book is only one part of the story.

It has been years since the promulgation of the eighth amendment to the Chinese Criminal Law. Based on the three amendments enacted after the eighth amendment, I made some updates in the concluding chapter of the book. The preventive doctrine continues to apply to terrorism-related offences and other offences against road safety, drug safety and environmental safety in China. At present, the Chinese academia is debating the appropriate response of criminal law to dangerous behaviors during the COVID-19 pandemic. Several people are faced with criminal charges for creating risks of spreading the virus, or refusing to be tested. How criminal law should maintain a balance between controlling risks and protecting human rights remains a long-lasting topic for legal scientists. My further research is still underway.

Acknowledgments

I am indebted to many people without whose help and encouragement this book would never have been published. This book is an update of my doctoral dissertation. I offer my gratitude to the faculty, staff and fellow students in Peter A. Allard School of Law of the University of British Columbia. Special thanks go to my supervisor, Professor Ben Goold. His guidance continually inspired me to advance through my studies. Without his support and understanding I would not have been able to finish this work. I also owe a debt of gratitude to my supervisory committee, Professor Pitman Potter and Professor Timothy Cheek, for working with me throughout the writing process. Professor Scott Anderson also offered constructive comments at the early stage of my reading and writing. Suggestions and inspirations from these great professors are of great value to me, being new to the research field.

I also would like to thank my colleagues in the School of Law in the University of International Business and Economics in China. They are always happy to share with me their experiences in teaching and doing research. I have benefited enormously from the time spent over the years as an assistant professor there. Besides my colleagues, I am grateful to my dear friends who helped me at home and abroad, Yue, Si and Joe. The staff of Routledge, Alison Kirk and Emily Summers, have also been central to bringing this to press and they must be thanked.

Finally, I am forever thankful to my parents. I deeply appreciate them for their love, patience and support. I could not love them more.

This book is supported by the Foundation of Ministry of Education of China (18YJC820027), Social Science Foundation of Beijing (17FXC021) and Foundation of University of International Business and Economics (16QD02).

1 Introduction

This book uses case studies as the main research method. The three case studies include revisions to the offences of drunk driving, manufacturing and selling fake medications and environmental protection in the eighth amendment. The eighth amendment reflects several trends in criminal law, and these three cases are the most explicit examples of proactive development. Based on these revisions, the book will be able to carry out an analysis of past events, which have an ongoing impact on the current society.

This book is about reasons for the preventive shift in Chinese criminal law, that is, the social, legal and political rationales of the shift. It is inspired in part by the eighth amendment of Chinese criminal law in 2011 which amended several penalties related to road, drug and environmental safety. The eighth amendment stemmed from a series of nationally known incidents that triggered widespread public dissatisfaction with the rules and functions of the Chinese criminal justice system. This dissatisfaction would eventually result in a crisis of the government and the legal system. Based on Kingdon's theory of the multiple streams—"problems, policies and politics"—this book seeks to explain the origins of the legislative process and its outcomes by examining the role of public opinion, policy experts and political actors in the making of Chinese criminal law. It argues that in authoritarian China, the prominence of risk control through criminal justice methods is a state response to uncertainties generated through reforms under the Chinese Communist Party (CCP)'s leadership. The process of criminal lawmaking has become more responsive and inclusive than ever before, even though it remains a consultation with the elites within the framework set by the CCP, including representatives of the Two Sessions (the National People's Congress and Chinese People's Political Consultative Conferences), government ministries, academics and others. The process enhances the CCP's legitimacy by not only generating popular expectations of legislative participation, but also by meeting the punitive demands of the public.

1.1 The Chinese landscape

Amendments to Chinese criminal law—as the most visible sign of change in the institutional arrangement of criminal policies and sanctions in China—provide a sound case study of Chinese criminal justice. Scholars usually argue that amendments are driven by multiple pursuits, such as adhering to the policy of combining justice with mercy, solving problems of public livelihoods and following international rules.[1] But a core characteristic of the eighth amendment is that it expands the boundary of criminal law by not only increasing the penalties for several existing offences, but also by criminalizing a number of minor offences. For instance, a prominent characteristic of this eighth amendment is that it comprises several minor offences justified by the requirement of crime prevention—particularly the rationale of risk control—symbolizing the further growth of preventive justice in the field of criminal justice in China.[2] The amendment also provides additional reasons for expanding state power in the name of public security governance.[3]

In this amendment, three changes constitute the present development of preventive justice in criminal law, in which the role of "result" in *actus reus* becomes less important. Most of the changes are focused on fields related to public well-being, such as road and drug safety, and environmental protection. The first and foremost change is the "crime of endangerment"; endangerment offenses criminalize the creation of unacceptable "risks."[4] This "risk-liability" (in contrast to harm-liability) includes offenses of explicit endangerment, such as impaired driving in Article 133(a): "A person who races with other automobiles when driving on the road or commits drunk-driving shall be sentenced to criminal detention and be concurrently given a fine, provided that the circumstances are grave."[5] Second, in the case of the crime of manufacturing or selling fake medications, the eighth amendment presumes that the behavior is risky, so committing the offence simply requires identifying behaviors rather than further evaluation of the seriousness (real harm) of the actions. Third is the amendment of the crime of discharging, dumping or disposing of radioactive waste, waste containing pathogens of infectious diseases or toxic substances. Committing serious environmental incidents was a compulsory element for this offence before, but in this amendment simply seriously polluting the environment is enough to receive the same sentences. That is, whether the action has generated a serious incident or not is unimportant. With the components of crime offences having been changed, "result-crimes" in criminal law are replaced by crimes manifested in a "behavioral" mode (as "conduct crimes").

The above changes share a few common features. First, the focus on the punishment of harms is replaced by risk prevention. The justification for criminal sanctions or increased criminal sentences is preventive, aiming to reduce the risks of such behavior. This differs from the traditional emphasis on punishing based on the harm already caused. Second, the role of the "result" is reduced when defining offences. With the increased number of "conduct crimes," an offence simply requires the existence of criminal conduct instead of a substantial result. In this way, the paradigms of criminal intent and acts are clearly different. For example, with the crime of endangerment, reckless crime without harm is criminalized.[6] Third, given that inchoate crimes, preparatory crimes, crimes of membership and crimes of possession are all acts falling short of causing actual harm, preventive offences are not new in Chinese criminal law. However, distinct from the other preventive designs, the changes all focus on risks directed at the general public's security. Such security involves road safety, drug safety and environmental safety, areas that are closely related to the public well-being. As a matter of fact, besides criminal law, this pursuit of public security can also be identified in Chinese criminal procedure law and administrative law, which keep introducing procedural restrictions on crime suspects who endanger national security or public security, or engage in terrorist activity.[7] Thus, in Chinese criminal law, the preventive amendments manifest the regulatory uses of Chinese criminal law that will give rise to the idea of prevention being the primary justification in the near future. It is possible that more changes will take place to "shift the orientation of crime control away from traditional, reactive strategies towards more prospective and preventive measures designed to maximize security."[8] The offense of risk creation in particular, which diverges from the other two in its explicit seeking to control "risk," has the potential to bring about theoretical and practical changes in the penal field; for instance, new definitions of the fault element in liability, new criteria for criminal behavior without traditional "harm," and the relationship between the seriousness of the criminal offense and the proportionality of the punishment.

Focusing on these transformations, this book seeks to analyze the reasons behind this preventive criminalization in the field of Chinese criminal justice. The book concentrates on explaining how risk, as a legal form of knowledge, has emerged in Chinese criminal law. How can such changes be explained in terms of transformations taking place within the state and social structure? By examining the social, legal and political rationales of the eighth amendment of Chinese criminal law, this book will shed light on key characteristics of the Chinese criminal justice system, as well as the landscape of contemporary society. The overall question this book will explore is: what are the rationales behind this preventive shift in Chinese criminal law? It examines the social, legal and political elements that contribute to the shift. The other two sub-questions that the book will examine contextualize the Chinese transformations in the global environment, since the preventive shift is not limited to China. What are the particular state and social structures that make Chinese lawmaking distinct from that of other countries? What are the similarities in legislation between China and the West, such as the UK and the US, even accounting for their social and political differences?

As a matter of fact, Western criminological scholarship from the UK and the US sheds light on similar changes in the context of Western criminal justice. Since the 1990s, some Western societies such as the UK and the US have been going through a preventive rise. A large part of Western criminological literature claims that crime prevention has become "increasingly prominent ever the past twenty years,"[9] and "central to the government's law and order policy."[10] For instance, in the UK, Anti-Social Behaviour Orders (ASBOs), control orders and serious crime prevention orders generate a variety of academic discussions about the shift in criminal justice. Besides Britain, "parallels can be drawn with developments elsewhere, not least the introduction of Control Orders (modeled closely on the British example) in Australia and the deployment of civil containment against sexual offenders in the US."[11] In the US, the preventive shift is shown not only through anti-terrorism laws, but also through civil orders against sexual offenders and violent offenders.[12] Western research provides background information on the criminal justice system in a general sense. A variety of comparative studies of criminal justice have been carried out between the US and the UK.[13] Rarely has the comparison been carried out between that of the West and China. Instead, China is commonly studied as an authoritarian country, whose political structure and social landscape are distinct from liberal democratic countries.[14] Thus examining Chinese criminal justice with a globalized view, using practices of the West as evidence, is a new attempt. Interpreting what others are actually trying to do is essential even if – or especially if – the social actors we are studying do not have, nor could have, all the answers to our – or even to their – problems.[15] On the one hand, comparative studies between Chinese and Western criminal justice shed light on the characteristics of the Chinese lawmaking and practices. On the other hand, a Chinese case study not only tests to what extent Western theorization could explain the experiences of other districts, but also complicates the global understanding of crime prevention and risk control due to its special social context consisting of the current complex development status, the authoritarian regime, the large population and other factors that are specific to developing countries or to China.

In all, focusing on how law and institutions have developed in China, the book will investigate the impact of multiple factors on criminal law in an attempt to understand the fundamental problems in Chinese society and potential future transformations. The next section will address existing literature on this topic, including from China and other countries such as the US, the UK and Australia. The literature review intends to provide an analysis of the literature of the preventive shift of criminal justice both in China and the West. Reviews of the Chinese literature summarize current Eastern scholarship on the preventive shift of Chinese criminal law. It not only exists as the theoretical foundation of the book—concepts and theoretical frameworks that have been used to examine the preventive shift of the law—but also uncovers the gap in the existing literature that the book will address through critical analysis. By contrast, reviews of Western scholarship, through examining "fundamental structural and cultural conditions that provide the broader context for policy formulation"[16] in the Western context, help to find out the socio-legal methodology that can be used to fill in the gap of Chinese legal studies.

1.2 Literature review

The growth in the preventive shift in criminal law has been a cause of controversy among Chinese scholars. The discussion is intertwined with debates about the role of criminal law in the risk society from 2007 until present. Since 2007, criminal law scholars in China have tried to use the risk society theory to interpret the social background of the preventive shift of criminal law, suggesting that criminal law was going through fundamental structural transformations.[17] These scholars employ the risk society to theorize not only Chinese reforms, but also the reforms of developed countries like Germany and Japan. However, after many debates, opponents started to refute the relationship between the risk society theory and the Chinese social landscape by claiming that the risk society theory is unable to interpret the Chinese social environment. Such debate continue now. The following section will document this history, identify the concerns of Chinese scholars, examine the theories they use and assess the strength as well as weakness of their arguments.

1.2.1 Chinese scholarship

In China, preventive criminal policy is not adopted from Western counterparts; rather, it is the introduction of the Western risk society theory that augmented Chinese scholars' interests in the relationship between risk control and criminal law. According to the China Knowledge Resource Integrated Database,[18] there have been more than 200 articles about the efforts of criminal law to control risk, as well as the threats of such efforts to civil liberties. Articles from top law journals number more than 30; most of them are based on doctrinal analysis rather than empirical study.

Dongyan Lao from Tsinghua University raised this topic first in her famous article "Public Policy and Criminal Law in the Risk Society" in *Social Sciences in China*.[19] The article initiated the debate about the new role of criminal law in the risk society. Drawing from Bernard Harcourt's article "The Collapse of the Harm Principle," Lao suggests that in China criminal law turns into a proactive tool of the government whose function has now been completely changed to risk management. That criminal law is increasingly subordinate to public policy pursuits has brought about eight significant transformations to coercive social control techniques, known as expanding the definition of "criminal action," adopting criminal law to censure risky behaviors, diversifying ways of taking criminal responsibility and broadening the criteria of establishing legal causation. As a conclusion, Lao insists that while it is normal to make legal innovations, one should not break the basic principles of criminal justice. Otherwise, any change cannot be justified.[20] After her article appeared, several papers were published in Chinese journals that examined the current and potential changes of the criminal justice system. In a short time, studies of so-called "criminal law and risk control" dominated academic discussions of Chinese criminal law, covering several topics such as endangerment crimes, negligent crimes and crimes against public security.[21] It seemed this theory had obtained a number of followers with significant academic enthusiasm. However, at the time, most researchers tended to accept the coming of the risk society as a reality without considering deeper conceptualizations of basic terms such as "risk," "risk control" and "risk society."[22]

Although it was insightful of them to be cautious of the dangers of preventive transformations of criminal law, they failed to identify whether the target they criticized was correct or not.

Discussions reached a peak in 2011 when a few noted scholars—including Xingliang Chen, Yanhong Liu and Hongjie Tian—published their articles together in *Studies of Law and Business*. These scholars are mostly skeptical of the legality of preventive methods in the criminal justice system, especially of risk control. Xingliang Chen claims that there is tension between maintaining social order and protecting individual liberty. Managing risk is not an excuse for expanding the boundaries of criminal law.[23] Yanhong Liu emphasizes that the "risk-oriented" reforms ought to be under strict scrutiny, since they may infringe on the foundation of criminal law. Hongjie Tian asserts that community correction and victim–offender reconciliation are better strategies than simply increasing criminal penalties. In addition, it is more appropriate to resort to civil and administrative law to deal with the increasing social risks.[24] In summation, it is clear that Chinese scholars share some basic views about the relationship between risk control and criminal justice. They all recognize that Chinese criminal law is undergoing certain transformations; they harbor concerns about the dangers of preventive justice in corrupting state power, and they believe it imperative to use criminal penalties cautiously while simultaneously searching for alternative methods of crime prevention. Their focus mainly lies on a normative analysis of the proactive function of criminal law and its challenges with the criminal law principles and human liberty.[25]

> This extension of criminal liability through pre-emptive laws raises serious questions about the elasticity of the boundaries of the criminal justice system, and whether so stretching the boundaries of the criminal law is desirable or indeed possible without fundamentally corroding the criminal justice system.[26]

In 2012, the eighth amendment of Chinese criminal law gave rise to more scholarly papers in the following year that used the amendments as evidence of preventive reform. Among the 50 papers[27] that directly or indirectly addressed such issues, one that was particularly noteworthy was "Critical Review of the Risk Criminal Law Theory," published in the *Criminal Law Review*.[28] Compared to the others, it conducted a deeper analysis of the theory of risk society, claiming that the current theory understood the risk society incorrectly. Criminal law itself was unable to deal with the globalized risks generated by the advent of the risk society. The limits of criminal law and its post hoc logic make it hard to handle the insecurity created by nuclear explosions, genetic engineering, environmental deterioration, economic crisis and terrorism.[29] This criticism demonstrated that Chinese scholars had started to question the appropriateness of using the risk society theory as the framework for examining reforms of contemporary criminal law.

Later in 2014, Dongyan Lao and Xingliang Chen separately wrote two more articles as follow-ups of their previous ones from 2011. Although holding opposite opinions, they both explored the relationship between risk society theory and changes to criminal law. In Lao's article "Risk Society and Changing Criminal Law Theory," she argues that the link between risk society theory and criminal law reform is the security (or safety) concern, which has enhanced the proactive role of criminal law to control the risks based on increasing public demands.[30] She highlights "security" and "prevention" as new key words of the ongoing discussion. Conversely, Chen's article "Critical Doctrinal Analysis of Risk Criminal Law Theory" is an overall rejection of the relationship between the risk society theory and reforms in Chinese criminal law.[31] He insists that the risks that criminal law intends to manage are not those described in the risk society theory. A detailed examination of the background and logic of negligent crimes, endangerment crimes and crimes of omission is required. Chen also claims that rather than changes that are enhanced by the risk society, amendments of the Chinese criminal law are signs of the re-arrangement of judicial and administrative (policing) powers in China, since more and more behavior regulations are now subject to legal procedures rather than police discretion.[32] Therefore, debates suggest that the key issue demanding further study lies in identifying the changes to Chinese criminal law and their driving forces.

The above studies are undoubtedly informative. Generally speaking, the theory of risk society can be applied to the Chinese social landscape in certain respects. On the one hand, Beck uses "world risk society" to refer to the politics of risk management among the other countries. With globalization, China—which will inevitably face insecurity—is part of the world risk society. On the other hand, China, as a country with a mix of pre-modern, modern and late-modern identities,[33] manifests certain features of late modernity demonstrated by the risk society theory. However, although many Chinese researchers agree that risk control is a "new" shift in criminal justice, current research lacks a perspective on how China varies from the other countries, even in the framework of the risk society. The key question of locating the Chinese landscape within international developments of crime control is not answered. For instance, scholars have not considered issues such as the following: is the rise of preventive justice a Chinese phenomenon or a worldwide trend? How does the Chinese practice exemplify and modify the general proactive shift? How will comparative studies with Western development of crime control highlight factors in Chinese rule of law?[34] More insight will be achieved if Western theories and practices are introduced into Chinese research. Thus examining discourses of the risk society theory is a good place to start, but there remains far more to be done.[35]

Second, as it has been noted, compared to the large amount of normative analysis seeking to restrict the use of preventive methods, little attention has been paid to the fundamental question about the way in which preventive justice came about and how well it fits into Chinese society. How can such changes be explained in terms of transformations taking place within the state structure?

This is a common problem for Chinese criminal justice research, which focuses on doctrinal analysis and pure legal reasoning without considering the social and political context of legal change. Such research limits the analysis to changes of statutes, rather than broader social reforms, how governmental activities and the effects of such unfold or how we think and act, individually and collectively with the government. Even though scholars have insisted over the years that equal attention should be paid to the social origins and impact of criminal law,[36] little progress has been made in this area. Introducing the risk society theory has been a fine start, but existing concerns are limited to the theory itself. It will be interesting if we are able to move concerns from the risk society theory into concerns of risk and crime prevention in the Chinese context. "Punishment is a social institution, which can be understood only within the social context, which gives it its practical meaning and determines its social effects."[37] In China, studies linking legal reforms with social environment remain limited. Articles that specifically examine characteristics of the society usually fail to document changes to criminal law, while those that study legal changes commonly lack specific analysis of the Chinese social context. Compared to a large variety of Western literature on socio-legal or sociological studies of criminal law,[38] Chinese research has considerable gaps.

Therefore, this book aims to examine these neglected problems in order to obtain an in-depth understanding of Chinese criminal justice. It considers whether risk-oriented crime prevention emerges in China's penal system and, if so, what the underlying social and political structures are that make the changes unique. Gaps will be filled by socio-legal studies and foreign literature on current penal research.

1.2.2 Western scholarship

Lucia Zedner and Andrew Ashworth are the two most influential scholars in the UK, working on coercive preventive justice. Since the 2000s, and particularly in the last five years, they have examined the undercriminalization effect of preventive orders like the ASBOs,[39] the impact of the Terrorism Act,[40] the implication of actuarial techniques[41] and the boundaries of punishment, among others.[42] They first identify the characteristics of preventive justice methods in the following three ways: a large part of their rationale is punitive; they aim to prevent the occurrence of harm or the risk of harm; and they are backed by the threat of coercive sanction (sanction of breach).[43] Similar to their Eastern counterparts, the two scholars emphasize that prevention makes good sense, but it is often carried out using regulatory strategies and authoritarian impulses. It is also questionable whether these penalties are proportionate to the breach alone. Accordingly, it is essential to hold coercive methods under rigorous principled restraint and appropriate procedural protection so that criminal justice will be capable of maintaining its legitimacy without depriving human liberty.[44]

Related literature on normative analysis of risk in other countries includes "Governing Risk" and "Risk, Crime and Prudentialism Revisited" by Pat

O'Malley, "Actuarial Justice: The Emerging New Criminal Law" by M. Feeley and J. Simon, *Against Prediction: Punishing and Policing in an Actuarial Age* and "The Shaping of Chance: Actuarial Models and Criminal Profiling at the Turn of the Twenty-First Century" by B. Harcourt, "The Limits of the Preventive State" by C. Steiker, "A Jurisprudence of Dangerousness" by C. Slobogin, "A Jurisprudence of Risk Assessment: Forecasting Harm Among Prisoners, Predators, and Patients" by J. Monahan, *Failure to Protect: America's Sexual Predator Laws and the Rise of the Preventive State* and "The Preventive State, Terrorists and Sexual Predators: Countering the Threat of a New Outsider Jurisprudence" by E. Janus and "Precaution, Precaution Everywhere: Developing a 'Common Understanding' of the Precautionary Principle in the European Community" by E. Fisher. The scholars have different analytical focuses within the framework of the preventive state, including preparatory laws mainly facilitated by the fight against terrorism and laws of forecasting harm among potential offenders, risky prisoners and mental illness patients, as well as actuarial techniques of prediction in sentencing and policing. First, scholars interpret the concept of prevention in either a broad or narrow sense, as a general shift or a specific model, with political or managerial significance. For instance, Ian Hacking traces the history of the probabilistic revolution in *The Taming of Chance*, and demonstrates how the laws of probability displaced in significant part the laws of necessity by the early twentieth century. B. Harcourt points out that "the concept of the actuarial connects with several strands of modern penalty—the emphasis on classification, risk assessment, preventative crime-control, and criminal profiling."[45] Feeley and Simon argue that "a new penology is emerging that shifts away from a concern with punishing individuals to managing aggregates of dangerous groups," characterized as an "actuarial language of probabilistic calculations and statistical distributions applied to populations."[46] Second, their concerns about the legality of the new strategies to be justified through legal principles are basically the same claims as those of the Chinese researchers. For example, in "The Preventive State, Terrorists and Sexual Predators," Janus claims that the sexual predator laws provide a model for undercutting these constitutional protections of liberty. In "A Jurisprudence of Dangerousness," C. Slobogin describes a jurisprudence of dangerousness by developing the psychological and prediction criteria to govern the state's implementation of its police power.[47]

> The paradigm of the criminal law and the criminal trial is being eroded by the state as it pursues other agendas such as greater regulation, an emphasis on prevention, and an authoritarianism linked closely with penal populism and the demand for public protection.[48]

Such literature "raise[s] basic questions about the right to punish, the limits on state power, the responsibility and dignity of the offender, the nature of criminality, the depiction of human nature."[49]

Besides the normative analysis discussed above, there is other work from scholars such as David Garland, Jonathan Simon and Pat O'Malley that contextualizes the reforms in broader social environments. Though compared with literature mentioned above, they are not particularly focused on crime prevention and risk control, the theories they raise—such as the risk society theory, the late-modern society theory and the governance theory—help us understand the reasons for and impact of the changes.[50] Such reasons consist of social unrest, the influence of social policies, public consciousness of risk and crime and shifts in the sphere of criminal justice. Conceptualizing the risk discourse is a primary focus of Western scholarship. "This seems a rather massive and long-term process, when many criminologists are more concerned to consider and deal with specific changes in crime control associated with risk frameworks."[51] Risk, as a very abstract concept, "is capable of multiple and very divergent realizations in institutional or governmental forms."[52] It is difficult to define risk since "there are numerous definitions that depend on the situational context, field of application and adopted perspective."[53] The way to view risk is shaped by social transformations and public policy alterations. For instance, researchers holding the "cultural perspective" argues that risk is socially constructed and that all knowledge about risk is dependent on belief systems and moral positions.[54] Risk is used to "reproduce and maintain concepts of selfhood and group membership,"[55] while sociologists adopting the "risk society" perspective are predominantly interested in the macro-social processes they consider characteristic of late-modern societies and their relation to concepts of risk.[56] Risk is a late-modernist vision of the world's chaos and conflicts. By contrast, "governmentality" scholars identify risk as a moral concept used to discipline future actions through rationalization and calculation. Individuals who are self-regulating moral agents take on the responsibility of self-protection from the government. Shifts in the meaning of risk or in risk itself reflect a change from welfare–social politics toward a neoliberal political rationality, and from a collective treatment of social problems to a prudential model of partnerships between the state and individuals.[57]

The above theories employ different angles to analyze risk and risk control techniques. Looking at the ways in which the concept of risk operates in Western societies invites us to examine a China-based understanding of risk-control methods. Western scholarship has remarkable value for Chinese criminal law research for the following reasons. Besides normative analysis of the preventive shift that is a common focus of both Western and Eastern scholars, first, the socio-legal method of Western studies inspires a similar study of China-based legal transitions. As Duff and Garland have argued, "Punishment is a social institution, which can be understood only within the social context, which gives it its practical meaning and determines its social effects."[58] Conceptualizing crime prevention cannot be separate from the broad social, political and intellectual contexts. In Western scholarship, crime prevention is used to exemplify radical changes in the configuration of both public and private governance in late-modern society under the influence of neoliberal or other policies. This literature exists as an example of the Chinese case study on the transformations taking place within the state and social structure. Such an understanding will shed light on how the

Chinese view not only themselves, but also the state, the society and the globalized world. It will also illuminate the public's rising risk awareness, the governance of the ruling party and China's authoritarian regime in an era of deepening reforms and exposure.

Second, contextualizing the Chinese preventive shift will enrich these arguments concerning crime prevention on an international level that are currently based largely on trends in Western countries. On the one hand, existing research suggests that both China and the West show some similar moves in criminal justice, such as the criminalization of minor behavior and the role of public opinion in policy making, all of which may provide some understanding of crime prevention and of social situations given the worldwide focus on security governance. On the other hand, Western knowledge can also "help us rethink our approaches to the possible sources of punitiveness and leniency rather than only reinforce what we already think and value."[59] In China, the expansion of crime includes several changes justified by the crime prevention requirement—particularly the rationale of risk control—symbolizing further growth of proactive techniques in the field of criminal justice in contemporary China, and additional reasons for expanding state power in the name of public security governance.[60] The party-state, which either hesitates or refuses to admit the state's capacity limits in crime control, strives to show the public that it is both willing and capable of sustaining a safe environment in the transformative era. Effective security control manifests the superiority of China's political system under the leadership of the party. Besides the social environment in which punishments are embedded, "A fuller understanding of penal-policy changes also requires a more detailed understanding of the purposive actions of key agents within the policy process, and the constraints and opportunities provided by the political systems within which they operate."[61] Through examining the social, legal and political rationales of the preventive shift of Chinese criminal law, the book will highlight the participants' beliefs and practices regarding the law, which helps to understand the politics, the dynamics and the future of the Chinese rule of law.

1.3 Methodology

Methodology describes how sources are chosen, what criteria are used for making assessments and what concepts are used to organize a project.[62] A research design is a blueprint dealing with at least four problems: what questions to study, what data are relevant, what data to collect and how to analyze the results.[63] In contrast to domestic research that focuses on normative analysis of the threats of preventive justice to civil liberties, this research will use the case study as the main research method. Many well-known case study researchers such as Robert E. Stake, Helen Simons and Robert K. Yin have written about case study research and suggested techniques for organizing and conducting the research successfully.[64] According to Yin, "the case study is not either a data collection tactic or merely a design feature alone but a comprehensive research strategy."[65] It is "an empirical inquiry about a contemporary phenomenon (e.g., a 'case'), set within its real-world context—especially when the boundaries between phenomenon and context are not clearly evident." It tends to explore the links between the "interventions" and the outcomes. Bogdan and Biklen identify case study as "a detailed examination of one setting, or a single subject, a single depository of documents, or one particular event."[66] Bruce L. Berg and Howard Lune define it as "a method involving systematically gathering enough information about a particular person, social setting, even, or group to permit the research to effectively understand how the subject operates or functions."[67] In general, these definitions suggest that case study is a qualitative social research method that describes, explains or explores the cases (as an individual, community, event or social phenomenon). It develops narratives of single or multiple cases through data-gathering techniques to examine human behaviors and their settings.

In this book, the case study is explanatory and traces the social, legal and political rationales for the preventive shift of Chinese criminal law. The book chooses the case study as the main research method for the following reasons. First, "this qualitative case study is an approach to research that facilitates exploration of a phenomenon within its context using a variety of data sources."[68] This book will be carried out through case studies, with the intention of locating them within both the Chinese and the global contexts. Besides, case studies consist of a detailed contextual analysis of a "limited" number of events or conditions and their relationships.[69] As to the number of cases, the three revisions of criminal law (drunk driving, manufacturing and selling fake medications and environmental pollution) provide sound cases with a "limited number" for a multiple-case study.

Second, mostly importantly, according to Yin, the case study is the preferred strategy when "how" or "why" questions are being posed, when the investigator has little control over events and when the focus is on a contemporary phenomenon within some real-life context.[70] This book, focusing on the rationales for the preventive shift in Chinese criminal law, explores the question of why the shift is emerging in the criminal justice system. Because the eighth amendment of criminal law was passed in 2011, the time passed makes it difficult to become involved in the discussion or to reassess the public's opinion, scholars' suggestions or demands of the officials through interviews or surveys. Using case studies, this book will be able to carry out an analysis of these past events, which have an ongoing impact on current society.

The key question for this book is what are the reasons behind this preventive criminalization in the field of Chinese criminal law. "The case is a unit, entity, or phenomenon with defined boundaries that the research can demarcate or fence in." The book is a multiple-case study. The three cases this book intends to explore from the eighth amendment of Chinese criminal law are revisions to the drunk driving offence, the manufacturing and selling fake medications and environmental protection. The eighth amendment reflects several trends in criminal law, and these three cases are the most explicit examples of proactive development. Each case aims to examine a complementary facet of the major research question.

Furthermore, "case study research is not limited to a single source of data."[71] A key strength of the case study method involves using multiple sources and techniques in the data-gathering process.[72] There are six common sources of evidence used for case studies: direct observations, interviews, archival records, documents, participant-observation and physical artifacts.[73] This book aims to use a combination of sources, relying on both Eastern and Western experiences to gain a clearer picture of the shift in Chinese criminal law. It will focus on the attitudes and practices of different actors toward preventive techniques by analyzing criminal law amendments, amendment drafts, official reports of the lawmaking body, legislative procedures, Supreme Court reports, the Supreme Procuratorate and the Ministry of Public Security, online comments, blogs and academic scholarship. Case studies rely on multiple sources of evidence including documentation, archived records, interviews and observations. The difficulty of conducting interviews in the Chinese social context stems from the challenges of gaining full access to the information within Chinese government ministries and legislative bodies. Without firsthand information, this book will collect documentation from the three cases as far as is possible. It also draws on firsthand experience, knowledge and observations obtained in my own daily life, as supplemental information.[74] "This (drawing on his or her own experience) can be necessary in areas from which we have no research findings, or the findings are too general for use in the specific instance."[75] The limits also manifest the Chinese characteristics of decision making which remains contained in elite cooperation without a high level of transparency to the public.

As to the research strategy, this book applies Kingdon's multiple streams approach (MSA) of agenda-making in the US as the theoretical framework for analyzing the Chinese process of lawmaking. Kingdon's multiple streams framework is an adaptation of the "Garbage Can Model."[76] It (the multiple streams approach) contrasts with "comprehensively rational" policy making in which—in this order—policy makers identify problems (or their aims), bureaucracies perform a comprehensive analysis to produce various solutions (or ways to meet those aims) and policy makers select the best solution.[77] According to Kingdon, "both ambiguity and time constraints render rational problem-solving models highly unconvincing."[78] In his book *Agenda Making, Alternatives and Public Policies*, Kingdon identifies three streams that lead to final policy outcomes: "problem, policy and political streams."[79] The three streams develop separately from each other with their own logic, but at some critical moments (when policy windows open), they are joined together, and this is where agendas are successfully set. Thus "collective choice is not merely the derivative of individual efforts aggregated in some fashion but rather the combined result of structural forces and cognitive and affective processes that are highly context dependent."[80]

Though Kingdon's model is based on interviews about the health and transportation reforms in the US, it has been applied to a wide variety of policy areas, ranging from energy policy,[81] environmental policy,[82] climate policy,[83] forestry policy,[84] educational policy,[85] privatization policy,[86] gender policy[87] and constitutional policy to foreign policy,[88] to name just a few.[89] His model has also been subject to modifications by other researchers in other social environments, such as the parliamentary systems.[90] However, as it is claimed, "MSA is rarely applied to policy making in developing and transition countries."[91] The book is a refinement of the MSA model in the Chinese context. Chapter 2 of the book will specifically explore the reasons (strengths and limits) for adopting this framework on China-related issues. In China, at times, rather than "comprehensive rationality," "policymaker aims and policy problems are ambiguous, and bureaucrats struggle to research issues and produce viable solutions quickly."[92] "Individuals sometimes behave rationally, but the process of making systemic decision often does not exhibit rational properties."[93] The Chinese legislation is not a fully rational process. The three-stream conceptualization clearly categorizes and summarizes the factors that contributed to the criminal law revisions. It also matches with the social, legal and political rationales of Chinese criminal law that this book examines. But at the same time, there are several aspects that make Chinese lawmaking distinct from the framework that Kingdon proposes. For instance, in the Chinese context, the policy and the political streams overlap. On the one hand, those who raise proposals in the policy stream are commonly experts, technicians and scholars working in government ministries. Their activities are inevitably influenced by political interests. On the other hand, in the political stream a number of experts are also the ones who carry out these proposal debates. Therefore, the book is both an application and modification of MSA. How the peculiarities of agenda making are related to the requirement and logic of risk management sheds light not only on the Chinese characteristics, but also on the differences between China and the US in issues of agenda making.

Lastly, throughout this book, Western theories and practices since the late 1990s will be used as supporting evidence to highlight the characteristics of their Chinese counterparts. This book views the development of the Chinese criminal justice system within the global context and situates the progress of laws and legal institutions in this historical and social context. Compared to other countries, more attention will be on the practices of the UK and the US, since these two countries are the key focus of Western criminological studies, offering rich data and theories about the political, social and cultural reasons for the changes in Western criminal justice. Statistics originate not only from reports and publications on official websites from the West (such as the Home Office of the UK, the FBI and the US Justice Department), but also from Western academic research, including literature on the rise of preventive justice in the UK and the US, the punitive turn in Western criminal justice after the 1970s, the coming of late-modern society and the impact of neoliberal politics on the penal realm. For instance, preventive justice in the UK has also generated hot academic debate. The research on the justifications for preventive justice in the UK starting from 2011 at the University of Oxford sets a great example for the study on Chinese pre-emptive methods. Though most Western undertakings are quite distinct from the Chinese experience, there are similarities between China and the West, such as the criminalization of minor behavior, preventive techniques in policing and the role of public opinion in policy making, all of which show hints of similar beliefs on crime prevention and social situations given the worldwide focus on security governance. Theorizing risk in the Western context through a socio-legal perspective also inspires similar criminological research on the Chinese experience. It fills the gap in current studies which focus solely on the philosophy of criminal law while ignoring what crime control rhetoric actually is.

1.4 Book structure

This book comprises eight chapters. Drawing on Western theories that are applicable to China, it examines both the macro and micro aspects of the process of law and policy making, and the major forces that have driven this shift. Based on three case studies of the eighth amendment of Chinese criminal law, it explores rationales of the preventive shift of Chinese criminal law through analyzing the problem, policy and political streams of the lawmaking processes.

After the introduction section, the second chapter examines the legislative changes to Chinese criminal law to identify what has emerged. It also lays the foundation for the entire book. Based on case studies of the changes in criminal penalties for food, drug and environmental safety and their implications for the Chinese criminal justice system as signs of pro-active reforms, it analyzes how risk discourse diverges and overlaps with the routine moral regulations of responsibility allocation. The hypothesis of this chapter is that current legislation shows evidence of preventive developments for the pursuit of public security. Accordingly, it first examines the changes in the eighth amendment to investigate if these changes are distinct from the other provisions of the amendment and the effects they have on Chinese criminal law, state power and civil liberty. Later provisions of all amendments before the eighth will be summarized to identify whether these changes illustrate a clear trend toward crime prevention, as well as the general public's pursuit of security governance. In addition, corresponding reforms in other fields enhance the validity of proposed changes in criminal justice. Legal changes to criminal procedural law and administrative law are also addressed as supporting evidence to examine the extent to which they indicate the growing emphasis on public security.

After that, "to understand how law matters in China, we have to unpack society and discover how different political, cultural, economic and personal experiences shape attitudes toward the law and lead to different forms of legal and political action."[94] In the third chapter, the book starts to examine the history of amending Chinese criminal law. It then explores the reasons for applying the "problems, policies and politics" framework of John Kingdon for US policy making to analyze the social, legal and political rationales for the preventive shift in Chinese criminal law. The chapter claims that Kingdon's MSA theory helps to classify the roles of the public, of proposal makers and of political actors in the eighth amendment. Kingdon's theory is also subject to revisions in the Chinese context.

In the fourth chapter, in order to assess the social justifications for legislative change, the book examines the "problem stream" of amending Chinese criminal law, emphasizing the demands of social forces in the "focusing events." In MSA, the problem stream includes multiple conditions that policy makers have to deal with. Policy makers discover the problematic conditions through indicators, focusing events and feedback. In the problem stream, focusing events are, for example, road accidents, terrorist actions or social crises. In the Chinese focusing events, the public's rising sense of security runs parallel to growing anxiety about social risk, which poses challenges to the governance of the CCP by eroding the "trust" between the state and society. The social forces manifest as an increase in media-stimulated public involvement under state censorship prior to the legislation. The inclusion of public opinion converges with "penal populism" documented in Western scholarship.

The fifth chapter will explore the "policy stream" in amending Chinese criminal law, including activities of government specialists, think tanks, lawyers, NGOs, representatives in the national congress and scholars. In MSA, the policy stream is a selection process. Ideas are created by specialists in various forms, such as conferences, papers, speeches, etc. Whether the ideas will be selected or not depends on their value acceptability, technical feasibility or resource adequacy.[95] In China, the wide participation in proposal making was mainly triggered by political and social pressures from the "focusing events." The involvement of the specialist is also an effort to consolidate or enhance individual power, which directly leads to changes in criminal law.

The sixth chapter examines the "politics stream" of amending Chinese criminal law by analyzing the status, attitudes and activities of the institutions. In MSA, the politics stream is "composed of such factors as swings of national mood, election results, changes of administration, changes of ideological or partisan distributions in Congress, and interest group pressure campaigns."[96] In the Chinese context, responses from various participants, including the CCP, the National People's Congress (NPC), the Supreme People's Court, the People's Procuratorate, the Ministry of Public Security and the media, are covered in this section. Law is a mechanism by which political power is exercised and protected. First of all, criminal law exists as an essential tool of the CCP to regain public trust and maintain social stability, especially with the rise in the sense of insecurity. On the one hand, the making of criminal law takes place within the framework set by the CCP. On the other hand, criminal law reforms reflect the CCP's governing characteristics by determining on a macro perspective which risks should be reduced and which ignored, deciding what constitutes unacceptable levels of risk, evaluating who should bear risk plus who should be protected from risk and what are acceptable ways of reducing risk. Second, the legislation is a co-operative model with internal conflicts among the agencies, which has indeed shown much progress toward legal and rational legislation.

Based on the three streams examined in the previous chapters, the seventh chapter makes a comparison between the role of the state in the West and in

China. Then the eighth chapter analyzes the "policy window" of amending criminal law when problem, policy and political streams have overlapped one another. The policy window is the time when the three streams are joined. "An open policy window is an opportunity for advocates to push their pet solutions or to push attention to their special problems."[97] In China, the dynamic between public support and political approval not only raises national attention for the agendas, but also largely affects the final result of the decision making.

The concluding chapter summarizes the above findings, claiming that the present Chinese criminal legislation has been more inclusive and responsive than ever before. It aims to create trust between the government and the public in the transitional era of modernization. The making of criminal law enhances this trust through a top-down approach in both procedural and substantial aspects; as has been shown, lawmaking procedures win mass support with responsive and participatory institutional arrangements. In addition, substantial changes to criminal law strengthen the government's legitimacy by "being harsh on crimes."

This preventive shift remains evident in revisions of Chinese criminal law after the enactment of the eighth amendment in 2011. The numbers of endangerment crimes, inchoate crimes and pre-inchoate crimes keep increasing. It is hoped that the government could give equal consideration to restraining criminal law. Otherwise, given that authoritarianism is more likely to lead to the expansion of the penal system, Chinese society will become more and more exclusive, which will eventually be detrimental to the establishment of a liberal society.

Notes

1 Shishi Li, "Explanation of the First Draft of the Eighth Amendment of Criminal Law", online: <http://www.npc.gov.cn/huiyi/lfzt/xfxza8/2011-05/10/content_1666058.htm>.
2 Minor offences justified by the requirement of crime prevention consist of offences of impaired driving, manufacturing and selling fake medications (without any actual harm) and environmental pollution (without any actual harm). The Chinese criminal justice system does not distinguish between minor and serious offences. Nor does it have the distinction of summary and indictable offences. "Minor offences" here refer to offences that are not commonly believed serious in Chinese criminal law.
3 See Wei Liu, "Trend of the Amendment of Criminal Law and Its Principles" (2011) 5 *Political Science and Law* 95–101.
4 Andrew Ashworth & Lucia Zedner, "Prevention and Criminalization: Justifications and Limits" (2012) 15 *New Criminal Law Review* 546.
5 Yaozhong Wang, "Legal Analysis of Impaired Driving" (2012) 5 *Science of Law* 124–125.
6 Bernard E. Harcourt, "The Collapse of the Harm Principle" (1999) 90 *Journal of Criminal Law & Criminology* 109.
7 Articles 83 and 148 of the new amendment stipulate that in cases concerning national security or terrorist activities, the police may not notify the family of the arrested person about the reason for the arrest and the place of custody if the notification may hinder the investigation process. In cases regarding crimes that violate national security, terrorist activities, organized crime, drug crime or any

other crime that seriously endangers society, the police may take special investigative measures.

8 Lucia Zedner, *Security* (London, UK: Routledge, 2009) 1–2.

9 Kevin D. Haggerty, "From Risk to Precaution, the Rationalities of Personal Crime Prevention", in Richard V. Ericson & Aaron Doyle, *Risk and Morality* (Toronto: University of Toronto Press, 2003) 193.

10 Gordon Hughes, *Understanding Crime Prevention* (Buckingham: Open University Press, 1998) 17.

11 Lucia Zedner, *Security* (London, UK: Routledge, 2009) 83.

12 See Bernard E. Harcourt, "Neoliberal Penalty: A Brief Genealogy" (2010) 14 (1) *Theoretical Criminology* 75; John Monahan, "A Jurisprudence of Risk Assessment: Forecasting Harm among Prisoners, Predators and Patients" (2006) 92 (3) *Virginia Law Review* 391–435; Alan Norrie, "Citizenship, Authoritarianism and the Changing Shape of the Criminal Law", in Bernadette McSherry, Alan Norrie & Simon Bronitt, eds, *The Re-Direction of Criminalization and the Futures of Criminal Law* (Oxford: Bloomsbury Publishing, 2008) 15; Corey Rayburn Yung, "Sex Offender Exceptionalism and Preventive Detention" (2011) 101 (3) *The Journal of Criminal Law and Criminology* 971.

13 See Trevor Jones & Tim Newburn, "Comparative Criminal Justice Policy-Making in the United States and the United Kingdom: The Case of Private Prisons" (2005) 45 *British Journal of Criminology* 58–80; David Hirschel, William Wakefield & Scott Sasse, *Criminal Justice in England and the United States* (Sudbury, MA: Jones & Bartlett Learning, 2007); Trevor Jones & Tim Newburn, *Policy Transfer and Criminal Justice: Exploring US Influence over British Crime Control Policy* (Berkshire: Open University Press, 2007). Besides, differences of harshness of punishments between the US and Europe has also been studied. See James Q. Whitman, *Harsh Justice: Criminal Punishment and the Widening Divide between America and Europe* (Oxford: Oxford University Press, 2003).

14 In criminal justice and criminological studies, literature on the comparisons between China and the West is really limited. One exception is Jerome Bourgon, "Chinese Executions: Visualizing Their Differences with European Supplies" (2003) 2 (1) *European Journal of East Asian Studies* 153–184.

15 David Nelken, "Comparative Criminal Justice: Beyond Ethnocentricism and Relativism" 6 (4) *European Journal of Criminology* 307.

16 Dario Melossi, "The Cultural Embeddedness of Social Control: Reflections on the Comparison of Italian and North-American Cultures Concerning Punishment", in Tim Newburn & Richard Sparks, eds, *Criminal Justice and Political Cultures* (Cullompton: Willan, 2001) 407.

17 Dongyan Lao, "Public Policy and Criminal Law in a Risk Society" (2007) 3 *Social Sciences in China* 126–127.

18 The database, Global CNKI, is the most commonly used academic database in China.

19 Dongyan Lao, "Public Policy and Criminal Law in a Risk Society" (2007) 3 *Social Sciences in China* 126.

20 Dongyan Lao, "Public Policy and Criminal Law in a Risk Society" (2007) 3 *Social Sciences in China* 126–127.

21 See Yanbing Hao, "Values and Role of Criminal Law in the Risk Society" (2009) 07 *Chinese Criminal Justice* 15–23; Yong Xia, "Responses of Criminal Law to Risks to People's Livelihood" (2001) 04 *Studies in Law and Business* 6–10; Hong Li, "Reflections on Criminal Law in the Risk Society" (2001) 3 *People's Procuratorial Semimonthly* 16–20.

22 For instance, they simply take the conception of "risk society" as a society full of risks. "Risk" is considered identical to road and food safety accidents in China.

Min Long, "Balances of Social Order and Freedom: Conflicts of Values of Criminal Law in the Risk Society" (2010) 9 *Journal of Gansu Institute of Political Science and Law* 145–149.

23 Xingliang Chen, "Criminal Law in the Risk Society and Risk of Criminal Law" (2011) 4 *Studies in Law and Business* 11.

24 Hongjie Tian, "Position of Criminal Law in the Risk Society" (2011) 4 *Studies in Law and Business* 20.

25 Yong Xia, "The Risk in Risk Society: Clarifying the Misunderstandings in Researches of Risk Control in Criminal Justice" (2012) 24 *Peking University Law Journal* 250–262; Yan Cheng, "The Target of Criminal Law in the Risk Society" (2012) 29 *Criminal Law Review* 283–300.

26 Tamara Tulich, "A View Inside the Preventive State: Reflections on a Decade of Anti-Terror Law" (2012) 21 (2) *Griffith Law Review* 235.

27 This number was collected from China National Knowledge Infrastructure (CNKI). In China, CNKI is one "key project of national informatization construction, which is dedicated to the mass digitalization of China knowledge resources, as well as creating the platform for global dissemination and value-added services."

28 Lianwei Nan, "Critical Analysis and Reflections on the Risk Society Theory" (2012) 4 *Chinese Journal of Law* 138–153.

29 Lianwei Nan, "Critical Analysis and Reflections on the Risk Society Theory" (2012) 4 *Chinese Journal of Law* 138–153.

30 Dongyan Lao, "Risk Society Theory and Shifting Criminal Law Theory" (2014) 1 *Peking University Law Review* 70–102.

31 Xingliang Chen, "Critical Doctrinal Analysis of Risk Society Theory" (2014) 1 *Peking University Law Review* 103–127.

32 Xingliang Chen, "Critical Doctrinal Analysis of Risk Society Theory" (2014) 1 *Peking University Law Review* 103–127.

33 Yihua Jiang, "The Pursuit of Modernity: Reconstruction of Thoughts in Contemporary China", in Qing Liu & Xiaochun Guan, eds, *Liberalism and Thoughts on the Chinese Modernity: Essays in the Conference of "Transforms of the Chinese Modern Thoughts"* (Hong Kong: The Chinese University Press, 2003) 120; Xiaotian Feng & Xiao Yuan, "Popular Culture and Values of the Chinese Youth, Thirty Years after the Economic Reform", in Kam-yee Law & Yushuo Zheng, eds, *Changed and Unchanged: Thirty Years of Reform in China* (Hong Kong: City University of Hong Kong Press, 2009) 281.

34 Lianwei Nan, "Critical Review and Reflection of the Role of Criminal Law in the Risk Society" (2012) 4 *Chinese Journal of Law* 138–153.

35 Most of them remain descriptive analysis of the theory and normative analysis of the preventive shift.

36 See Huaizhi Chu, *Outline of Criminal Sciences Integration* (Beijing: Peking University Press, 2007).

37 Antony Duff & David Garland, "Introduction: Thinking about Punishment", in Antony Duff & David Garland, eds, *A Reader on Punishment* (Oxford: Oxford University Press, 1995) 43.

38 See Philip Smith, *Punishment and Culture* (Chicago, IL: The University of Chicago Press, 2008); Richard V. Ericson & Aaron Doyle, eds, *Risk and Morality* (Toronto, ON: University of Toronto Press, 2003); Roger Matthews & Jock Young, eds, *New Politics of Crime and Punishment* (Devon, UK: Willan Publishing, 2011); Vanessa Barker, *Politics of Imprisonment: How the Democratic Process Shapes the Way America Punishes Offenders* (Oxford: Oxford University Press, 2009); Les Johnston & Clifford Shearing, *Governing Security: Explorations in Policing and Justice* (London, UK: Routledge, 2003); David Garland, *Punishment and Modern*

Society: A Study in Social Theory (Chicago, IL: The University of Chicago Press, 1993).

39 Lucia Zedner, "Pre-Crime and Pre-Punishment: A Health Warning" (2010) 81 *Criminal Justice Matters* 25.

40 See Lucia Zedner, *Security* (London, UK: Routledge, 2009).

41 Lucia Zedner, "Against Prediction: Profiling, Policing, and Punishing in an Actuarial Age" (2008) 11 *New Criminal Law Review* 359–362.

42 Andrew Ashworth & Lucia Zedner, "Defending the Criminal Law: Reflections on the Changing Character of Crime, Procedure, and Sanctions" (2008) 2 *Criminal Law and Philosophy* 21–51; Lucia Zedner, "Pre-Crime and Pre-Punishment: A Health Warning" (2010) 81 *Criminal Justice Matters* 24–25; Carol S. Steiker, "The Limits of the Preventive State" (1998) 3 *The Journal of Criminal Law and Criminology* 771–808.

43 Andrew Ashworth & Lucia Zedner, "Preventive Orders: A Problem of Under-Criminalization?", in R. A. Duff, ed, *The Boundaries of the Criminal Law* (Oxford: Oxford University Press, 2010) 62; Andrew Ashworth & Lucia Zedner, "Just Prevention: Prevention Rationales and the Limits of the Criminal Law", in R. A. Duff & S. Green, eds, *Philosophical Foundations of Criminal Law* (Oxford: Oxford University Press, 2011) 302.

44 R. A. Duff & Stuart Green, *Philosophical Foundations of Criminal Law* (Oxford: Oxford University Press, 2013); R. A. Duff et al., *The Boundaries of the Criminal Law* (Oxford: Oxford University Press, 2010).

45 See Bernard Harcourt, "The Shaping of Chance: Actuarial Models and Criminal Profiling at the Turn of the Twenty-First Century" (2003) 70 *University of Chicago Law Review* 105–128.

46 See M. Feeley & J. Simon, "Actuarial Justice: The Emerging New Criminal Law", in David Nelken, ed, *The Futures of Criminology* (London: Sage, 1994) 173–201.

47 See Christopher Slobogin, "A Jurisprudence of Dangerousness" (2003) 98 *Northwestern University Law Review* 1–62.

48 Lucia Zedner, *Security* (London, UK: Routledge, 2009).

49 David Garland, *Punishment and Modern Society: A Study in Social Theory* (Chicago, IL: University of Chicago Press, 1993) 8.

50 In the book *Governing Through Crime*, Jonathan Simon argues that crime has become central to the exercise of authority in America. It is a central theme through which all other problems are interpreted, framed and addressed. This "bold" theory is criticized for its exaggeration of the social reality at some points, but he successfully points out the punitive change the US has been experiencing since the 1970s, which not only creates the fear of crime but also intensifies social isolation. See Jonathan Simon, *Governing Through Crime: How the War on Crime Transformed American Democracy and Created a Climate of Fear* (New York: Oxford University Press, 2007).

51 Pat O'Malley, "Neoliberalism and Risk in Criminology", in T. Anthony & C. Cunneen, eds, *The Critical Criminology Companion* (New South Wales: Federation Press, 2008) 55–67.

52 Pat O' Malley, "Risk and Restorative Justice: Governing Through the Democratic Minimization of Harms", in Ivo Aertson, TomDaems & Luc Robert, *The Institutionalization of Restorative Justice* (Portland, OR: Willan Publishing, 2006) 216–236.

53 Stephen A. Webb, "Risk", online: (2006) 4 (2) *Social Work and Society International Online Journal* <http://www.socwork.net/sws/article/view/166/555>.

54 Deborah Lupton, *Risk Key Ideas* (London, UK: Routledge, 1999) 30.

55 Deborah Lupton, *Risk Key Ideas* (London, UK: Routledge, 1999) 30.

56 Deborah Lupton, *Risk Key Ideas* (London, UK: Routledge, 1999) 26.
57 For Keynesian welfarism, risk is regarded as a problem, as a product of pathology or incompleteness. Social engineering can and should be directed to correct these problems and eliminate the risks they generate. Pat O'Malley, "Risk and Responsibility", in Andrew Barry et al., *Foucault and Political Reason: Liberalism, Neo-Liberalism, and Rationalities of Government* (Chicago, IL: University of Chicago Press, 1996) 203. Most risks are regarded as pathologies, and scientifically guided government should eventually eliminate them or neutralize their effects.
58 R. A. Duff & D. Garland, "Introduction: Thinking about Punishment", in R. A. Duff & David Garland, eds, *A Reader on Punishment* (Oxford: Oxford University Press, 1995) 43.
59 David Nelken, "Comparative Criminal Justice, Beyond Ethnocentricism and Relativism" (2009) 6 (4) *European Journal of Criminology* 299. David also argues that, "When it comes to the evaluation of criminal justice practices, whether actors think they are being tolerant or punitive is not the end of the matter. It can make sense in some contexts to describe people as tolerant even if they do not intend to be (and vice versa)." David Nelken, "Comparative Criminal Justice, Beyond Ethnocentricism and Relativism" (2009) 6 (4) *European Journal of Criminology* 308.
60 See Wei Liu, "Trend of the Amendment of Criminal Law and Its Principles" (2011) 5 *Political Science and Law* 95–101.
61 Trevor Jones & Tim Newburn, "Comparative Criminal Justice Policy Making in the United States and the United Kingdom: The Case of Private Prisons" (2005) 45 *British Journal of Criminology* 59.
62 Patricia Cochran, *Common Sense and Legal Judgement: Community Knowledge, Political Power and Rhetorical Practice* (Montreal; Kingston; London; Chicago: McGill-Queen's University Press; 2, 2017) 53.
63 Robert K. Yin, *Case Study Research: Design and Methods* (Los Angeles, CA: Sage Publications, 2013) 20.
64 "The Case Study as a Research Method: Uses and Users of Information -- LIS 391D.1 -- Spring 1997", online: The University of Texas at Austin School of Information <https://www.ischool.utexas.edu/~ssoy/usesusers/l391d1b.htm>.
65 Robert K. Yin, *Case Study Research: Design and Methods* (London, UK: Sage Publications, 2013) 14.
66 R. C. Bogdan & S. K. Biklen, *Qualitative Research for Education: An Introduction to Theories and Methods*, 4th ed. (New York: Pearson, 1998) 54.
67 Bruce L. Berg, *Qualitative Research Methods for the Social Sciences* (New York: Pearson, 2008) 325.
68 P. Baxter & Susan Jack, "Qualitative Case Study Methodology: Study Design and Implementation for Novice Researchers" (2008) 13 (4) *The Qualitative Report* 544.
69 "The Case Study as a Research Method: Uses and Users of Information -- LIS 391D.1 -- Spring 1997", online: The University of Texas at Austin School of Information <https://www.ischool.utexas.edu/~ssoy/usesusers/l391d1b.htm>.
70 See Robert K. Yin, *Case Study Research: Design and Methods* (Thousand Oaks: Sage Publications, 2013).
71 Robert K. Yin, "A (Very) Brief Refresher on the Case Study Method", in Robert K. Yin, *Applications of Case Study Research* (Los Angeles, CA: Sage Publications, 2008) 10.
72 "The Case Study as a Research Method: Uses and Users of Information -- LIS 391D.1 -- Spring 1997", online: The University of Texas at Austin School of Information <https://www.ischool.utexas.edu/~ssoy/usesusers/l391d1b.htm>

73 Robert K. Yin, "A (Very) Brief Refresher on the Case Study Method", in Robert K. Yin, ed, *Applications of Case Study Research* (Los Angeles, CA: Sage Publications, 2008) 10.
74 Resorting to the personal experience of the researcher is common in social research. "They (practitioners) may draw on experience gained from practice or from their life in general ... the experienced practitioner is liable, therefore, to draw upon those three areas—formal knowledge, specifically social research, practice experience, and life experience—to provide them with guidance in relation to any particular practice issue or problem." Michael Sheppard, *Appraising and Using Social Research in the Human Services: An Introduction for Social Work and Health Professionals* (London: Jessica Kingsley Publishers, 2004) 28. However, at the same time, the researcher has to try to be objective, and manage to collect as much information as possible to support the arguments.
75 Michael Sheppard, *Appraising and Using Social Research in the Human Services: An Introduction for Social Work and Health Professionals* (London: Jessica Kingsley Pub, 2004) 28.
76 Michael Cohen et al., "A Garbage Can Model of Organizational Choice" (1972) 17 (1) *Administrative Science Quarterly* 1–15.
77 Paul Cairney, "Policy Concepts in 1000 Words: Multiple Streams Analysis", online: Paul Cairney: Politics & Public Policies <https://paulcairney.wordpress.com/2013/10/31/policy-concepts-in-1000-words-multiple-streams-analysis/>.
78 Zeimut Zohlnhofer & Friedbert Rub, "Forum Section: Theoretically Refining the Multiple Streams Framework" (2015) 54 *European Journal of Political Research* 412.
79 MSA is a revision of the "Garbage Can Model" developed by Michael Cohen, James March and Johan Olsen. See Michael D. Cohen et al., "A Garbage Can Model of Organizational Choice" (1972) 17 (01) *Administrative Science Quarterly* 1–25.
80 Nikolaos Zahariadis, "Ambiguity and Multiple Streams", in Paul A. Sabatier & Christopher M. Weible, eds, *Theories of the Policy Process*, 3rd ed. (Boulder, CO: Westview Press, 2014) 26.
81 Ian H. Rowlands, "The Development of Renewable Electricity Policy in the Province of Ontario: The Influence of Ideas and Timing" (2007) 24 (3) *Review of Policy Research* 185–207.
82 M. V. Simon & L. R. Alm, "Policy Windows and Two-Level Games: Explaining the Passage of Acid-Rain Legislation in the Clean Air Act of 1990" (1995) 13 (4) *Environment and Planning C: Government and Policy* 459–478.
83 Sabine Storch & Georg Winkel, "Coupling Climate Change and Forest Policy: A Multiple Streams Analysis of Two German Case Studies" (2013) 36 *Forest Policy and Economics* 14–26.
84 Jessica E. Boscarino, "Surfing for Problems: Advocacy Group Strategy in US Forestry Policy" (2009) 37 (3) *Policy Studies Journal* 415–434.
85 Michael K. Mclendon, "Setting the Governmental Agenda for State Decentralization of Higher Education" (2003) 74 (5) *Journal of Higher Education* 479–515.
86 Nikolaos Zahariadis, "Selling British Rail: An Idea Whose Time Has Come?" (1996) 29 (4) *Comparative Political Studies* 400–422.
87 Daniel Beland, "Gender, Ideational Analysis and Social Policy" (2009) 16 (4) *Social Politics* 558–581.
88 R. Travis & N. Zahariadis, "A Multiple Streams Model of US Foreign Aid Policy" (2002) 30 (4) *Policy Studies Journal* 495–514.

89 Zeimut Zohlnhofer & Friedbert Rub, "Forum Section: Theoretically Refining the Multiple Streams Framework" (2015) 54 *European Journal of Political Research* 414.
90 N. Herweg, "Straightening the Three Streams: Theorizing Extensions of the Multiple Streams Framework" (2015) 54 (3) *European Journal of Political Research* 436.
91 Zeimut Zohlnhofer & Friedbert Rub, "Forum Section: Theoretically Refining the Multiple Streams Framework" (2015) 54 *European Journal of Political Research* 414.
92 Paul Cairney, "Policy Concepts in 1000 Words: Multiple Streams Analysis", online: Paul Cairney: Politics & Public Policies <https://paulcairney.wordpress.com/2013/10/31/policy-concepts-in-1000-words-multiple-streams-analysis/>.
93 Nikolaos Zahariadis, "Ambiguity and Multiple Streams", in Paul A. Sabatier & Christopher M. Weible, *Theories of the Policy Process*, 3rd ed. (Boulder, CO: Westview Press, 2014) 30.
94 Neil J. Diamant, Stanely B. Lubman & Kevin J. O'Brien, eds, "Law and Society in the People's Republic of China", in Neil J. Diamant et al., *Engaging the Law in China: State, Society and Possibilities for Justice* (Stanford, CA: Stanford University Press, 2005) 16–17.
95 Nikolaos Zahariadis, "Ambiguity and Multiple Streams", in Sabatier Paul A. & Weible Christopher M., *Theories of the Policy Process*, 3rd ed. (Boulder, CO: Westview Press, 2014) 30.
96 John W. Kingdon, *Agendas, Alternatives and Public Policies, Update Edition, with an Epilogue on Health Care*, 2nd ed. (New York: Pearson, 2010) 162.
97 John W. Kingdon, *Agendas, Alternatives and Public Policies, Update Edition, with an Epilogue on Health Care*, 2nd ed. (New York: Pearson, 2010) 203.

2 Reforms in Chinese criminal law and their implications

This chapter argues that there are tensions between these revisions and the basic principles of criminal law. The preventive shift raises concerns about the challenges posed by "prevention" to the dominance of "just desserts" as the central rationale in penal theory. Because criminalization entails the imposition of public censure and the infliction of the pains of punishment, it requires stronger justification. But in practice it is difficult to impose normative restraints on the expansive criminal law. It is also difficult to conceptualize "security." Restraints on the Chinese style of preventive justice remain weak.

Based on the eighth amendment of Chinese criminal law, the second chapter of this book will document reforms to the statutes of the law in order to lay the foundation for the book as a whole. Through a comparison between the Chinese and Western preventive models of the criminal justice system, the first section examines the reasons the book uses the three legislative changes as case studies. Then the second section analyzes these three changes in detail by highlighting their characteristics as preventive shifts. The third section argues that solely relying on the risk society theory as the analytical framework for the preventive shift of Chinese criminal law is not enough. This book aims to fill the resulting gap.

2.1 Conceptualization of "crime prevention"

2.1.1 Crime prevention in the Chinese context

In China, the concept of "prevention" can be analyzed with diverse analytical frameworks, relying on what it refers to in each circumstance: first, prevention has a similar utilitarian function as "deterrence"[1]: aiming to prevent offenders or potential offenders from committing crimes in the future. Crime prevention justifies the expansion of the whole Chinese criminal justice system. Since the 2000s, there has not only been continuous criminalization of new behavior in the law, but also increased policing input in crime prevention and security governance (such as the relentless war against deviance and crime), as well as widespread use of surveillance technology all over the country.[2]

As rationales for criminal penalties—and in parallel with retribution, deterrence and rehabilitation—"prevention" refers to the exertion of criminal penalties without actual harm being committed, such as inchoate crimes which include attempt, conspiracy and incitement. In Western scholarship, Andrew Ashworth and Lucia Zedner identify seven preventive offences in which prevention is the primary rationale for the criminalization, including inchoate crimes, preparatory or pre-inchoate offences, crimes of membership and crimes of endangerment.[3] At present in China, inchoate crimes are routinely criminalized. Articles 22–24 and 25–29 of the criminal law (as general rules applied to all offences) have detailed provisions of inchoate crimes of attempt, conspiracy and solicitation.

Besides existing as a justification for substantial criminal law, "prevention" can also serve as a rationale of criminal procedure, which implies intense policing and broader surveillance management. The Ministry of Public Security, the Ministry of State Security and private security forces keep strict surveillance of the society both openly and secretly. In the amended Criminal Procedure Law in 2011 and 2018, although much progress has been made to restrain police authority, police power keeps extending its surveillance and investigation of serious crimes such as terrorism, crimes against state security and crimes endangering social order, the definitions of which remain quite blurred.[4] On terrorist crimes and certain offences against public or state security, the amendments of criminal procedure law also developed special restrictive provisions, criticized by lawyers and foreign commentators as "secret detention."[5] The expansion is also shown in the penal system, where the number of prisoners incarcerated and that of convicted offenders are on the rise every year.[6]

But changes to Chinese criminal law are not simply limited to those discussed above. There are three techniques in the eighth amendment of Chinese criminal law to make criminalization even more preventive on crimes of drunk driving, manufacturing and selling fake medications and environmental pollution. The three change categories are signs of the law's preventive move in the Chinese punitive criminal justice system. "Prevention" refers to the techniques justified by controlling conduct risk for the prevention of future harm, rather than punishing existing harm. The shifting focus from harmful results to risky behavior is a signal that criminal law itself is moving even further from the emphasis on harmful wrongdoing. Compared to the concept of "just desserts," the law is increasingly moralized through the need for risk control.

Therefore, on one hand, in the Chinese context, fighting serious crimes (a long-lasting focus of Chinese criminal justice), like terrorist activities, is a factor that keeps promoting changes to the legal system. On the other hand, there are minor offences that violate public well-being as well, like driving infractions, fake medications and environmental pollution. These social problems that emerge in modernization have been attracting attention and debate. The proactive techniques of Chinese law reflect the Chinese legislative pattern and social conditions.

Indeed, over the past ten years, a number of countries such as the US, the UK and Australia have also witnessed a preventive turn in criminal justice.[7] Though Western penal practices have divergences among them, they nonetheless share an overall developing trend.[8] Treating the West as a whole,[9] the next part of this section will analyze the distinctions between the Chinese and the Western models, with the aim of shedding light on the Chinese characteristics of the preventive shift.

2.1.2 Crime prevention in the Western context

In the West, the concept of crime prevention is not clear. Under the umbrella of "crime prevention" there is a set of theories and practices ranging from criminal law statute transformations and new policing approaches, to the emergence of atypical penalties such as preventive orders and civil commitments. "Crime prevention" can be conceptualized in at least two dimensions. Used in a utilitarian perspective, "all correctional ideologies can be legitimized by the rhetoric of prevention,"[10] and constitute key parts of the expansion of the state apparatus. The rise in crime prevention refers to the expansion of the coercive state through the criminal justice and policing systems, which also comprise approaches of situational crime control, multi-agency cooperation and community participation programs. While in another perspective, preventive methods tend to govern the future through criminalizing "risk," rather than imposing punishment on existing harmful wrongdoing, which implies the use of restrictive methods on risky behavior based on recidivism, mental illness or summary offences. Preventive methods themselves are also subject to various interpretations. They are not limited to terrorist offences, encompassing a broad range of social policies and regulatory endeavors, such as the proliferation of preventive offences like inchoate crimes, civil preventive orders, the courts' preventive role, preventive detention of dangerousness and preventive counter-terrorism laws.[11]

These dimensions of the prevention concept overlap on some occasions; they are essentially "in stark contrast to the traditional retrospective orientation of the criminal justice system"[12] but, at times, will be discussed separately by researchers who each have a distinctive focus. For instance, in the US, changes to criminal justice focus mostly on criminal conduct associated with terrorism and violent crimes. First, the Model Penal Code penalizes a person who "recklessly engages in conduct which places or may place another person in danger of death or serious bodily injury."[13] Because reckless endangerment under this provision could be based on any act or failure to act that creates the requisite danger, these statutes are routinely upheld by the courts against challenges of ambiguity.[14] Second, since 2000, anti-terrorism laws have tremendously extended state power. The USA Patriot Act of 2001 as well as its Extension Act of 2011 gave the FBI much more discretion in terms of search and surveillance, even without a court order.[15] The provisions have generated a great deal of controversy about the Act's constitutionality since they may abuse the privacy of not only the suspects but also of innocent people.[16] Third, in the US there is civil detention of sexual crime offenders as well as prolonged detention/continued supervision of criminals with risky personalities. For instance, the Supreme Court in Kansas v. Hendricks (1997) and Kansas v. Crane (2002) upheld sexually violent predator statutes that provided for the post-imprisonment civil commitment of sex offenders who have a "mental abnormality" (but not a major mental disorder such as schizophrenia) which results in their becoming "likely to engage in repeat acts of sexual violence."[17] Fourth, the US has also enacted preventive orders to restrict gang-related activity, particularly violent crimes and drug trafficking. A case in point is that, in 2011, the city of Chicago revised the Chicago Municipal Code 8-4-015 (1992) to make anti-loitering laws constitutional.[18]

In the UK, besides concerns over public security, the state aims to crack down more on minor crimes and anti-social behavior. The preventive shift is most evidently shown in a series of preventive orders—including Anti-Social Behaviour Orders, control orders (which have been repealed), sexual offence prevention orders and serious crime prevention orders—which were enacted to control minor behavior for the prevention of more serious crimes such as terrorist acts and sex crimes. Freed from the restraints of criminal procedure law, these civil orders allow the government to "avoid the rigorous procedural protections of the criminal law and perhaps eventually replace criminal justice altogether."[19] The pre-trial detention and investigative stops by police often—or always—depend upon dangerousness assessments as well.[20] There are also cases of the expansion of inchoate and anticipatory offenses, as well as preventive detention of mentally disordered persons, all of which constitute the so-called "preventive justice," manifesting how the state governs and the nature of criminal justice in the United Kingdom.[21]

UK and US practices have had enormous influence on other Western countries.[22] In more and more countries all over the world, the prediction of dangerousness and the attempt to preempt future harm through deterrence, rehabilitation and incapacitation are becoming well-established pillars of punishment. A great variety of crimes are based on the prediction of harm, even without the proof of any harm. For instance, Australia has witnessed the pervasion of the term "prevention" in its anti-terror policy[23] as it introduced control orders into its legal system.[24] Other commonwealth countries also added new penalties for crimes of solicitation and crimes of conspiracy.[25] In civil law countries like Germany, the legal system has not only attached increased importance to environmental interests, but also added new endangerment crimes and offences of weapon possession, as well as inchoate and conspiracy actions of terrorism crimes.[26]

Western experience shows that the fight against terrorism is one of the main driving forces of the preventive shift in its criminal justice system. But in addition to anti-terrorism laws, each country also has its own features. For instance, the US demonstrates the most intense control of terrorist behavior, while the UK focuses more on minor offences. In China, the expansion of crime prevention can be addressed in a variety of dimensions. Similar to that of the West is the expansion of the overall system and the increase in preparatory offences to commit terrorist attacks.[27] Differences lie in the control of political risk and criminal law amendments as indications of the proactive trend of punitive law on crimes against public well-being. For instance, the three legislative changes to criminal penalties on minor misbehavior in the eighth amendment of Chinese criminal law—having been officially written in criminal law—represent the largest number of such proactive legislative changes. Anti-terrorism laws are mostly decided by the deciding bodies themselves, while these three changes illustrate more of the interplay between the public and the state, the law and the policy. Accordingly, this book will use these three changes as case studies, with the other reforms as supporting evidence. Preventive techniques can be understood in the context of a broader transformation of governance and society. "Crime is not only about the imposition of actual criminal sanctions but is also descriptive of situations in which crime provides the metaphors and narratives in which efforts to govern are cast."[28] It is "a mechanism for viewing the institutions, practices and personnel of government."[29]

2.2 Three case studies: Based on the 2011 eighth amendment of criminal law

In China, enacting the Criminal Law Amendment Act as the major method of revising criminal law was designed to meet the needs of a rapidly developing society while maintaining the stability and predictability of the law. It is also one of the signs of progress in China's criminal justice system. After the 1997 Criminal Law replaced the 1979 Criminal Law, the Chinese state made eight amendments up until 2011. In 2011, the eighth amendment, which is acknowledged as the most important amendment by a number of commentators, came into force with 50 provisions that changed the penalties for a variety of crimes that endanger public security, economic order and property rights.[30] It is difficult to use one term to categorize the changes since the changes reflect multiple pursuits. The abolishment of 13 capital punishments (for the first time in Chinese history) was recognized as showing respect for liberal values.[31] New community correction practices have also been introduced to address minor crimes or offenders ascribed with less responsibility, such as juveniles. Compared to former amendments, these changes reflect the progress in Chinese law towards more lenient and diversified penalties,[32] while at the same time, the boundary of criminal law has been continuously expanded to criminalize new conduct, especially those acts closely associated with public well-being (the livelihood of the people).[33] Penalties for violent crimes—such as terrorist attacks, gang crimes, crimes against state security and their associated minor offences—have been increasing over time. In criminalization, three changes manifest a preventive trend of crime control. This section will identify these changes and examine their similarities.

2.2.1 Three offences in Chinese criminal law

2.2.1.1 Crime of drunk driving

The first of the changes establishes impaired driving as a crime. Impaired driving is an offence in many countries like the US, the UK and Canada.[34] In China, drunk driving or speeding without causing an accident was punished with administrative penalties.[35] However, with the eighth amendment of criminal law in 2011 it became a criminal offence against public security.[36] Making the shift from an administrative offence to a criminal offence is a crucial transformation in China's legal system. Only offences that seriously violate the public interest are "crimes."

The imposition of public censure as well as the deprivation of liberty by criminal law is much more intense than the other punishments. Furthermore, due to the Chinese drinking culture, drunk driving, which was assumed to be a minor problem, is commonly regarded as a non-criminal offence in the public mind.[37] The Chinese people are apt to worry about the expansion of state power if such endangerment behavior continues to be criminalized in the future.

In the jurisprudence of criminal law, drunk driving is preventive for several reasons. First, drunk driving is an endangerment crime that criminalizes the creation of an unacceptable risk of harm.[38] "The driving is not itself harmful, and need not be directed toward increasing the risk of injury to others; it is criminalized primarily because it does increase that risk."[39] The primary purpose of establishing this as a crime is to prevent road accidents (the potential result of drunk driving); however, there is yet no established harm result for the crime itself. Though "modern criminal law is characterized by 'bringing forward of criminal law in the sphere of endangerment',"[40] it is new in Chinese criminal law.

Second, this kind of "negligence/recklessness + risk" combination, which is distinct from the "negligence/recklessness + harm" model, applies more restrictions on the freedom of ordinary people. An offender is found guilty as a person with common consciousness who, even though without intent, leaves others at excess risk in road safety. The risks have become so grave that criminal law can no longer tolerate them.

Third, without "harm" as the defining rule, assessing risk must rely more on actuarial techniques. For instance, according to the Law on Road Traffic Safety, driving with an alcohol content in the blood that is 20–80 mg/100 ml is "driving after drinking," while that exceeding 80 mg/100 ml is "drunk driving." The judges also have to consider other circumstances such as the time and the place where the offences were committed to assess whether the conduct posed a risk to the public. Based on Article 13 of Chinese criminal law, "an act that is clearly of minor importance and little harm shall not be considered a crime"; if it is impossible for the conduct to generate any injury or property loss, then it is not a crime.

Before the enactment of the eighth amendment, it was the Road Traffic Safety Law of the People's Republic of China and other associated regulations that penalized drunk driving without causing road accidents. Article 88 of the law establishes several administrative penalties such as warnings, fines, suspending or withholding the driver's license, or taking the driver into custody. Regulation on the implementation of the law specifies the details of carrying out the penalties. However, since 2003, officials report that cases of drunk driving and speeding have separately exceeded 19 and 1 million per year nationwide, and the public's awareness is growing.[41] Since 2009, with the rising number of drunk-driving infractions and a series of notable cases that produced fatal accidents, some local courts found the offenders guilty of "crimes against public security through other dangerous means," since under such circumstances they could be charged with detentions of more than ten years rather than less than seven years.[42] At the same time, both internet comments and journal papers began to argue that existing administrative penalties for the offences were not compatible with the risks they actually generated, and demanded harsher punishments to prevent potential injuries.[43] Under these circumstances, in order to prevent drunk driving more effectively under the amendment in 2011 (and besides the existing "traffic offence causing bodily harm or property damage") a second provision was added to Article 133 as an offence of "dangerous driving"; that is, "A person who chases with other automobiles when driving on the road or commits drunk-driving shall be sentenced to criminal detention from one to six months and be concurrently given a fine, provided that the circumstances are grave."[44] The crime of drunk driving fills the gap in the former system that maintained the harm result as one requirement of committing a crime. With the crime of drunk driving, current traffic offences consist of the offence of drunk driving, traffic offences causing inquiry or property damage and using drunk driving conduct as the means to endanger public security. In this way, Chinese criminal law regulates road safety more efficiently by criminalizing drunk driving, both with and without road accidents, and with intention, negligence or recklessness.[45]

It may be suggested that drunk driving criminalization is a common practice all over the world. For instance, Canadian driving offences include Drive Disqualified, Dangerous Driving (no injury), Dangerous Driving (injury occurs), Driving or Care or Control while Impaired or Over 80 mgs, Impaired Driving Causing Bodily Harm and Impaired Driving Causing Death. In the UK, the Highway Code sets penalties for a variety of offences, such as causing death by dangerous driving, dangerous driving, careless and inconsiderate driving, driving while disqualified, speeding and traffic light offences. Other countries or districts, including Japan, Germany, Korea, Finland and Hong Kong, also have corresponding penalties for drunk driving.[46] While it may be true that drunk driving is common, this cannot be an argument for the crime of drunk driving not being preventive in the Chinese context. The concern lies in the shift from an administrative penalty to a criminal penalty in China, rather than having a penalty or not. In addition, as the first endangerment crime in criminal law, it is a sign that creating risk without a purpose (which is distinct from traditional models focusing on either guilty intention or harm) can be criminalized as well.

2.2.1.2 Crime of manufacturing and selling fake medications

Another example of this shift in criminal law is found in the changes concerning manufacturing and selling fake medications. Before the eighth amendment, Article 141 of the criminal law stipulated that those

> Manufacturing or selling fake medications, which is serious enough to endanger public health, shall be sentenced to imprisonment of less than 3 years or criminal detention, and be given a fine with 50% to twice amount of gross sales concurrently or un-concurrently.

This offence was one of the "crimes with risks."[47] The *mens rea* of manufacturing and selling fake medications was intention, but for the endangerment of public health it was negligence/recklessness. Controversy ignited over the meaning of "serious enough to endanger public security." It was debated whether simply manufacturing or selling fake medications without generating income constituted an offence. It was also uncertain whether manufacturing or selling fake medications but without producing bodily harm constituted committing this crime.[48] In 2009, the Supreme Court and the Supreme People's Procuratorate made a judicial interpretation using five examples of "seriousness" for local courts to follow.

The eighth amendment avoids the above controversy by eliminating the condition "serious enough to endanger public security," and changing the offence to "whoever manufactures or sells fake medications shall be sentenced to imprisonment of less than 3 years, or criminal detention, and be concurrently given a fine." This is a shift from the offence of concrete endangerment (which presupposes the causation of danger or harm) to abstract endangerment (which presupposes that the conduct at least typically causes danger).[49] Since the amendment presumes the risk of the behavior itself, judges no longer have to evaluate the seriousness of the risks like they did before. Rather, the act becomes one of the offences that are charged through behavior identification without risk assessment, which makes criminal trials easier.[50] At the same time, by removing the condition (serious enough to endanger public security) that was used to restrain the scope of this offence, the boundary of criminal law is accordingly expanded to behavior producing minor risks. The significance of the changes lies in the shift from "crime with risks" to preventive crimes; it is not compulsory to identify precise wrongful harm or risk in the offense.[51]

2.2.1.3 Crime of environmental pollution

The third case in the amendment is the crime of discharging, dumping or disposing radioactive waste, waste containing pathogens of infectious diseases= or toxic substances. Before the eighth amendment, Article 338 of Chinese criminal law stated

> whoever, in violation of the regulations of the state, discharges, dumps or treats radioactive waste, waste containing pathogens of infectious diseases, toxic substances or other hazardous waste on the land or in the water bodies or the atmosphere, thus causing a major environmental pollution accident which leads to the serious consequences of heavy losses of public or private property or human casualties, shall be sentenced to fixed-term imprisonment of no more than three years, and be concurrently or separately fined. If the result is extremely serious, he/she shall be sentenced to fixed-term imprisonment of three to seven years and be concurrently fined.[52]

The *mens rea* of this offence is intentionally violating the state regulation by discharging, dumping or treating dangerous waste; however, it was uncertain whether the mental state involved in causing an accident was negligence or recklessness.[53] Many scholars claimed that it was an offence of negligence; otherwise, causing environmental accidents on purpose was an offence against public security.[54]

The eighth amendment of Chinese criminal law made essential changes to this environmental crime by eliminating the "result" of "a major environmental pollution accident," the key component of the offense, and replacing it with "seriously polluting the environment." It is preventive since the focus on risk has started to replace results of harm. The name of the offence was changed accordingly from "crime causing major environmental accident" into "crime of environmental pollution." Eliminating the "results" of serious environmental accidents means that lawmakers believe it is too late to take action once an accident happens. Criminalizing behavior causing minor harm or risk will prevent more accidents from happening. However, it is not an overall transformation from result-oriented to behavior-oriented, since according to judicial interpretation this offence is a balance of harmful results with risky behavior. In 2003, the Supreme People's Court and Procuratorate jointly issued a judicial interpretation with precise criteria for convictions and sentences to make the amendment more enforceable, from which 14 rules were developed based on the concept of "seriously polluting the environment."[55] In the 14 rules, less than one-half focus on dumping waste of more than three tons, or discharging waste to Grade 1 areas of water supply or natural reserves. The rest (more than one-half) are characterized as bodily injury or property loss. However, compared to the old statute, the number of behaviors that do not cause harm has still increased as the sole elements of committing the crime.[56] This shift from the post hoc responses with a "harm done" perspective, to a more proactive focus on "harm prevention," expands the boundary of criminal law even further.

2.2.2 Similarities among the changes

The currently used criminal law in China is the 1997 Criminal Law, which replaced the 1979 Chinese Criminal Law to meet the needs of rapid social and economic developments. The 1997 Criminal Law made several breakthroughs at that time, including introducing new offences, removing old ones and establishing new fundamental principles of the law, as stipulated in Articles 3–5. After that, China enacted seven amendments to the 1997 Criminal Law, before the eighth amendment, in 1999, 2001, 2002, 2005, 2006 and 2009 with around 70 articles.[57] At present, Chinese criminal law has 11 amendments in total. The 1997 Criminal Law adheres to the post hoc nature of criminal law, with limited exceptions.

The 1997 Criminal Law, just like the criminal law of most other countries, aims to punish behaviors that have caused harm or substantial threats to society. Criminal law mainly focuses on behaviors with unacceptable harm. For instance, in crimes such as murder, kidnapping, robbery and economic crimes, the results are measurable, and the causations are easy to detect. It is justified to apply proportionate punishments to the offenders for the sake of distributive and deterrent effects. In contrast, in Chinese criminal law, offences without real harmful results include inchoate crimes, possession crimes, crimes of membership, etc. Such behaviors are usually criminalized when associated with crimes of grievous harm, like organized crimes, gang crimes, drug crimes, etc. Most of them are crimes against public security and order. The exceptional risks they generate subject them to criminal penalties. But the number of these offences is quite limited, due to the difficulties of risk assessment and the boundary of criminal law.

It is hard to calculate the ratio of crimes based on harm to those based on risk among all the offences in the Chinese criminal law. But criminal punishments are the harshest penalties in China. Considering the last-resort nature of criminal law, offences of a preventive nature are commonly kept within a relatively small scope.

Compared with existing offences in Chinese criminal law, the three cases above share at least four common features. First of all, the element of "harm" has become increasingly less important. With the rising number of crimes that create risks, criminal law intervenes proactively to control behavior before harm is done. The role of "harm" as a core justification of criminal penalties is collapsing. For example, in offences of drunk driving, manufacturing or selling fake medication and discharging, dumping or disposing of waste, it is now unnecessary for the offender to cause criminal results (that is, traffic, drug or environmental accidents). The behavior constituting the offence exists as the primary justification of a criminal penalty. By penalizing risk to prevent potential harm, such offences diverge from the traditional paradigm of "harm plus culpability." It may also be argued that such conduct causes "social harm" by damaging social order or hurting public feelings of security, but in this case, an over-extension of the concept of "harm" may violate legal certainty through its ambiguity and thus infringe upon the fundamental spirit of criminal law.

Second, the scope of legally protected interests is expanding.[58] Legally protected interests are mainly materialized benefits including the physical integrity of the body and the value of property. However, at present "these interests are becoming 'magic words' whose conceptions are more and more blurred,"[59] including conceptions that are commonly claimed by officials as objectives of their policies, such as the security of society, the peace of the community or even the well-being of future generations without concrete victims or losses.[60] On the one hand, the general words are subject to a wide range of interpretations. Some of them are even subjective "feelings," violations of which ought not to be criminalized. On the other hand, compared to other crimes, the distance between protected interests and the offences are much further apart, and the "cause result" relationships are more indirect. In the case of drunk driving, fake medications and dumping waste, Chinese criminal law has started to punish behavior that remains far from real and concrete harm.

Third, criminal behavior turns into the main focus for these criminal penalties. By criminalizing "risk" rather than "harm," criminal behavior replaces criminal results as the criterion for substantial crime. Not only has the number of conduct crimes increased in Chinese criminal law, but in existing conduct crimes some requirements have shifted from risk assessment to behavior identification, making it easier for prosecutors to charge offenders. The boundary of criminal law is accordingly expanded by penalizing the rising number of behaviors that are with or without minor "harm" results. In this aspect, it is justified for the Supreme People's Court and the Procuratorate to work out judicial interpretations of the law on ambiguous concepts, such as the criteria of the amendments, to assess how much risk the criminal behavior produces.

Fourth, the *mens rea* of these offences with respect to causing risk is either recklessness or negligence. It involves the pursuit of a course of action while consciously disregarding the fact that the action gives rise to a substantial and unjustifiable risk, or failing to exercise the care that a common prudent person should exercise in like circumstances. In Chinese criminal law, there is no concept of recklessness. In the US, the Model Penal Code sets out five different modes of culpability: negligently, recklessly, knowingly, purposely and strict liability. "Recklessly" is a level of *mens rea* that is similar to oblique intention and negligence with overconfidence in the Chinese legal system. Different from direct intention, both recklessness and negligence require some degree of objective testing to establish the minimum requirements of foresight. The greater the risks that exist, or the more they can mature into a foreseen injury, the greater the degree of blameworthiness, and subsequently, the greater the sentence rendered. In this way, the mental states of recklessness and negligence demand individuals to be more cautious of risks, for the protection of public safety.

Such a shift raises concerns about the challenges posed by "prevention" to the dominance of "just desserts" as the central rationale in penal theory. Adhering to just desserts is a basic principle of Chinese criminal law. Article 5 of Chinese criminal law stipulates that "The degree of punishment shall be commensurate with the crime committed and the criminal responsibility to be borne by the offender."

> Whereas uncertainty once spoke of incalculability, of an unknown future impossible therefore to control or of a lack evidence sufficient for prosecution for criminal offences, it has now become a developed set of discourses and techniques through which state action is both warranted and required.[61]

Preventive measures not only penalize risks, but also censor risk creators with a negligent or reckless mindset. The utilitarian characteristic is much more explicit, particularly when it is employed for the pursuit of public security. Considering that "just desserts" remains a central justification of criminal law in China, the risks that criminal law prevents must be grave enough. "Unless the individual engages in conduct that causes legally-defined harm or that is otherwise obviously risky, the government should not be permitted to intervene preventively."[62] The further the system travels from the paradigm of the "harm plus culpability" model of criminal offences, the stronger the justifications should be for invoking criminal law with its censures and punishments.[63] This is the legitimate line beyond which preventive methods cannot step.

2.2.3 Weak constraints of the law

In practice it is difficult to impose normative restraints on the expansive criminal law. The foremost issue is whether the offences are defined in broader terms that criminalize a wide range of activities remote from actual harm and "stretching their predictive capacity beyond safe reliance."[64] While it is quite proper for criminal law to punish risky behavior, there should be a boundary within which the restriction is both justified and effective. To be justified commonly means that the restriction adheres to the fundamental principles of criminal law.[65] In order to be proportionate to the seriousness of the wrong involved, and as the last resort when civil, administrative and other regulatory measures have failed, "the more remote an offense becomes from the actual infliction of harm, the higher the degree of fault necessary to justify criminalization."[66] To be effective means it is capable of meeting the demands of the retributive and deterrent effects it seeks, which is the common primary reason for criminalization. Working well in doctrinal analysis, both of these two criteria are complex when tested in actual practice. On the one hand, ambiguous principles coupled with the prevention function are open to the interpretations of legislators and judges in deciding how significant the risk of serious harm is, whether other means will be ineffective and which kind of sanctions are appropriate. On the other hand, it is difficult to assess the long-term effects of criminal sanctions. Most of the public believes in the positive correlation between an increase of criminal penalties and their deterrent effects. In legislation concerning crimes against public safety (or security), support for efficient prevention measures will prohibit an accurate calculation and rational response to unknowable and incalculable risks.

It is also difficult to conceptualize "security." Conflict between the pursuit of public security and human rights is the deciding factor for the rationales of preventive methods. The number of revisions on crimes endangering economic order was the greatest in Chinese criminal law amendments from 1999 to 2011.[67] This reflects the development of Chinese crime rates, where crimes compromising economic order contribute most to their growth, while rates of traditional crimes as homicide, injury and rape have not changed substantially in the past 20 years. However, criminal law has always been associated with the pursuit of security. Besides adding new offences, the law continues to increase the harshness of criminal penalties for traditional serious crimes. There are wars to ensure road, food and drug security every year. In the Chinese context, "feelings of insecurity may encapsulate a much larger set of concerns, coalescing perhaps around security of the environment, of health, employment, and the economy."[68] Personal safety concerns make the public much more sensitive to road accidents, food and drug scandals exposed by the media, and the expanding internet. This sensitivity may eventually have an impact on laws and state policies. However, the rising focus on security does not parallel a clear understanding of the concept. The concept of "security" is subject to expansive interpretation and application. The concept's boundaries become even broader when "safety" and "security" refer to the same Chinese character.[69] Furthermore, "the effect of applying the label security is to foreclose debate, to legitimize emergency powers and thus to depoliticize questions of social and political power."[70] Thus, it is commonly insisted that "security" should be used very cautiously and with solid evidence. It ought to be balanced against liberty, freedom and justice to have its proper place.[71] Meanwhile, in countries such as the United States, Canada, Germany and South Africa, those safeguards have constitutional guarantees. In other countries, such as the United Kingdom and several other European jurisdictions, the rights are reinforced by protection from the European Convention on Human Rights (ECHR).[72] In China, such restraints remain weak.

In all, highlighting key words such as "risk," "conduct" and "recklessness/negligence," these changes are signs that Chinese criminal law has become increasingly preventive, characterized as a special proactive technique of criminal law for intense regulation of misbehavior for the better pursuit of public safety. Compared to criminal behavior resulting in harm, such risky behavior is of minor seriousness to society. Compared to behavior with the intention of harm, a reckless or negligent mindset is less condemned as well. In Chinese criminal law, inchoate crimes and weapon possession crimes punish behaviors that simply cause risks. The above changes in the amendment are preventive shifts of the statues. But in China preventive techniques are never limited to those in the law. As has been claimed, there are other initiatives in criminal procedures and policing that can be characterized as preventive methods. In the West, crime prevention is intertwined with risk discourse and is not only based on the degree to which the methods reflect the pursuit of risk control, but also on how risk discourse in the changed social environment shapes the pattern of crime prevention.[73] In China, current changes are subject to the legislation politic among different participants with distinctive risk awareness, and this sheds light on society's power relationships in the long journey of socialist modernization.

2.3 Analytical framework of risk society and its limitations

As has been addressed, Chinese scholars who recognized the preventive shift in Chinese criminal law interpreted the legislative changes through the risk society theory (mainly Ulrich Beck's theory) almost seven years ago.[74] Until now the whole debate has been carried out within this framework. The debate is mainly about whether it is appropriate to apply this theory in the Chinese context, whether Chinese criminal law is transforming into a "risk-oriented" tool and how to cope with associated challenges of the basic principles of criminal law and human rights protection. The eighth amendment is also assessed using this approach.

In this discussion, Chinese researchers introduce the risk society theory as a theoretical framework to analyze the proactive shift, with the eighth amendment as one of the main pieces of evidence for their arguments.[75] Not only do they employ it to theorize the Chinese reforms, but also those of developed countries like Germany and Japan. Supporters such as Dongyan Lao claim that it is the coming of the risk society—characterized as a rising number of road accidents, drug accidents, environmental accidents, violent crimes and acts of terrorism—that enhances the role of risk control in criminal law.[76] The link between the risk society and changes to criminal law is "security," although in the Chinese context, the link may be referred to as either "safety" or "security."[77] It seems that growing demands for security due to rising risk awareness that the risk society theory advocates has successfully interpreted current public sentiments of the Chinese society. This has made the theory increasingly popular not only in the field of criminal justice but also in research in other legal fields.[78] Opponents like Xingliang Chen insist that it is essential to draw a distinction between the "risks" in the risk society theory and "risks" that criminal law has to cope with. Whether these two concepts are identical or not reflects on the rationale of the changes. In two of his articles, Chen also suggests that the shift should be viewed as the progress of the rule of law in China.[79] According to him, with criminal penalties taking the place of administrative ones, administrative power will consistently be restrained.

As the debate goes on, the understanding of basic concepts keeps being developed. Debates move to examining whether China is a risk society, and whether criminal law can control the "risks" described in this theory.[80] Discourses set by the risk society theory emphasize individuals' reflexivization on risk (an enhanced level of risk awareness) and world-historic pessimism of scientific expertise. "The risk society is fraught with new risks and hazards that we ourselves have manufactured."[81] Failure to manage these hazards that scientific development creates generates an endemic sense of insecurity all over the world. Facilitated by the anxieties about everyday risks and uncertainty, "welfare sanctions and penal modernism, aimed at reforming and reintegrating offenders" were replaced with mass incapacitation and exclusion in the name of risk reduction.[82] However, what the Chinese scholars understand of the risk society theory is far from enough, since confined to the risk society theory, they ignore the discourse of "risk" in other Western literature. The risk society theory is simply one way to view the discourse of risk. Some Western researchers also raise criticisms that the risk society theory is too "speculative, making broad and loose speculations about structural and organizational processes, without grounding these specifically enough in the actual processes and experiences of institutional and everyday life."[83] Understanding of penal transformations calls for a detailed study of the actions of the participants and the scope of the institutional environment in which they are involved. In addition to risk society theory, scholars from the US, the UK and Australia analyze the shift in a variety of different analytic frameworks such as the neoliberalism theory and the late modernity theory.[84] For instance, "it is widely accepted that the rise of crime prevention is linked with a convergence of social forces associated with the 'risk society' and the ascendancy of neo-liberal governance from the 1970s forward."[85] In the neoliberal framework, the emergence of neoliberal politics in the 1970s in the US and the UK "seeks to make the techniques and mentalities of the business sector—both risk-taking and risk management—into the guiding rules for the public sector."[86] Based on this, the field of crime control witnessed not only the normalization of crimes as everyday risks, but also "the emergence of an individually focused framework of governing risk—a new prudentialism,"[87] which fostered community-based crime prevention, or situational crime prevention that reflected the vision of neoliberal politics. Besides the two theories, "an increasing number of social theorists have taken up the challenge of relating developments in crime prevention and risk management to the large-scale, historical shifts highlighted in this grand theorizing on late modernity."[88] Late modernity theory characterizes the era "with uncertainty and ambivalence related to constant change and flux, cultural fragmentation and the breakdown of norms and traditions."[89] The shift away from modernity gives rise to a growing fear of risk. Preventive methods are state responses to the late-modern social transitions to fight crimes, secure public support and maintain security.

The above theories have distinct interpretations of the rise of crime prevention and risk control in Western countries. However, they overlap on several aspects, even supporting each other on sketches of major social reforms in late-modern Western society since the 1970s.[90] In general, they argue that major changes in the governance of crime have shifted the orientation of crime control away from traditional, reactive strategies towards more prospective and preventive measures designed to maximize security. The current era is a break from the past modern and welfare state, in which risk anxiety shapes collective and individual behavior. Furthermore, the theories go on to examine the shifts of governance, trends in the contemporary era and unpacking new modes of government intervention and public involvement. "As a cutting edge of a much broader contemporary social transformation in which risk was displacing other forms of governance,"[91] crime prevention is taken to exemplify radical changes in the configurations of both public and private governance in late modern society under the influence of neoliberal or other policies. The theories all address the state's capacity to control in the era of transition when there is a crisis of public trust due to rising crime rates. This is the reason why crime prevention has generated so much concern among scholars.

These Western theories inspire a similar study to contextualize risk operation in China. Criminal behavior cannot be understood apart from the cultural context in which it occurs. The concept of prevention changes based on how it is interpreted in practice. "Without clarification of the specific meanings of the terms in the context in which they are used, the discourse has little explanatory or analytical power, and hampers discussion of broader legal implications."[92] Considering that "law making is the result of the work of a multitude of institutions and actors, ranging from the national legislature to the local level, and from professional law-drafters to the general public,"[93] this book seeks to contextualize the changes in Chinese criminal law through a study of the shaping power between the state and the public in the legislation. Compared to the era before the 1980s when poverty was a main social issue, the current Chinese state is suffering from multiple side effects of extensive economic growth and social unrest. The coexistence of rapid economic ascendance, far-reaching open-up policy and slow political reform brought about many challenges and much imbalance. The Chinese state has been increasingly resorting to criminal law as a risk-control method in various social aspects to regain public trust. Criminal law becomes a sound justification for the Chinese party-state to manage these political, economic, social and cultural uncertainties. Thus, this book not only re-conceptualizes "crime prevention" and "risk," but also highlights the broader transformation of governance and society. Methods in different countries originate from distinctive social backgrounds and political regimes with different aims and effects. The models are "relied on by legislators, sentencing-guideline drafters, and judges in the formulation, interpretation and application of the rules and doctrines of criminal law and the determination of sentencing guidelines and individual sentences."[94] It is a complex picture that is still being formed and constantly changing.

Lastly, the preventive shifts in Chinese criminal law developed simultaneously with preventive techniques of political risk. Chinese preventive restraints are also strict on those posing political risks to the regime of the party-state. To secure its authority, the party-state never stops intense censorship and suppression. "A grand theory of law in a book seldom explains the behavior of law on the streets of China."[95] It is known that preventive techniques for political aims are widely used in Chinese social governance, even though it is sensitive to publicly address some of the issues on the mainland. Crime is used as an excuse to enact legitimate interventions that have other motivations. For instance, to maintain "harmonious" social order, the rights to free association are remarkably restricted to avoid potential mass incidents. The Ministry of State Security and Public Security monitors public activities and speeches that may "endanger the state security" or "pick quarrels and provoke trouble." Expression or activity the Ministry of State Security considers to be risky to the governance of the Communist Party will be censored, let alone actual preparatory acts. It is difficult to assess whether such prisoners have actually committed the crime of subversion of state power (the definition of which is broad), leaving much room for state discretion. Furthermore, people who have been consistently petitioning have been secretly detained by both central and local authorities for the so-called stable social order to prevent them from appealing.[96] Police patrols and surveillance are also increased in large cities to deter misbehavior, crimes, petitions and those who are ostensibly against the government. The total number of political prisoners significantly increased from 2004 to 2014.[97] Such methods to prevent political risk (unrest) rather than punish existing harms are seriously criticized by liberals for their disregard of procedural justice, distortion of legal norms and infringement on human rights.[98] They are no less burdensome than punitive sanctions, and they truly sidestep legitimate procedures with low or even no standard of proof of risk or harm. Though this book will not address these sensitive issues in authoritarian China, it is important to keep in mind that there are far more underground illegal realities, both within and beyond criminal procedure.

Notes

1 As to the justifications of penal punishments, there are hybrid principles for the existence and distribution of criminal sanctions, including different models of combining retribution, deterrence, rehabilitation, incapacitation, prevention and restorative justice. Researchers Ludwig Andreas Feuerbach, M. E. Mayer, H. L. A. Hart, Herbert L. Packer, Ernest van den Haag, Andrew von Hirsch and Paul Robinson have independently constructed theories about the dynamic of these combined purposes functioning within one criminal justice system. They advocate a hybrid system to balance the "just desserts" concerns and utilitarian purposes, though they each adopt a different approach to distribute sentencing. "Code drafters are choosing to further different purposes in different contexts." See Stephen Shute & A. P. Simester, *Criminal Law Theory: Doctrines of the General Part* (Oxford: Oxford University Press, 2002) 83.

2 Lena Y. Zhong & Peter N. Grabosky, "The Pluralization of Policing and the Rise of Private Policing in China" (2009) 52 (5) *Criminal Law and Social Change* 448.

3 Andrew Ashworth & Lucia Zedner, "Prevention and Criminalization: Justifications and Limits" (2012) 15 *International and Interdisciplinary Journal* 544–546.

4 There exists an unequal structure of police power over offenders' and lawyers' rights. Ira Belkin, "China's Criminal Justice System" (2000) 6 (2) *Washington Journal of Modern China* 61. "Revisions of the Chinese Criminal Procedure Law, April 2018–September 2018", online: National People's Congress <http://www.npc.gov.cn/zgrdw/npc/lfzt/rlyw/node_34734.htm>.

5 Duihua Human Rights Journal, "China's New Criminal Procedure Law: 'Disappearance Clauses' Revised", online: Duihua <http://www.duihuahrjournal.org/2012/03/chinas-new-criminal-procedure-law.html>. *Criminal Procedure Law of People's Republic of China*, RS2012, Articles 73, 83 and 148 of the Criminal Procedure Law of China all impose looser rules in the stage of investigation of suspects of crimes against state security, crimes of terrorism, gang crimes, serious drug crimes or corruption.

6 Lei He, "Prison Population and Chinese Criminal Law Reforms" (2013) 8 *Chinese Criminal Law Science* 104–108.

7 See Andrew Ashworth & Lucia Zedner, *Preventive Justice* (Oxford: Oxford University Press, 2014).

8 In Western scholarship, "that contemporary penal policy and practice is complex and capricious is generally agreed. Whether the transformations it appears to be undergoing can be explained by reference to a larger master pattern is more controversial. And which particular master pattern this might be is more controversial still." Lucia Zedner, "Dangers of Dystopias in Penal Theory" (2002) 22 *Oxford Journal of Legal Studies* 341–366.

9 The book treats the West as a whole for the convenience of research, but at the same time, it also recognizes the differences among these countries. In the book, the West consists of Anglo-American countries, the UK and Western Europe, excluding continental Europe. While studies have shown similarities and transplantations of criminal polices between the US and the UK, or between the UK and the Commonwealth, the policy distinctions between the US and continental Europe are evident. Some researchers even use "American Exceptionalism" to refer to the apparent differences between America and continental Europe in their approaches to justice generally. See James Q. Whitman, *Harsh Justice: Criminal Punishment and the Widening Divide between American and Europe* (New York: Oxford University Press, 2005) 41–68; Carol S. Steiker, "Capital Punishment and American Exceptionalism" (2002) 81 *Oregon Law Review* 97–130; Matthew B. Kugler et al., "Differences in Punitiveness across Three Cultures: A Test

of American Exceptionalism in Justice Attitudes" (2013) 103 (4) *Journal of Criminal Law & Criminology* 1071–1114.

10 Gordon Hughes, *Understanding Crime Prevention* (Berkshire: Open University Press, 1998) 18.

11 Andrew Ashworth & Lucia Zedner, *Preventive Justice* (Oxford: Oxford University Press, 2014) 2.

12 Tamara Tulich, "A View Inside the Preventive State: Reflections on a Decade of Anti-terror Law" (2012) 21 (2) *Griffith Law Review* 2.

13 Daniel E. Hall, *Criminal Law and Procedure*, 7th ed. (New York: Delmar Cengage Learning, 2014) 666.

14 Christopher Slobogin, "A Jurisprudence of Dangerousness" (2003) 98 (1) *Southwestern Law Review* 21.

15 See Stewart A. Baker & John Kavanagh, eds, *Patriot Debates: Experts Debate the USA Patriot Act* (Chicago, IL: American Bar Association, 2005).

16 Michael T. McCarthy, "USA Patriot Act" (2002) 39 *Harvard Journal on Legislation* 435.

17 John Monahan, "A Jurisprudence of Risk Assessment" (2006) 92 (3) *Virginia Law Review* 394.

18 Aaron B. Overton, "Federal Gang Laws: A New Tool against a Growing Threat or Overbroad and Dangerous" (2008) 9 *Rutgers Race & Law Review* 432.

19 Christopher Slobogin, "A Jurisprudence of Dangerousness" (2003) 98 (1) *Southwestern Law Review* 6. The UK as a united nation has distinct systems of law: English law (England and Wales), Northern Ireland law and Scots law. Specifically, England and Wales ASBOs have mostly been via the Anti-Social Behaviour Act of 2003, in Northern Ireland through an Order in Council and in Scotland with the Antisocial and Sexual Behavior, etc. (Scotland) Act of 2004. In practice, the growth in the use of ASBOs in England and Wales has been more rapid, and stands well above the rate (relative to household population) in Scotland.

20 Christopher Slobogin, "A Jurisprudence of Dangerousness" (2003) 98 (1) *Southwestern Law Review* 32.

21 See G. R. Sullivan & Ian Dennis, eds, *Seeking Security: Pre-empting the Commission of Criminal Harms* (Oxford: Hart Publishing, 2012).

22 Lucia Zedner, "Fixing the Future: The Pre-emptive Turn in Criminal Justice", in Bronnit, S., McSherry, B. & Norrie, A., eds, *Regulating Deviance: The Redirection of Criminalization and the Futures of Criminal Law* (Oxford: Hart Publishing, 2009) 53.

23 Tamara Tulich, "A View Inside the Preventive State: Reflections on a Decade of Anti-Terror Law" (2012) 21 (2) *Griffith Law Review* 9.

24 An anti-terrorism control order is a civil order that imposes obligations, prohibitions and restrictions on an individual, such as reporting to police and abiding by a curfew. A control order is issued by a court where the court is satisfied, on the balance of probabilities, that making the order "would substantially assist in preventing a terrorist act" or the person provided or received training from a listed terrorist organization.

25 Lucia Zedner, *Security* (London, UK: Routledge, 2009) 83.

26 Mingxiang Liu, "The Risk of Criminal Law of Risk Control and Its Regulation" (2011) 4 *Studies in Law and Business* 16–19.

27 Zoe Scanlon, "Punishing Proximity: Sentencing Preparatory Terrorism in Australia and the United Kingdom" (2014) 25 (3) *Current Issues in Criminal Justice* 763–783.

28 See Johnathan Simon, *Governing Through Crime: How the War on Crime Transformed American Democracy and Created a Climate of Fear* (New York: Oxford University Press, 2007).

29 Tamara Tulich, "A View Inside the Preventive State: Reflections on a Decade of Anti-Terror Law" (2012) 21 (2) *Griffith Law Review* 22.
30 *Criminal Law of the People's Republic of China*, RS 2011.
31 Liying Li, "The Death Penalty for Economic Crimes in Reformed China", in Xiaobing Li & Qiang Fang, eds, *Modern Chinese Legal Reform: New Perspectives* (Lexington, KY: University Press of Kentucky, 2013) 171–188.
32 Kechang Ma, "Position of Criminal Policy of Combining Justice with Mercy" (2007) 4 *China Legal Science* 117–122.
33 Shishi Li, "Explanation of the First Draft of the Eighth Amendment of Criminal Law", online: NPC <http://www.npc.gov.cn/huiyi/lfzt/xfxza8/2011-05/10/content_1666058.htm>; see Jianping Lu, "On Strengthening Criminal Law Protection for the People's Livelihood" (2010) 12 *Law Science Magazine* 10–13.
34 Zhiqiong Yang, "Drunk Driving in the US" (2011) 2 *Law Science Magazine* 35–44.
35 In China, administrative penalties are usually issued by the police or the other departments from the government. They do not involve with court decisions, and are commonly believed to be less harsh than criminal penalties. Typically, administrative penalties include but are not limited to fines, revocation of licenses and detention of less than 15 days. To change from an administrative penalty to a criminal penalty is an increase of the seriousness of penalties in China.
36 As stipulated in Article 133(1) of the Chinese Criminal Law, the official name of the crime is impaired driving. The ninth amendment enacted in 2015 introduced further revisions of this article to punish more risky behaviors against road safety.
37 Yi-lang Tang et al., "Alcohol and Alcohol-Related Harm in China: Policy Changes Needed" (2013) 91 *Bull World Health Organ* 270–276.
38 Andrew Ashworth & Lucia Zedner, "Prevention and Criminalization: Justifications and Limits" (2012) 15 *New Criminal Law Review: An International and Interdisciplinary Journal* 546.
39 A. P. Simester & Andrew Von Hirsch, "Remote Harms and Non-constitutive Crimes" (2009) 28 (1) *Criminal Justice Ethics* 90.
40 Gordon Woodman & Diethelm Klippel, eds, *Risk and the Law* (New York: Routledge-Cavendish, 2008) 80.
41 Bingzhi Zhao & Bin Yuan, "Discussion on Main Issues of Drunk Driving" (2011) 3 *Criminal Law Review* 159.
42 Liangyuan Mo, "Use of Law in Hot Discussed Cases: Based on 7 Cases of Drunk Driving" (2012) 8 *Legal Science Monthly* 133–134.
43 Guangquan Zhou, "Necessity of Creating the Offence of Impaired Driving in Our Criminal Law", *Social Sciences in China*, 2009-08-18, A7. Zhou claims that penalties of drunk driving are too lenient in China. Creating this new offence in criminal law will not only decrease such offences, but also clarify the distinction between traffic crimes and intentional crimes against public security. In this respect, the Japanese experience serves as a good example for Chinese legislation; Ling Jia & Qimei Bi, "On Criminalizing Drunk Driving" (2010) 09 *Law Science Magazine* 86–89. Jia and Bi insist that criminalizing drunk driving is the trend in criminal law all over the world. It meets the public's demands in China as well.
44 Yaozhong Wang, "Legal Analysis of Impaired Driving" (2012) 5 *Science of Law* 124–125.
45 Under this circumstance, the boundaries of these three crimes are as follows: the crime of drunk driving is negligently or recklessly creating risks that are serious enough to generate road accidents; drunk driving that leads to real road accidents by negligence or recklessness is a traffic offence causing injury or property damage; using the conduct of drunk driving as a means to endanger the general public is an intentional crime against public security through other dangerous means.

The Law on Road Traffic Safety was also revised in 2011 to serve as a supplement of criminal law by raising the administrative punishments of drunk driving and driving after drinking. The new amendment of this law adds revoking the driver's license as well as depriving the driver of the eligibility to regain it in five years as associated punishments. As such, the overall penalties for drunk driving are both harsher and more complete.

46 Bingzhi Zhao & Bin Yuan, "Discussion on Main Issues of Drunk Driving" (2011) 3 *Criminal Law Review* 163–165.

47 See Maosheng Li, "Lectures on General Principles of Criminal Law", online: NTU College of Law <http://www.law.ntu.edu.tw/main.php?mod=document&func=show_document&show_edu=main&site_id=0&show_folder=24>.

48 Xihui Li & Wenhui Dong, "Research on the Revisions of Crime of Environmental Pollution" (2011) 9 *Law Science Magazine* 8–11.

49 Petter Asp, "Preventionism and Criminalization of Nonconsummate Offences", in Andrew Ashworth et al., *Prevention and the Limits of the Criminal Law* (Oxford: Oxford University Press, 2013) 23–46.

50 Mingkai Zhang, "Crime with Risks" (1998) 1 *Tsinghua Law Review* 118–142.

51 Forthcoming judicial interpretations may clarify that minor violations will not be criminalized, but a change in the law itself is an official declaration prohibiting any such behavior.

52 *Criminal Law of the People's Republic of China*, RS 2011, c6, s338.

53 Zegang Jin & Yi Yan, "Why Identical Cases Have Different Verdicts: Reflections on the Water Pollution case of Yancheng and the Chemical Major Pollution Case of Yixin in Corporation" (2011) 2 *Journal of Shanghai Jiaotong University* 31–32.

54 However, in these 14 rules of the explanation, besides clarifying the place, times and types of waste that may pollute the environment, the court still uses certain minor results as defining criteria of "seriously polluting the environment." Thus, in general, this is a behavior-oriented arrangement, but the "harm" result still plays some part in defining crimes.

55 "New Judicial Interpretations of Offences of Environmental Pollution Promulgated", online: Xinhua <http://news.xinhuanet.com/legal/2013-06/18/c_124871016.htm>.

56 The amendment also replaces the concept of "hazardous waste" with "harmful substances."

57 The second and third amendment were enacted in the same year of 2002.

58 Xingliang Chen, "Critical Doctrinal Analysis of Risk Theory Society" (2014) 1 *Peking University Law Review* 103–127.

59 Zhiming Gao, "History of the Concepts of Legally Protected Interests: Based on German Theories", (Master book, Taiwan National University Law Faculty 2001) [unpublished].

60 David Nelken, "Comparative Criminal Justice, Beyond Ethnocentricism and Relativism" 6 (4) *European Journal of Criminology* 307.

61 Lucia Zedner, "Fixing the Future: The Pre-emptive Turn in Criminal Justice", in Simmon Bronnit, Bernadette McSherry & Alan Norrie, eds, *Regulating Deviance: The Redirection of Criminalization and the Futures of Criminal Law* (Oxford: Hart Publishing, 2009) 55.

62 Christopher Slobogin, "A Jurisprudence of Dangerousness" (2003) 98 (1) *Southwestern Law Review* 21.

63 R. A. Duff & Stuart Green, eds, *Philosophical Foundation of Criminal Law* (Oxford: Oxford University Press, 2013) 12.

64 Lucia Zedner, "Fixing the Future: The Pre-emptive Turn in Criminal Justice", in Simon Bronnit, Bernadette McSherry & Alan Norrie, eds, *Regulating Deviance: The Redirection of Criminalization and the Futures of Criminal Law* (Oxford: Hart Publishing, 2009) 55.

65 *Criminal Law of the People's Republic of China*, RS 2011, c1, s 3–5. Articles 3–5 of Chinese criminal law outline the principles of Chinese criminal law. Article 3 stipulates, "For acts that are explicitly defined as criminal acts in law, the offenders shall be convicted and punished in accordance with law; otherwise, they shall not be convicted or punished." Article 4 states, "The law shall be equally applied to anyone who commits a crime. No one shall have the privilege of transcending the law." Article 5 stipulates that "The degree of punishment shall be commensurate with the crime committed and the criminal responsibility to be borne by the offender."
66 Andrew Ashworth, *Principles of Criminal Law* (Oxford: Oxford University Press, 2009) 456.
67 This conclusion is drawn based on the calculations of all the amendments to Chinese criminal law from 1999 to 2011.
68 Lucia Zedner, *Security* (London, UK: Routledge, 2009) 18.
69 The Chinese character for safety and security is the same (pinyin: an quan). In China the distinction between safety and security is blurred.
70 Lucia Zedner, *Security* (London, UK: Routledge, 2009) Introduction.
71 Lucia Zedner, *Security* (London, UK: Routledge, 2009) 155.
72 R. A. Duff & Stuart Green, *Philosophical Foundation of Criminal Law* (Oxford: Oxford University Press, 2013).
73 See Pat O'Malley, *Crime and Risk* (Los Angeles, CA: Sage Publications, 2010).
74 These Chinese scholars include Dongyan Lao, Xingliang Chen, Hong Li, Yong Xia, Yanhong Liu, Lianwei Nan, etc.
75 See Hongjie Tian, "Position of Criminal Law in the Risk Society" (2011) 4 *Studies in Law and Business* 20; Lianwei Nan, "Critical Analysis and Reflections on the Risk Society Theory" (2012) 4 *Chinese Journal of Law* 138–153.
76 Dongyan Lao, "Public Policy and Criminal Law in a Risk Society" (2007) 3 *Social Sciences in China* 127–128.
77 Dongyan Lao, "Risk Society Theory and Shifting Criminal Law Theory" (2014) 1 *Peking University Law Review* 81.
78 Dongyan Lao, "Risk Theory Society and Shifting Criminal Law Theory" (2014) 1 *Peking University Law Review* 97.
79 Xingliang Chen, "Criminal Law in the Risk Society and Risk of Criminal Law" (2011) 4 *Studies in Law and Business* 11; Xingliang Chen, "Critical Doctrinal Analysis of Risk Theory Society" (2014) 1 *Peking University Law Review* 103–127.
80 There are controversies about the accurate meaning of "risks." Some insist that the risks are post-modern risks of disasters like nuclear explosions, or genetic disorders that criminal law is unable to manage. Some claim that the risks are exactly everyday risks that criminal law should be conscious of and cope with.
81 David Garland, "The Rise of Risk", in Richard V. Ericson & Aaron Doyle, eds, *Risk and Morality* (Toronto, ON: University of Toronto Press, 2003) 48–86.
82 M. Feeley & J. Simon, "Actuarial Justice: The Emerging New Criminal Law", in D. Nelken, ed, *The Futures of Criminology* (London: Sage Publications, 1994) 173–201; David Garland, *The Culture of Control* (Chicago, IL: University of Chicago Press, 2001).
83 Deborah Lupton, *Risk Key Ideas* (London, UK: Routledge, 1999) 85.
84 See Pat O'Malley, ed, *Crime and the Risk Society* (Aldershot: Ashgate, 1998); David Garland, *The Culture of Control* (Chicago, IL: University of Chicago Press, 2001); Emma Bell, *Criminal Justice and Neoliberalism* (Basingstoke: Palgrave Macmillan, 2011).
85 Pat O'Malley & Steven Hutchinson, "Reinventing Prevention, Why Did 'Crime Prevention' Develop So Late?" (2007) 47 (3) *British Journal of Criminology* 373.
86 Pat O'Malley, "Governing Risk", in A. Sarat, ed, *The Blackwell Companion to Law and Society* (Oxford: Blackwell Publishing, 2005) 292–308.

87 Pat O'Malley, "Governing Risk", in A. Sarat, ed, *The Blackwell Companion to Law and Society* (Oxford: Blackwell Publishing, 2005) 292–308.
88 Gordon Hughes, *Understanding Crime Prevention* (Buckingham: Open University Press, 1998) 135.
89 Deborah Lupton, *Risk Key Ideas* (London, UK: Routledge, 1999) 11.
90 The formation of social work was shown to take place in a complex system that includes a social dimension, that of risk society; a political dimension, that of advanced neoliberalism; and a cultural dimension, that of reflexive or late modernity.
91 Pat O'Malley, "Reinventing Prevention: Why Did 'Crime Prevention' Develop So Late?" (2007) 47 (3) *British Journal of Criminology* 375.
92 Tamara Tulich, "A View Inside the Preventive State: Reflections on a Decade of Anti-Terror Law" (2012) 21 (2) *Griffith Law Review* 4.
93 Jan Michiel Otto & Yuwen Li, "Overview of Law-Making in China", in Jan Michael Otto et al., *Law-Making in People's Republic of China* (The Hague: Kluwer Law International, 2000) 1–18.
94 Paul Roberson, "Hybrid Principles for the Distribution of Criminal Sanctions" (1987) 82 *Northwestern University Law Review* 19–24.
95 Kam C. Wong, *Chinese Policing: History and Reform (New Perspectives in Criminology and Criminal Justice)* (New York: Peter Lang Publishing, 2009) 6.
96 "China: Secret 'Black Jails' Hide Severe Rights Abuses", online: Human Rights Watch <https://www.hrw.org/news/2009/11/11/china-secret-black-jails-hide-severe-rights-abuses>. Frank Langfitt, "For Complainers, A Stint in China's 'Black Jails'", online: NPR <http://www.npr.org/2012/11/01/163949720/for-complainers-a-stint-in-chinas-black-jails>.
97 Congressional-Executive Commission on China, "List of Political Prisoners, Detained or Imprisoned as of October 2014", Political Prisoner Database.
98 R. Munro, "Judicial Psychiatry in China and Its Political Abuses" (2000) 14 (1) *Columbia Journal of Asian Law* 1–128.

3 The history of lawmaking and the multiple streams approach

This chapter claims that John Kingdon's "multiple streams approach" to policy-making provides a sound framework for analyzing the Chinese model. The three-stream framework of "problems, policies and politics" helps to classify the roles of the public, of proposal makers and of political actors. The theory is also subject to revisions in the Chinese context to fit with Chinese criminal justice. In China, with the increase of multiple factors in the policy-making process, such as the media, the public and scholars, the system is filled with uncertainty and irrationality.

The second chapter of the book examined the preventive shift in Chinese criminal law. In the third chapter, the first section will document the history of making the eighth amendment to Chinese criminal law through three case studies. Examining the legislative history is like "processing tracing," a method used to search for causal inference through the "unfolding of events or situations over time."[1] "Process tracing, to reiterate, is an analytic tool for drawing descriptive and causal inferences from diagnostic pieces of evidence—often understood as part of a temporal sequence of events or phenomena."[2] A central concern (of process tracing) is with the sequences and mechanisms in the unfolding of hypothesized causal processes.[3] In order to examine the rationale for the preventive shift of the law, this book will identify the causal relationship between the reasons and the shift using evidence, while the sequences and mechanisms can only be identified through legislation history. During the process of lawmaking, the crime of drunk driving (with the contested nature of drunk driving overall) gave rise to diversified attitudes among departments, officials and the public. The other two cases, which are less radical, were selected for complementary purposes. After that, the second section of this chapter examines the approach of applying John Kingdon's multiple streams policy-making theory to Chinese legislation. This section argues that the MSA Kingdon proposes can be used as the theoretical framework for analyzing the current process of criminal lawmaking in China.

3.1 Legislative initiative, bill passing and final amendments

This section will examine the drafting process of the three amendments of Chinese criminal law to identify the legislation's stages and participants. In China, lawmaking is now a far more important part of the policy-making process, is far more conflictual and is fought out among a far greater array of institutions and arenas than ever before. By providing background information for the "multi-stage and multi-arena"[4] process, this section lays the foundation for the rest of the book.

3.1.1 Amendment on the crime of drunk driving

Before the enactment making drunk driving a crime, there was a series of nationally known cases in 2008 and 2009.[5] When the media exposed the series of cases of drunk driving with bodily harm it quickly drew the public's attention, producing mixed feelings of anxiety, pity and anger.[6] Some of the news was first broadcasted by traditional media, including newspapers and TV, while some was disclosed by the netizens in blogs or forums. The internet discourses were, in turn, documented in newspapers, magazines and journals. For instance, China Daily, Guangming Daily, Xinhua Daily and CCP newspapers also followed the developments of the cases and expressions of public attitude from the internet.[7] News on traditional media and the internet quickly gave rise to hot topics throughout the country. Residing in a country with a long history of paternalism, citizens tended to blame the government for neglect of duty, such as lenient penalties or failure of policing. The criticisms undoubtedly put pressure on the CCP's governance.

The first direct effect of establishing traffic violations was the launch of a national war against drunk driving by both the Ministry of Public Security and local police starting in August 2009. "The Chinese police departments have been very busy waging specific campaigns targeted against special crimes that are prominent, almost one campaign after another."[8] In a short period with huge police input, cases of drunk driving declined significantly in a variety of provinces and districts.[9] In August 2009, the Standing Committee of the National People's Congress (NPC), China's top legislature, added amending criminal law to the 2010 legislation plan just a few months after amending it in February 2009.[10] It was claimed that making drunk driving a crime was a key focus of this amendment, which had not only gained support from the people's representatives, but also from the party's senior leaders and the government. The Road Traffic Safety Law and Regulations on Road Traffic Safety Violations on Penalties Points were also revised to match the increased penalties after the criminal law amendment. The government also upgraded the enforcements in 2013, specifying details on the definition of drunk driving and related administrative penalties in a new regulation against behaviors violating road traffic safety.[11]

With the growing amount of personal automobile ownership, departments in both the central and local police have had to fight drunk driving behavior, particularly since 2007.[12] However, "conditions must deteriorate to crisis proportions before the subject achieves enough visibility to become an active agenda item."[13] Although indicators from government agency monitors had already shown there was a problem, it was not until August 2009 that the series of well-publicized cases took place and the war began.[14] Before that, public reports from the Ministry of Public Security rarely saw drunk driving as an issue requiring special resolution. Data before 2007 on such offences were limited, while since then there have been monthly and yearly statistics on drunk driving accessible both nationally and provincially. For instance, in 2009 the number of drunk driving cases increased by 22%, and in 2010 it decreased by 22.3%.[15] The rise in 2009 was mainly due to an increase in police investigations, while the decline in the following year resulted from the temporary deterring effects of the war on drunk driving. The cases reinforced the pre-existing perception of the problem. By disclosing and following the cases, more and more national attention was called to drunk driving until officials deemed it to be a widespread condition that needed special attention.

3.1.2 Amendment on the crime of manufacturing and selling fake medications

Fake medications are not a new problem and have been haunting Chinese society for decades. Since 2000, there have been cases of manufacturing and selling fake medications every year, but national attention was only raised after fatal cases in 2006.[16] Evidence suggests that a complete and transparent information system on fake drugs has emerged in China in response to these crises.[17] "At the national level, Ministry of Health, State Administration of Traditional Chinese Medicine, and State Food and Drug Administration issued many policies on strengthening drug safety management in pharmacy,"[18] with the aim of promoting drug safety. Although data available to the public mostly consist of scattered statistics from departments in different provinces and time phases (which makes it difficult to assess the seriousness of the problem), the China Food and Drug Administration Bureau website has statistics on manufacturing and selling fake medications in China from 2008 onward. Police data remain limited. Table 3.1 shows that the number of cases developed at a slow pace with minor ups and downs until 2011 when it witnessed a sudden rise.

In May to July 2009, six departments and bureaus—including the Ministry of Health, the Ministry of Public Security, the Ministry of Industry and Information Technology, the Food and Drug Administration Bureau, the Industry and Commerce Administration Bureau and the Traditional Chinese Medicine Administration Bureau—passed the Agenda on Drug Safety Management Program, from which began a planned timeframe of two years of intense control of national drug safety. In 2010, these six agencies started comprehensive work on drug safety,[19] which is part of the reason the offences in Table 3.1 increased significantly in 2011. From 2011 to 2012, the Ministry of Public Security and the Food and Drug Administration Bureau cooperated to fight the manufacturing and selling of fake medications, giving rise to even higher commissions in 2012. In 2013, the Ministry of Public Security continued the war.

Meanwhile, in 2009 the Supreme Court and the Supreme People's Procuratorate enacted the Interpretations on Issues Concerning the Application of Law in the Trial of Criminal Cases of Production and Sale of Medicine.[20]

Table 3.1 Number of nationwide cases tackled by the Food and Drug Administration Bureau from 2008 to 2012

	Cases tackled	*Business suspension for rectification*	*License revocation*	*Sent to the police*	*Sentenced with criminal sanctions*
2008	326	547	212	223	92
2009	273	445	73	259	88
2010	285	703	112	262	49
2011	441	1015	126	763	173
2012	833	1274	236	2160	425

In 2010, the Good Manufacture Practice of Drugs was revised. In 2011, the Measures for Supervision and Administration of Drug Safety were put in place. In addition, the eighth amendment of the criminal law, which was revised in 2010, was put into effect in 2011. It was uncertain to what degree these initiatives were triggered by the fatal cases, but the campaign-like activities were clearly influenced by such. "Problems are brought to the attention of people in and around government by systematic indicators, by focusing events like crises and disasters, or by feedback from the operation of current programs."[21] National incidents such as fake drug scandals, by generating national awareness of the problem, lead to emerging consensus and agreement on solutions or proposals. The number of cases disclosed is also influenced by the resources that the state devotes to the problem. The more attention that is put into investigations, the more the problem will be discovered. Police officials have argued that they had not expected there to be so many problems in this area after the war started.[22]

3.1.3 Amendment on the crime of environmental pollution

Since 2000, cases of serious water pollution have been striking different Chinese provinces almost every year. "Despite China's comprehensive system of environmental laws and standards, poor water quality is widespread."[23] To date, the "violation of environmental law remains a pervasive problem and law enforcement, while improving, is still weak."[24] It is argued that "Difficulties with environmental enforcement in China point to fundamental systemic problems relating to inappropriate institutional arrangements, inadequate resourcing, and unclear legislative drafting."[25] In China, "Of all the classes of environmental accidents, water pollution accidents are the most frequent, and they have become more frequent between 1997 and 2003."[26] Most cases involve chemical companies that discharge pollutants into the rivers, either damaging drinking water for days, or causing property and bodily harm to nearby residents. In 2007, more than 80 provisions of the Law on the Prevention and Control of Water Pollution were changed through a new amendment, increasing administrative penalties for both offenders and regulatory agencies.[27] However, national attention increased mainly after the pollution of Lake Tai in 2007 and the polluting of drinking water in Yancheng City in 2009 due to their negative impact on thousands of households.[28] The public also expressed doubts about the effects of existing administrative and criminal penalties, some of which even led to protests.[29]

After the crisis, in 2010 the Legislative Affairs Committee (LAC) proposed to the Standing Committee of the National People's Congress to expand the boundary of criminal law for tougher treatment concerning violations of environmental protection. The proposal turned into part of the eighth amendment of criminal law in 2011. To match with the amendment, in 2013 the Supreme Court and Supreme People's Procuratorate worked out an "Explanation of the Application of Law on Criminal Cases of Environment Pollution."[30] Considering that a bill usually takes years to draft, this explanation was impressive for its speed and detailed specifications. According to one official who participated in this legislation, this was primarily due to demands from the CCP and the state council: "this top-down approach shows that the high rankings are really concerned about the wellbeing of the people."[31] Furthermore, in 2013 the Ministry of Environmental Protection and the Ministry of Public Security announced an official agreement to enhance cooperation in environmental protection, for which seven mechanisms were designed to fight against criminal behavior.[32] The 12th Five-Year Plan, and its subordinated plan, the "General Planning for the Development of Environmental Protection Legislation and Environmental Economic Policies," not only sets impressive sustainability targets for water pollution management, but also lists key fields in which to improve environmental legal systems and the eco-compensation mechanisms.[33] Therefore, a war was waged in China in the field of environmental protection.

3.2 Applying John Kingdon's theory in the Chinese context

This book will identify the social, legal and political rationales of the preventive shift of Chinese criminal law by examining the legislative model from which it was generated. Rationales for the shift are embodied in the procedures of criminal lawmaking. On one hand, law making itself as an organized national activity is an essential part of the rule of law, shedding light on a large portion of the features of Chinese society. Ever since the 1978 Third Plenum of the Eleventh Chinese Communist Party Central Committee called for more rapid development of a "socialist democracy" and rule by law, lawmaking has become an increasingly large, important and contentious part of policy-making.[34] This book considers legislation as an approach to explore the beliefs of the Chinese public and its elites with regard to criminal law and crimes. On the other hand, it is impossible for one book to cover all the aspects of criminal justice, considering there have been diverse national and local practices before and after the promulgation of criminal law. Thus, this book does not examine the final stage: the implementation of criminal law. Rather, it takes legislation as a springboard for future research.

Although Chinese Legislation Law has stipulated the rule of lawmaking in China, there remains a lack of study on the actual participants and processes of it. It is argued that

> the result of this fundamental lack of understanding about how policy is made, for whom, by whom and the constraints that policy makers and policy doers operate under, led otherwise perfectly able students to make unfounded criticisms of current arrangements and put forward unachievable utopian suggestions for policy advances.[35]

Among the limited literature concerning Chinese legislation, it is suggested that the Chinese legislative model follows the approach of "setting an agenda, inter-departmental assessment, approval by senior politicians, parliamentary procedure and implementation."[36] It is also claimed that "each law moves through approximately five different stages: agenda-setting; inter-agency review; top leadership approval; NPC debate and passage; and the explication, implementation or adjudication of the law as policy."[37] However, these models commonly fail to examine the activities of external participants like the public, the media and scholars, which have been newcomers to Chinese decision making. "Efforts to explain such rapid changes within an organizational politics paradigm often seem to require the analyst to invoke actors, events and situations which actually fall well outside the core elements of the organizational paradigm."[38] Shaoguang Wang's 2013 book *The Chinese Model of Consensus Decision Making: A Case Study of Healthcare Reform* is an effort to incorporate such external participants. Based on empirical research on how the new Chinese healthcare policy is formed, it argues that rather than being decided upon by one leader or a group of entrepreneurs, the policies are debated by government officials, think tanks, interest groups and the public. Not only has the government intentionally eliminated the barriers to participation in decision making, but the proceedings have also been reformed to be more democratic, with multiple rounds of reviews and negotiations. Wang's book, as up-to-date research of the Chinese model of agenda making, provides data to prove that the process and the people involved are indeed different from decades or years ago. However, considering that some of the arguments in the book are exaggerated, their credibility is downgraded to some extent.[39]

In contrast, the "garbage can model" is another theory frequently mentioned by scholars in the last 20 years. In the book *The Politics of Lawmaking in Post-Mao China*, Tanner summarizes existing models of Chinese lawmaking with the following: the command model, the leadership struggle model and the organizational or bureaucratic politics model.[40] He applies the garbage can model to the politics of Chinese legislation.[41] Zhenglai Deng, a well-known scholar, has also indicated his support for this pattern of policy-making in China.[42] Authors of the garbage can model suggest three or four more or less independent streams: problems, potential solutions and opportunities for choice. "Problems are worked upon in the context of some choice, but choices are made only when the shifting combinations of problems, solutions and decision makers happen to make action possible."[43] Kingdon's MSA theory is a revision of the garbage can model as well. In the book *Agenda, Alternatives and Public Policies*, Kingdon examines the reasons why some subjects rise and others fall as governmental agendas (see Figure 3.1). The "agenda" is conceived to be "the list of subjects or problems to which governmental officials, and people outside of government closely associated with those officials, pay some serious attention at any given time."[44] Based on interviews with people close to decision making in health and transportation, Kingdon identifies three process streams: problems, policies and politics. In brief, he claims that the "problem stream" refers to problems pressing in on the system (such as the focusing events), indicating the prominence of certain social problems. The "policy stream" refers to a gradual accumulation of knowledge among specialists in a given policy area. It focuses on the generation of policy proposals by researchers, career bureaucrats and consultants, among others. The "political stream" consists of events, such as swings in national mood, vagaries of public opinion, election results, administration changes and congress turnover, that may set the agenda. According to Kingdon, the three streams are largely independent of one another, but at some critical junctures when a policy window is open, the three streams are joined into a single package through which the final policy changes are made.[45] The most interesting part of this model is how the streams are coupled together. Why are specific problems addressed at specific moments? Is there a deciding factor that leads to the outcome?

Kingdon's book *Agenda, Alternatives and Public Policies* was first published in 1984, but the theory still has explanative power for contemporary policy-making not only in the US but also in other Western countries. The second edition of the book came out in 2010 with new case studies from the 1980s and 1990s and argues that the concepts still work well in those empirical studies, even beyond areas of health and transportation reform. In the last decades, the three-stream framework he adopts has still been used by Western researchers to analyze changes to criminal policy in the US, the UK and Europe, such as in gun control,

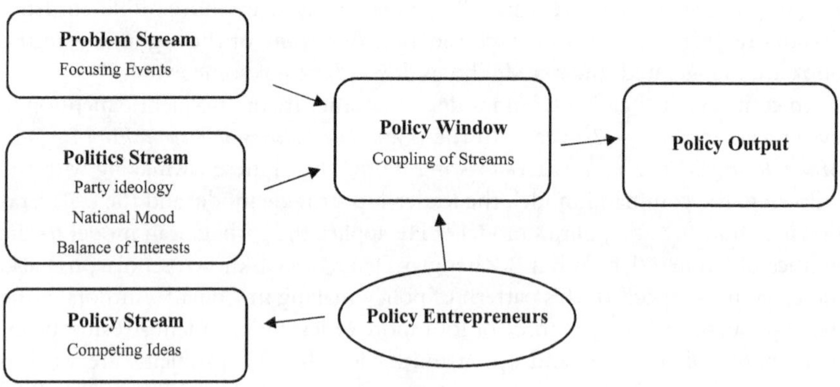

Figure 3.1 Multiple streams framework (MSF).

counter-terrorism and other punitive strategies.[46] Even the number of papers systematically applying the MSA is remarkable. Jones, in a recent meta-review, found no less than 311 English-language peer-reviewed journal articles applying the MSA since the year 2000.[47] Furthermore, this theory has been subject to broad application, discussion and modification. According to Kingdon, the theory itself is not all-inclusive; rather, it is open to revisions in different contexts. Even in some circumstances in the US, rather than the three streams merging with each other, some focusing events can become so dramatic that they directly lead to the final results. For instance, the 9/11 terrorist attacks turned into the "policy window" for a number of preventive offences and policing strategies.

Legislative initiative can be one option in a set of agendas. In this respect, Kingdon's MSA model of policy-making provides a sound framework for analyzing the Chinese model of criminal law. MSA "explains how policies are made by government under conditions of ambiguity."[48] It argues that policy makers are commonly under time constraints, so rather than a linear decision-making process—identifying problems, formulating solutions and making a choice, the whole process is complex and chaotic. The theory points out some of the basic nature of policymaking, though it originally focuses on the participants and processes of US policy formation. In China, on the one hand, power has been decentralized in the past 20 years during the legislative process. On the other hand, due to the rise of public opinion, the press and policy think tanks, proposals are less tied to government ministries. With the increase of multiple factors in the policy-making process, such as the media, the public and scholars, the system is filled with uncertain and irrationality. Therefore, this book uses MSA as a primary framework for Chinese lawmaking. Tremendous bureaucratic development remains responsible for lawmaking, but the bureaucratic politics is unable to fully illustrate the current Chinese legislation. At the same time, the model will also be revised in several aspects to fit with Chinese criminal justice. For instance, in the first dimension, the Chinese participants include the CCP, government bureaucracy, the media, scholars/think tanks and the public. How they act and relate to each other in China are different from what Kingdon presents in the multiple streams model about the president, congress and interest groups of the US. In the second dimension, the distinction between policy and political stream is not very clear in the Chinese context. The proposals that have more social influence are made by those within state institutions, or at least those in close relationships with the institutions. Policy drafts, presentations and acceptation can never be set apart from political considerations and bureaucratic competition. This adaption not only develops MSA but also sheds light on the Chinese characteristics of policy-making.

Specifically, the pattern of making the above three revisions to Chinese criminal law converges with this "problem + policies + politics" model of agenda making in a number of ways. An examination of the three streams, public demands, professional opinions and political willingness, will be addressed in the framework. In the problem stream, the focusing event reveals the development of public demands, which serves as one of the major trigger factors for criminal law expansion. Security concerns are the main booster for legal activism. Criminology scholars have mentioned the distinction between what is truly threatening and what is perceived to be threatening.[49] Among the dangers that have been detected by the public, those that successfully turn into focusing events require the coexistence of multiple factors to maintain continuous national attention. In the policy stream, institutions' proposals solve technical issues, including legal rationales of the change and the utilitarian use of criminal law by examining criminal law principles and the compatibility of criminal penalties with the others, such as administrative ones. Events are institutionalized through professionals both inside and outside the bureaucratic paradigm, which "means that further 'securitization' is facilitated as events and new problems can then be interpreted within the framework of established threat images."[50] Furthermore, in the political stream, bureaucratic cooperation, bargaining and political support finally make the change possible. "It is impossible for a threat image to gain salience if it has not been given some sort of form for decision-makers." The problem and political stream matter most to the agenda's chances of changing criminal law, with visible participants such as the public, the CCP and the NPC. However, the policy stream remains important as a bridge between the other two streams, based on the efforts of policy entrepreneurs. The growing awareness of problems, the rise of adequate policies and political acceptance all contribute to the final Chinese legislation. However, one challenge of this book is the difficulty of examining the policy stream without directly gaining access to the policy community, which is comprised of government staff, NPC representatives, People's Political Consultative Conference members, think tanks and scholars. Lacking primary sources is a common problem for research on Chinese issues. Under this circumstance, the book has to rely on second-hand information such as news broadcasts, journal papers and public speeches related to revisions of the law. A mixed-methods approach helps us to triangulate measurement strategies. However, when it is hard to obtain first-hand data, the research focuses will be more on the validity and reliability of the data, techniques of understanding existing data and ways of drawing the conclusion. Besides second-hand data, the book also relies on the personal observation and experience of the researcher as evidence. Compared with the other data, personal views only serve a supplementary role in this research.

All in all, the rest of this book will use John Kingdon's MSA as the theoretical framework to interpret Chinese legislation. As a preliminary sketch, the process of problem recognition, generation of policy proposals and political evaluations will be analyzed successively. First, problem recognition and definition affect outcomes significantly. Focusing events, including drunk driving, deadly fake medications and water pollution in Yancheng and Wuxi City, captured the attention of personnel in and around government. These actors indicated to officials that the crises had become so pressing that rapid settlements were required; otherwise the trust between the government and the public would deteriorate. Second, "policy entrepreneurs invest considerable resources bringing their conception of problems to officials' attention, and trying to convince them to see problems their way."[51] The specialists make proposals to revise both administrative and criminal laws. Representatives from the Two Sessions and staff from the State Council including the Ministry of Public Security, the Ministry of Health and the Ministry of Environmental Protection, as well as lawyers and NGOs kept claiming that current penalties were too lenient, making it difficult for the law to function. Their proposals provided solutions to emergent social problems. Third, in the political stream, criminal lawmaking re-establishes the public's trust in the CCP. "Events within government itself like administrative change bring with them marked changes in policy agendas."[52] The long-lasting politic of the CCP to maintain its governing capability and legitimacy by emphasizing people's livelihoods stands as the political environment for amendments to criminal law. Road and drug safety, together with environmental safety, constitute part of the "Chinese dream," a slogan promoted by General Secretary Xi Jinping in 2013. The party's central decision-making actors (the Politburo, the Secretariat, etc.), and other factors including jurisdiction competition and inter-agency consensus building, also operate as impetuses (or at least not as constraining factors) of the legislation. Finally, "the probability of an item rising on a decision agenda is dramatically increased if all three elements—problem, proposal and political receptivity—are coupled in a single package."[53] When the opportunity to amend criminal law emerged in 2009, changes took place accordingly.

Notes

1 David Collier, "Understanding Process Tracing" (2011) 44 (4) *Political Science and Politics* 824.
2 David Collier, "Understanding Process Tracing" (2011) 44 (4) *Political Science and Politics* 824.
3 Andrew Bennett, "Process Tracing and Causal Inference", in Henry Brady & David Collier, eds, *Rethinking Social Inquiry: Diverse Tools, Shared Standards*, 2nd ed. (Plymouth: Rowman and Littlefield, 2010) 1.
4 Murray Scot Tanner, "How a Bill Becomes a Law in China: Stages and Processes in Lawmaking" (1995) 141 *The China Quarterly* 39.
5 Zhaoxin Wang et al., "The Underestimated Drink Driving Situation and the Effects of Zero Tolerance Laws in China" (2015) 16 (5) *Traffic Injury Prevention* 430.
6 Loretta Chao, "China Drunk-Driver Case Hits a Nerve: Driver in Fatal Crash Faces Mild Charges, Sparking Abuse-of-Power Allegations", online: The Wall Street Journal <http://www.wsj.com/articles/SB100014240527487040626045761058733459207888>.
7 Yuqiong Zhou & Patricia Moy, "Parsing Framing Processes: The Interplay between Online Public Opinion and Media Coverage" (2007) 57 *Journal of Communication* 79.
8 Jinfeng Du, "Police-Public Relations—A Chinese View" (1997) 30 (1) *Australian and New Zealand Journal of Criminology* 87. About the strong enforcement of approach against drunk driving, see Ying Li et al., "The Drink Driving Situation in China" (2012) 13 (2) *Traffic Injury Prevention* 105.
9 "The prevalence of total fatalities did not change significantly in the period of 2011 to 2013. But the proportion of traffic fatalities that accounted for total fatalities decreased from 1.57% to 1.06%, showing a smooth declining

tendency." Zhaoxin Wang et al., "The Underestimated Drink Driving Situation and the Effects of Zero Tolerance Laws in China" (2015) 16 (5) *Traffic Injury Prevention* 431.

10 "2010 Legislative Plan of the Standing Committee of the National People's Congress", online: NPC <http://www.npc.gov.cn/npc/xinwen/2010-07/06/content_1581057.htm>.

11 The new 2013 regulation introduces a number of harsher administrative penalties against drunk driving offences, like revocation of driving licenses, fines and detentions. For instance, for those who drive after drinking alcohol or driving while intoxicated, causing a major accident, besides criminal offenses, the driver will lose their driving license for the rest of their life. These administrative penalties are used as supplements to increased criminal penalties.

12 This can be shown from news reports of road safety from the websites of the Ministry of Public Security before 2007, though data before 2007 were really limited. Researchers have argued that the Ministry of Public Security underestimated the seriousness fatalities caused by drunk driving in the late 2000s. See Zhaoxin Wang et al., "The Underestimated Drink Driving Situation and the Effects of Zero Tolerance Laws in China" (2015) 16 (5) *Traffic Injury Prevention* 431. Some researchers also point out the lack of thorough and reliable data on drunk driving as a common problem for low- and middle-income countries, including China, Colombia, Mexico, Nigeria, Russia and Vietnam. See Kathryn Stewart, David Silcock & Fred Wegman, "Reducing Drink Driving in Low-and Middle-Income Countries: Challenges and Opportunities" (2012) 13 (2) *Traffic Injury Prevention* 93–95.

13 John W. Kingdon, *Agendas, Alternatives and Public Policies, Update Edition, with an Epilogue on Health Care*, 2nd ed. (New York: Pearson, 2010) 95.

14 The fatal cases mainly include cases of Weiming Sun in 2008, Bin Hu in 2008 and Mingbao Zhang in 2009, which all caused huge levels of bodily injuries and property damage. Details of the cases will be discussed in the next chapter.

15 "Zero-Tolerance on Drunk Driving: Comments of Officials from the Bureau of Road Traffic Safety of the Ministry of Public Security on the Amendment to Road Traffic Safety Law", *Guang Ming Daily* (28 April 2011).

16 Among the fatal cases of counterfeit medications in China in 2006, the scandal of Qiqihar No 2 Pharmaceutical Company, which led to 13 deaths, was the most noted one. The other cases include but are not limited to fake Clindamycin Phosphate Glucose Injection (Xinfu Clindamycin) from Huayuan Co., Ltd. in Anhui province, fake Viagra in Zhejiang province, etc.

17 In China, "The SFDA oversees an extensive network of drug safety 'watchdogs,' including the China National Center for ADR Monitoring and 32 regional centers throughout China." Wenmin Du et al., "Drug Safety Surveillance in China and Other Countries: A Review and Comparison" (2008) 11 *Value in Health (Supplement 1)* 131.

18 Liyang Tang, "China's Regional Inequity in Pharmacist's Drug Safety Practice" (2012) 11 *International Journal for Equity in Health* 38.

19 Xiaoxi Huang, "Cooperation on the Fights against Drug Safety", *China Police Daily* (12 December 2009) 01.

20 Interpretations on Issues Concerning the Application of Law in the Trial of Criminal Cases of Production and Sale of Medicine, 2013, s1-12.

21 John W. Kingdon, *Agendas, Alternatives and Public Policies, Update Edition, with an Epilogue on Health Care*, 2nd ed. (New York: Pearson, 2010) 19.

22 Chaoxin Chu, "Fake Medications that Being Lost Control", *Southern Weekly* (25 November 2011).

23 Rebecca Nelson, "Water Pollution in China: How Can Business Influence for Good?" (2008) 7 *Asian Business & Management* 489.
24 Benjamin van Rooij, "The People vs. Pollution: Understanding Citizen Action against Pollution in China" (2010) 19 (63) *Journal of Contemporary China* 55. A case in point is the exposure and public outrage in the case of the chemical pollution of the Songhua River in 2005.
25 Rebecca Nelson, "Water Pollution in China: How Can Business Influence for Good?" (2008) 7 *Asian Business & Management* 492.
26 Mark Wang et al., "Rural Industries and Water Pollution in China" (2008) 86 *Journal of Environment Management* 651.
27 *Law on the Prevention and Control of Water Pollution of the PRC*, 2007.
28 See Jia Feng, "The Case of Yancheng Water Pollution: Problems in Judicature", online: Brill online <http://referenceworks.brillonline.com/entries/chinese-research-perspectives-online/the-case-of-yancheng-water-pollution-problems-in-judicature-C9789004183025_015>.
29 Kathleen A. Cannon, "Water as a Source of Conflict and Instability in China" (2006) 30 (2) *Strategic Analysis* 317–318.
30 *Explanation of the Application of Law on Criminal Cases of Environment Pollution of the PRC*, 2013.
31 Ma Jie, "Controlling Pollution: Coming of Harsher Penalties?", *Southern Weekly* (4 July 2013) online: Southern Weekly <http://www.infzm.com/content/92067>.
32 Jie Feng, "Inside Story of the Judicial Interpretation of the Offense of Drunk Driving: The Era of Harsher Penalties?", *Southern Weekly* (4 July 2013) online: Southern Weekly <http://www.infzm.com/content/92067>.
33 Liping Dai, "Tackling Diffuse Water Pollution from Agriculture in China: Drawing Inspiration from the European Union" (2014) 10 (2) *Utrecht Law Review* 139.
34 Murray Scot Tanner, *The Politics of Lawmaking in Post-Mao China: Institutions, Processes, and Democratic Prospects* (Oxford : Clarendon Press, 1998) 6.
35 Adrian Barton & Nick Johns, *The Policy-Making Process in the Criminal Justice System* (London, UK: Routledge, 2013) 1.
36 Jan Michiel Otto et al., *Law-Making in People's Republic of China* (The Hague: Kluwer Law International, 2000) 7.
37 Murray Scot Tanner, "How a Bill Becomes a Law in China: Stages and Processes in Lawmaking" (1995) 141 *The China Quarterly* 39.
38 Murray Scot Tanner, *The Politics of Lawmaking in Post-Mao China: Institutions, Processes, and Democratic Prospects* (Oxford : Clarendon Press, 1998) 27.
39 For instance, solid evidence is lacking to prove that public opinions are truly valued and reflected in the final result of policy-making. See Mingyu Yang, "Surpassed Fragmented Authoritarianism? Reviews of *The Chinese Model of Consensus Decision Making: A Case Study of Healthcare Reform*" (2014) 7 *Journal of Shandong Academy of Justice* 4.
40 See Murray Scot Tanner, *The Politics of Lawmaking in Post-Mao China: Institutions, Processes, and Democratic Prospects* (Oxford : Clarendon Press, 1998).
41 See Murray Scot Tanner, "How a Bill Becomes a Law in China: Stages and Processes in Lawmaking" (1995) 141 *The China Quarterly* 39–64. Specifically, these are independent streams of policy problems, proposed solutions (such as proposed legislation), political balances of power or "moods" and opportunities or vehicles for making decisions. Also see Michael Cohen, James G. March & Johan P. Olsen, "A Garbage Can Model of Organizational Choice" (1972) 17 *Administrative Science Quarterly* 1–26.

42 Zhenglai Deng, "Civil Society and Reconstruction of the State System of Knowledge Administration" (2000) 3 *Open Times* 15.
43 Michael D. Cohen, James G. March & Johan P. Olsen, "A Garbage Can Model of Organizational Choice" (1972) 17 *Administrative Science Quarterly* 16.
44 John W. Kingdon, *Agendas, Alternatives and Public Policies, Update Edition, with an Epilogue on Health Care*, 2nd ed. (New York: Pearson, 2010) 3.
45 John W. Kingdon, *Agendas, Alternatives and Public Policies, Update Edition, with an Epilogue on Health Care*, 2nd ed. (New York: Pearson, 2010) 19.
46 See Johan Eriksson & Erik Noreen, *Setting the Agenda of Threats: An Explanatory Model* (Uppsala, Sweden : Dept. of Peace and Conflict Research, Uppsala University, 2002); Karen Callaghan & Frauke Schnell, *Framing American Politics* (Pittsburgh, Pennsylvania: University of Pittsburgh Press, 2005).
47 Michael D. Jones et al., "A River Runs Through It: A Multiple Streams Meta-Review" (Paper delivered at the workshop on "Ambiguity and Public Policy", 14–15 November 2014), [unpublished].
48 Nikolaos Zahariadis, "Ambiguity and Multiple Streams", in Sabatier Paul A. & Weible Christopher M., eds, *Theories of the Policy Process*, 3rd ed. (Westview Press, 2014) 25.
49 Andrea Schoepfer, Stephanie Carmichael & Nicole Leeper Piquero, "Do Perceptions of Punishment Vary between White-Collar and Street Crimes" (2007) 35 *Journal of Criminal Justice* 151–152.
50 See Johan Eriksson & Erik Noreen, *Setting the Agenda of Threats: An Explanatory Model* (Uppsala, Sweden : Dept. of Peace and Conflict Research, Uppsala University, 2002).
51 John W. Kingdon, *Agendas, Alternatives and Public Policies, Update Edition, with an Epilogue on Health Care*, 2nd ed. (New York: Pearson, 2010) 198.
52 John W. Kingdon, *Agendas, Alternatives and Public Policies, Update Edition, with an Epilogue on Health Care*, 2nd ed. (New York: Pearson, 2010) 150–153.
53 John W. Kingdon, *Agendas, Alternatives and Public Policies, Update Edition, with an Epilogue on Health Care*, 2nd ed. (New York: Pearson, 2010) 195.

4 Problem stream for Chinese criminal lawmaking

This chapter argues that the development of the internet and increased public participation facilitate the amendment of Chinese criminal law. Willingness of expression on the internet and anxiety over social safety create demands for rapid responses from the government. While keeping tight control of the internet on political issues, the party-state tolerates some social pluralism on the discussion of non-political problems, as long as it maintains ultimate control over agendas and outcomes. State strategies on internet censorship and crime fighting have succeeded in maintaining the public sense of security at a relatively high level.

This chapter will examine the "problem stream" that has driven the amendments to the criminal law with the aim of examining the role the public plays in generating the "problem." Criminal law is the most public face of the state security function. While it is often argued that both Chinese bureaucratic administration and lawmaking lack public participation, criminal law legislation seems to be different, especially when it has a direct impact on the safety of the greater population. On the one hand, it is common to develop criminal lawmaking in response to intense public emotions and criticisms—feelings of insecurity, anger toward offenders and sympathy for victims. On the other hand, the use of criminal law usually shapes the public's assessment of the state's security capabilities, which is a key focus of governance. Thus, compared to other laws, criminal law stands as a case study of the interplay between a state trying to maintain its legitimacy and a public increasingly seeking to voice its demands.

The first section of this chapter examines the focusing events, which pose challenges for the public trust in the government. The second section argues that in the focusing events, collective forces from emotional, negative online voices empower the public who have been unable to express themselves properly. The internet, which provides the platform for information transmission and open discussion, shapes the development of such events. Then the third section analyzes survey results concerning public emotions as a comparison to online discourse. Surveys show that in China the fear of crime is low, but anxiety concerning risk has seen a significant increase. Anxiety partly explains the overwhelmingly negative online expression.

In this chapter, drunk driving is selected as a representative case due to its huge national influence, and the other two cases, which involve fewer conflicts, are used as the supplements. Evidence is collected from documentation and archival records. Documentation includes news broadcasts, journal articles and cyber blogs. Archival records are composed of charts, survey data, etc. It is noted that most documentation and records are produced for a specific purpose and a specific audience, so the contents of such evidence have to interpreted with enough caution.[1] Thus this chapter relies on both official announcements and cyber discourses, and survey data from both Chinese and foreign organizations as evidence.

4.1 Studies of nationally known cases as focusing events

> Problems are often not self-evident by the indicators. They need a little push to get the attention of people in and around government. That push is sometimes provided by a focusing event like a crisis or disaster that comes along to call attention to the problem, a powerful symbol that catches on, or the personal experience of a policy maker.[2]

The same happens in China. In concrete terms, governments constantly face a stream of problems, some of which are viewed as especially urgent or ripe for solution at any given time, some of which go largely unnoticed for long periods.[3] "It is a process of problem recognition that serves as an impetus."[4] This section examines high-profile cases as focusing events prior to the drafting of the amendments.

4.1.1 Three case studies

That drunk driving and speeding gained national online attention in 2008 and 2009 is deemed by a number of people as the main reason for the eighth amendment of criminal law. Serious traffic accidents have been the media's focus, but none have generated so much interest as a series of such accidents in 2008 and 2009. In December 2008, Weiming Sun killed four people and wounded one by crashing into four cars while driving drunk. In June 2009, Mingbao Zhang killed five people and injured four while driving drunk. Newspapers unavoidably set the stories together for more attention. Bloody crime scene photos and stories of grieving relatives rapidly grabbed national attention, giving rise to overwhelming expressions of sympathy and anger on the internet.[5] In May 2008, Bin Hu killed a young man while speeding with other cars. The accident enraged the public since the victim was said to be a decent, diligent man with a bright future, while the offender was a spoiled youth from a rich family who did not appear to feel any guilt about his offence. That the police first claimed his driving speed was 70 miles per hour—which was far below his actual speed—also intensified suspicions of a possible trade-off between the offender's wealthy family and the police.[6]

> Populist responses to crime are strongest and would seem most likely to influence policy when they are focused on a common enemy, a group of

> criminals who seem utterly different from the rest of the population, and a common enemy whose activities only add to the pervading sense of anxiety and tension characteristic of everyday life.[7]

In the process, the internet and traditional media have shaped the discourses of each other in following the developments of these cases. Online discussions are more emotional, critical and pessimistic, while traditional media like newspapers and TVs are balanced with detailed storylines, officials' opinions and public claims.

The cases of Mingbao Zhang and Bin Hu were voted into the top-ten influential cyber incidents in 2008.[8] With wide discussions online, the cases challenge the authority's management skills; not only is there anger toward the offenders, but the public keeps expressing demands for stricter governance of traffic offences, as well as voicing their suspicion of the injustice that the police and the judiciary may generate. "An idea has a history. When one starts to trace the history of a proposal or concern back through time, there is no logical place to stop the process."[9] Even though the cases are never a perfect illustration of the divide between a good and a deteriorating traffic situation, they emerge as crises of policing and social governance through pressures from society.

A similar situation arises in cases of fake medications. Since 2006, counterfeit medications have been a nightmare for China. Serious cases happened every month of every year in China before 2006, but it was still not a pressing "problem" that required timely response. The reasons why it changed into an urgent problem were: (1) consistent media exposure of similar fatal cases, particularly on the internet; (2) victim deaths; (3) growing public panic of unseen threats; and (4) loss of confidence in local governments. All of these reasons transformed the problem of fake medications into a national crisis. For instance, in 2006, the fake medicine scandal of Qiqihar No 2 Pharmaceutical Company in Heilongjiang province killed 13 patients. This scandal lasted for two years until the offenders were sentenced to life in prison in 2008.[10] After that, in the 2010 Shanxi vaccine scandal, a reporter for the *China Economic Times* disclosed that improperly stored vaccines administered by the Shanxi Provincial Center for Disease Control and Prevention had killed 4 children and injured more than 70 others between 2006 and 2008.[11] As the news quickly spread on the internet and other media, the panicked public not only called for a fast response from the government about the truth behind the vaccines, but also refused to take any vaccine provided by the government. This deep suspicion and fear can also be easily found in the Chinese opinion of food safety, instigated by the 2008 milk powder scandal.[12] Slow action from the Shanxi provincial government and a refusal to admit a problem with the investigation left the government heavily criticized by the public. The deaths by fake medications, particularly from government-owned enterprises, challenged the governing capacity of the party-state.

Environmental cases such as water pollution have also become increasingly serious since the 2000s. The 2007 Report of Cyber Opinions in China claimed that environmental protection was becoming an essential public concern.[13] In the 2008 report, it was suggested that environmental problems were one of the top social problems as well.[14] In 2007, the bloom of cyanobacteria in Lake Taihu that contaminated the drinking water of Wuxi City, and the 2009 water pollution in Yancheng City by carbolic acid emitted by a local factory which affected the daily lives of millions of people, were only two in a series of water pollution cases in the Jiangsu, Shandong and Fujian provinces from 2009 to 2011. Netizens who first discovered the news posted it on local forums and personal micro-blogs, complaining about the lack of timely information on water pollution.[15] Public anxiety quickly expanded to other provinces in China. Local governments swiftly dispatched emergency response and inspection teams to restore clean water to the cities. But even after restoring normal water supply, complaints and worries continued. "Crises, disasters, and focusing events reinforce some preexisting perception of a problem, focus attention on a problem that was already in the back of people's minds."[16] It has not only been the affected citizens, but also others who learn about stories through the media, who have increasingly stressed the urgent need for environmental protection. Through these cases, the public have also begun to recognize the price of extensive economic development. As surveys indicate, though satisfied with rising living standards, citizens are becoming more and more anxious about environmental, medication, food and traffic safety in China, most of which they believe is the result of government incompetence.[17]

4.1.2 The public, the media and the government

The above problems become the so-called "focusing events" for Chinese criminal lawmaking.[18] The dynamic looks different from what it used to be in the 1990s or before. First, the problems are prominent daily issues for Chinese citizens. John W. Kingdon suggests that compared to health issues, traffic problems (including car accidents and airplane crashes) generate more public attention, pushing the issue of traffic regulation onto the agenda.[19] Traffic, medication and environmental problems, which are a part of everyday public experience and perception, are easier to detect, especially when they challenge the governance capacity. Central and local governments must therefore react quickly to avoid social unrest. These challenges also show that China, which is still in the process of modernization, differs from late-modern Western societies where environmental, food or drug security issues have ceased to be top social concerns.[20]

Second, the public views the government's neglect of duty as a main reason for the above social problems. Trust in the government is consistently being challenged. It has become a characteristic of Chinese society to blame local or central governments for creating injustices, lacking modern management skills or being irresponsive to public demands. They "make that translation by evaluating conditions in the light of their values, by comparisons between people or between the US and other countries, and by classifying conditions into one category or another."[21] Although only a fraction of those who care about the issues write about it online, being brave and having the consciousness to complain have already been improvements of the traditionally obedient Chinese. The tendency to blame the government is partly because of the paternalistic tradition in Chinese society. The all-inclusive government has manipulated too many social fields, making it seem as though the government is responsible for all the problems. At the same time, the criticisms are also intensified when a large number of people start to view themselves as rights holders rather than subordinates of the government. Shifts in the roles and relationships between the government and the citizens empower the citizens to fight for their rights.

Third, one key reason for the rising attention toward problems is the media's function of sharing news and molding public opinion. It is through the internet and traditional media that information is exposed and discussed. Some news is first posted by netizens themselves; some is forwarded for more awareness. "People discuss and debate about these issues in online bulletin boards and online communities, thus taking the issues beyond the officially guided coverage of the mainstream mass media."[22] In several cases, broadcasting news through micro-blogs and forums demonstrates remarkable value since local governments are forced to respond quickly to satisfy not only the interested parties, but also bystanders. Whatever online or offline methods the government adopts, the goal is to minimize the effect of such social unrest, which could damage their reputations and careers within hours. Conflicts are rapidly mitigated rather than being continuously ignored.

Chinese society is extremely diverse with multiple participants and dynamics, and can never be fully described through a single aspect. It is a "field" in the theory of Pierre Bourdieu,[23] in which people on the inside relate and struggle with each other through complex social relations, developing the "habitus" as a subjective structure for their actions and thoughts. Both in the physical and virtual fields, the party-state that remains authoritative faces new challenges from the bottom, both about its legitimacy and its ability to govern. The media operates between government censorship and market drivers, but rather than a watchdog, it also strives for profit and independence. When public thoughts and activities are clearly influenced by the media and the restrictions imposed by the government, citizens also develop their own judgments and consciousness with the growing access to information. This necessarily impacts others with less media and internet access, shaping the entire Chinese society. The public, the media and the government develop the habitus for their own interests. If the participants can successfully arouse general attention, if the media deems something newsworthy and, most importantly, if the story is not a sensitive issue that will seriously undermine the government's legitimacy, the problem is more likely to be settled within the bureaucratic system or enter into the stream of legislation. Missing one single factor—for instance, government approval/support, public initiation or consistent follow-up from the media—may lead to a lack of government engagement. Whether public opinion is uninformed or not, or whether it boosts nationalism or populism or not, will not change this dynamic.

Considering the role of the media, and especially of the internet, in contributing to the focusing events, the next section will analyze netizens' opinions about these cases. Netizens who are concerned about such issues express themselves online by commenting on, forwarding and supporting (liking) the news. Their collective use of the internet initiates the so-called "focusing events."

4.2 Opinions of netizens on focusing events and Chinese criminal law

4.2.1 Rapid growth of the Chinese internet: Social background

The public needs to find ways to access information and voice their demands. Since 2000, the internet has become a new method for them to not only obtain the latest news, but also to communicate with the government and others in a much more efficient way. In China, according to the laws and policies,[24] there are multiple ways for the public to express their opinions, including through representatives of the National People's Congress or People's Political Consultative Conference, local party organizations, the petitioning system, public hearings and surveys. But these traditional approaches usually fail to provide space for enough "authentic" public voices. It is also difficult to determine the extent to which statistics are shaped by political considerations. Newspaper articles and TV programs are commonly filled with government guidelines or intellectual arguments, rather than those from the masses. The limited venues conflict with the soaring demands for expression and communication in the Chinese modernization process where "citizens intend to participate more and more in political, economic and social affairs for their rights and interests."[25] Lacking enough independence and power, the National People's Congress remains far from the Western understanding of parliament. Furthermore, the petitioning system is continuously being criticized for its ineffectiveness, abuse and illegal imprisonment of petitioners.[26] Non-government organizations also grow slowly due to the strict environment, with registration conditions, fund raising and their own problems. Public surveys organized by the government, research institutes and business corporations, which are much more numerous than before, are good ways to trace public opinion. But compared to the internet, surveys are still less responsive and convenient. New media outlets allow the voice of the general public a much more direct airing.[27] Cyber discourse is a crucial source for viewing the emotions and attitudes of the masses.

According to the thirty-third report of the Chinese Internet Network Information Center (CNNIC), at the end of December 2013 China had 618 million internet users, a 9.5% increase over the year before, and a penetration rate of 45.8%.[28] By March 28, 2020, the number of internet users increased to 904 million, with internet penetration reaching 64.5%.[29]

In 2011, according to a survey carried out by Sohu.com, a noted Chinese internet company, and the Horizontal Research Consultancy Group, a well-known professional research and consulting firm at that time, blogs, micro-blogs and online forums were the first choices for voicing complaints, compared to traditional means of making phone calls, writing or going directly to the agencies.[30] After that, since the middle of 2010s, WeChat gradually took the place of blogs and forums as the major means of communication for the Chinese public. Cyber opinions are generated and broadcasted every day in China, especially through mobile internet users. Those willing to meet in virtual arenas and daring enough to air their discontent with social and political problems are definitely on the increase.[31] There is also evidence that internet venues have influenced the verdicts of judges, party officials and the overall news agenda.[32]

Therefore, although cyber opinions are not fully representative of the views of the general public, the internet remains a low-cost way to assess public attitudes, especially those contrary views or findings that the authorities commonly dislike.

4.2.2 Netizen opinions on focusing events

The internet is commonly filled with negative opinions. Before the enactment of the eighth amendment, in Tianya Club, one of the most popular online forums in China at that time, news related to drunk driving could get millions of hits and thousands of comments.[33] With the exception of feedback with ambiguous meaning, a majority of replies were short and full of resentment toward offenders and the government. They often argued for retributive "eye for an eye" justice as well as tough treatment. The supposed lenient criminal penalties had always been a focus of cyber critics. For instance, in Tianya Club, on the cases of Mingbao Zhang, Weiming Sun and Qiming Li, there were three posts addressing them separately. They each had around 1000 replies. The case of Mingbao Zhang, who killed five, injuring four, gained the greatest number of angry relies. Even relies showing a little sympathy toward the offender were overwhelmingly berated. Among relies of the other two cases, around 25% argued that the offender should be sentenced with the death penalty. Around 23% were skeptical of justice since it looked to them that compensation to the victims' family could reduce sentences. Around 28% were focused on other legal problems, such as judicial discretion, gaps in the legal system and so on.[34] Compared to posts on drunk driving and speeding, posts addressing fake medications and environmental protection focused much more on poor governance. Comments on other websites such as www.163.com and www.weibo.com were similar. There were also numerous concerns about social disorder after news of serious offences. This may support the argument that cyber sentiment is sometimes emotional,[35] but a high number of comments represent the actual beliefs of a large portion of the public about the society's political, economic and social aspects—beliefs filled with dissatisfaction. Without the internet, such voices would not be reflected. It also appears as though most known cyber cases are created by the collective strength of such "nonsense" arguments. "Growing media diversification and consumption clearly increased public confidence in media and nurtured citizen-initiated political participation, pro-Western feelings, a sense of political efficacy and civic values."[36] The internet empowers the public; broad sections of the public that have regularly demanded the right to be involved in matters of governance are no longer satisfied with this (decision making) being decided on their behalf behind the scenes.[37] When the society starts to/dares to re-consider the legality, legitimacy and ability of state governance, the party-state will pay more attention to public demands.

The online discourse of criminal justice in China converges with the "penal populism" of the West.[38] For instance, in China "most people have a strong intuition that deterrence works."[39] The retributive and deterrent demands of the public on criminal law are not unique to Chinese society. The public in Western countries, including the US and UK, also expect strong punitive measures and criticize lenient sentences.[40] This idea that "desperate diseases must have desperate remedies" is almost a human instinct. "It is usually the rights of the public at large to safety and security, and the withdrawal of rights from those very groups (immigrants, asylum seekers, criminals, prisoners) on whose behalf other social movements are campaigning for."[41] Besides, the media "have the effect of shaping, solidifying and directing public sentiment and opinion on crime and punishment."[42] The media are prone to focus more extensively on stories of violent crimes and series of crimes, which make crime seem all too prominent and close to each individual (no matter how removed). Furthermore, both in the East and West, in criminal justice the politics appear more in tune with the ideas and expectations of the public. The internet not only provides a platform for individual expression and open communication, but also creates a new type of social participation[43] in which everyone can be the news receiver and broadcaster, with wider freedoms than ever before. Both the public and the authorities agree (officially, at least) that the public can and should have a strong influence on penal affairs, so punishment should be turned into a public spectacle rather than taking the form of a bureaucratic accomplishment hidden from public view. One aspect in which the Chinese scenario is distinctive from that of the West is public suspicion of judicial injustice. In the West, "the desire for longer, more punitive prison sentences was inextricably linked to the desire to curtail the power and authority of those members of the establishment who seemed to want to defend the criminal rather than protect innocent victims."[44] In China, by contrast, the desire for stronger punishments is based on the desire to prohibit those in power from exercising judicial inequality, which they believe will only segregate the powerless. Defending an advantaged criminal is what the Chinese largely believe happens in reality. Therefore, most Chinese still tolerate vulnerable criminals in some specific cases. The relatively open cyber arena gives rise to an explosion of emotions and demands. "Since political reform started in the late 1970s, openness has simultaneously brought a market economy, liberalism, and democratic ideas."[45] China is still in the process of establishing the institutions that define modernity, such as a market economy, professionalized bureaucracy and autonomous legal and political systems,[46] so that late-modern crises of the West are less prominent in China. The lack of independent victims' rights and citizen-based lobby groups forces individuals to directly face the government. What they mostly criticize is the unfairness in both the judiciary and the administration, which favor the powerful and the rich.

It is interesting that cyber pessimism is slightly different from the results of public surveys. Limited survey results on attitudes toward the eighth amendment of Chinese criminal law converge with online discourses, while surveys on the public's sense of security show a different picture. The last section of this chapter aims to explore surveys disseminated by the government, private companies and foreign research groups as comparisons of negative online discourses.

4.3 Public sense of security in the surveys

The surveys are taken by national bureaus, national research centers, government-owned magazines, civil organizations and market research companies in China. There are very few surveys on nationwide topics carried out by individual researchers. To increase the reliability of the information, this section also relies on survey data from a foreign project, Pew Global Attitudes Project, as a comparison with the Chinese data.

4.3.1 Public sense of security: Based on survey results

There have been a few surveys about public opinion specifically on the eighth amendment of criminal law. In 2009, the Horizon Research Consultancy Group conducted a survey on drunk driving; 73.7% of respondents believed drunk driving was very dangerous; more than half claimed that the penalties for driving after drinking were too lenient; more than 30% suggested that stricter enforcement and harsher penalties would help improve the situation.[47] However, surveys on fake medications and environmental protection are more scattered. The Canton Public Opinion Research Center, an independent civil organization, has been conducting surveys since 2011 all over China. After 2003, attitudes toward environmental protection within Guangdong province moved up and down, but in general people have recognized the pollution problem as becoming increasingly serious and damaging to their health. More than 80% of residents agreed that lack of regulation is the main reason for the deteriorating environment.[48] In online surveys on medicine safety and environmental pollution, negative opinions appear much more often than those on other topics. Increasing penalties is usually considered to be the most desirable solution.

However, surveys on the public's sense of security since 2000 tell a different story. For instance, statistics from the National Bureau of Statistics since 2001 suggest that although there was a minor decline in the number of people who believed the overall society was "quite safe" or "safe," that number has grown from 37.1% to 63.6% since 2005. If there were the option of choosing "basically safe," 90% of respondents would have chosen it. After 2008, the China Statistical Information and Consultancy Service Center replaced the National Bureau in administering the surveys, and the public's feelings of security in each province were above 95%.[49] Scholars like Yijun Pi from the China University of Political Science and Law raised doubts about the authenticity of the data,[50] but his doubts remained personal suspicion lacking academic counter-evidence.

There are still no independent academic surveys on the public sense of security today.

Survey results conflict with the rising crime rate in China. Rapid social development has been accompanied by rising crime rates that are unprecedented in Chinese history.[51] Crime rates in the 2000s were much higher overall than those before the 1970s, despite the ups and downs.[52] Especially after the economic reforms, both violent crimes and victimization rates increased, until around 2002 and 2003 when rates began to develop at a slow and steady speed.

Considering "Chinese public opinion via sample survey has come under increasing scrutiny, in a growing number of mass-based studies,"[53] there are other resources to help confirm the credibility of official data. Existing studies all suggest that the Chinese citizens agree that living in China feels relatively safe. The result is supported by surveys taken by the journal *Insight China* from 2007 to 2020.[54] But *Insight China* is a semi-monthly magazine that is affiliated to *Qiushi*, the party-run magazine in Beijing; even though it claims to voice public opinion, discussing affairs regarding Chinese politics and social culture, its data are inevitably influenced by political considerations. It is believed that "Information supplied by the Chinese government deserves careful reading, with attention to its possible incompleteness, omission, distortion, misrepresentation and bias." A public sense of security is a crucial factor to show the party's governing capacity.[55] "The state in China has sought to maintain its own legitimacy and authority by using poll reports in the news media to justify its performance and thus to influence Chinese people's fundamental political attitudes."[56] Table 4.1 also shows that national surveys may be more or less shaped by the preferences of Chinese officials in China.

In contrast to domestic surveys, overseas ones may test the survey results mentioned above. The Pew Global Attitudes Project conducts research around the world on a broad array of subjects ranging from people's assessments of their own lives, to the current state of the world and important issues of the day. Several surveys have been conducted on the views and concerns of the Chinese population.[57] Although the research design, sample size and representativeness of each survey are different, the Pew Global Attitudes Project was sponsored by an overseas organization and may help verify some official data on China. A 2007 report entitled "A Rising Tide Lifts Mood in the Developing World" found that the Chinese people are much more satisfied with national conditions than they were in 2002 (83% now vs. 48% then). The Chinese also give near universal support to the national government; fully 89% say the national government has a very good or somewhat good influence on the way things are going in the country. The 2008 report on China notes that the citizens who were polled rated many aspects of their own lives favorably.

> Concern about crime is down considerably, however, from 2002, when 89% said it was a big problem and 40% rated it very big. About six-in-ten Chinese think crime is a big problem in the country and 17% rate it a very big problem.[58]

Table 4.1 Comparisons of survey results regarding public sense of security

Data	*Data sources*	*Surveyor*	*Presenter*	*Data results*	*Feature of surveyors*
National Surveys of Fear of Crime (2002–2007)	Residences nationwide (more than 1 million samples)	National Bureau of Statistics (NBS)	NBS	≥ 90% of surveyees are satisfied	Directly or indirectly associated with the government and the Communist Party
Provincial Surveys of Fear of Crime (2008–)	Residents of every province	Provincial Bureau of Statistics (PBS)	PBS and NBS	≥95%	Directly or indirectly associated with the government and the Communist Party
Safety Index of the Chinese (2004–2013)	Based on multiple existing research results	Journal (*Insight China*) owned by the government/CCP	*Insight China*	65–75%	Directly or indirectly associated with the government and the Communist Party
Public Top 10 Concerns (2002–2014)	Netizens	http://www.people.com.cn	The media	Safety—not as top concerns	Directly or indirectly associated with the government and the Communist Party
Living Quality Reports of the Chinese (2000–2013)	Residents of ten provinces (2000–5000 samples)	Horizon Research Group (HRG)	HRG and China Academy of Social Sciences	60–70%	Independent business corporation with regular co-operation with the government

These findings are more or less consistent with Chinese domestic survey results.

Therefore, it may be superficial to argue that the data are solely the result of government manipulation. The results seem to be opposed to the abundant pessimism on the internet. The following part of this section will explore the reasons why the public who were surveyed have been generally satisfied with their safety in the past 10–15 years.

4.3.2 Reasons for public satisfaction and divergence from internet sentiment

Chinese policing strategies such as consistent wars against crimes and misbehaviors are effective in reducing the public's fear of crime. They may prohibit a decline in the sense of security despite the crime rate growth. Comprehensive management of public security—"strike hard" campaigns against violent crimes—has meant increased police patrols and the number of private security guards, as well as mass surveillance systems.[59] These measures have raised public confidence in personal safety, at least with regard to serious crimes. Since the 1990s, national comprehensive management of public security has aimed to control and prevent crime through the cooperation of multiple agencies and the public.[60] The Ministry of Public Security launches campaigns against serious crime every year; in May 2013, the state also held several conferences to continue these campaigns for the maintenance of public security.[61] Public fear is significantly decreased by such police endeavors. Surveys conducted by Pew Research Center suggest that most Chinese citizens don't think crime is a big problem within the country.[62] Surveillance technology and private security that are accessible to ordinary people also help decrease their fear of crime. For example, since 2014, with a number of terrorist offences on the mainland and random killings of the innocent,[63] the people's fear of crime started to grow, but after increased police patrols and media broadcasting of wars against serious crimes, public confidence was consistently reinforced, and the fear has faded.

In addition, as Pew reports show, rapid economic growth and growing social prosperity create much support for the government. Such support influences judgments on other aspects of governmental administration. In China, most Chinese (especially the elderly who have experienced past wars), have a deep-rooted fear of lawlessness and chaos.[64] There is strong support for a government that maintains law and order and forcefully metes out severe punishment to those who break the law.[65] With such firm popular sentiment, "harsh punishment proves to the public that the government is 'doing something' about the negative consequences of economic reforms."[66] In three surveys conducted by the National Bureau of Statistics from 2005 to 2007, respondents in favor of such campaigns rose from 42.5% to 58.1%.[67] But the National Bureau of Statistics failed to take similar surveys after 2007, making it hard to follow the development of the result. Such data suggest that the public is basically confident about the government's role in crime fighting, which helps maintain some form of good reputation for the government. A punitive sanctioning system and the popularity of harsh anti-crime campaigns help the regime gain support in an insecure environment of transition.

Furthermore, rapid urbanization and growing social inequality have led to soaring crimes against people and property rights. The rise in the crime rates from 1995 to 2010 suggests that the number of crimes against property has been far greater than those against people (see Figure 4.1). On the one hand, most people have become used to the threat of minor offences like theft and fraud, assuming them to be common risks of everyday life. Though they are wary of such crime, most people do not believe it is a big issue. On the other hand, serious life threats still seem a bit removed from the lives of regular people. Data from the Chinese Yearbook from 1987 to 2010 indicate that crimes such as larceny, fraud and smuggling have grown the most, while crimes such as murder, rape and injury have developed relatively slowly. Statistics from the National Bureau of Statistics and bluebooks of Chinese society (*Society of China, Analysis and Forecast*) suggest that, from 2003 to 2012, the number of cases of murder, rape and robbery has actually declined, with larceny, fraud and smuggling rising rapidly (see Figure 4.1).

Overall, it is difficult to determine whether and to what degree the statistics and media broadcasts concerning crime rates are misleading, so it remains uncertain exactly how much the government has manipulated public opinion. However, based on existing findings, it can be assumed that in the past ten years, the general public has been basically satisfied with the safety of their living environment. The state's tough measures on crime play a crucial role in this respect. In the West,

Figure 4.1 Categories of police-filed cases from 1995 to 2010 per 100,000.

penal populism consists of a set of penal policies aimed at winning votes rather than reducing crime or promoting justice. Penal populism does not exist in the one-party China; what is taking place also has a strong resonance "between governments and various extra establishment individuals, groups and organizations which claim to speak on behalf of 'the people' in relation to the general development of penal policy."[68] The Communist Party always argues for adherence to the rule of "mass line" to serve the people's interests, and wars against crime are good opportunities for them to enhance governing legitimacy by strengthening the party–people relationship. If the statistics are correct, the Chinese landscape varies from what penal populism describes about the state's declining authority and its representatives in the West. Statistics suggest that the Chinese still hold positive views of the government's ability to fight crime, even though they have serious doubts about the state's other abilities. The "responsibilization" strategy, as well as multi-agency partnership with the West, is also nothing new in China. Under the CCP's monitoring, even the courts assume security governance duties similar to the police. All stand as an intact bureaucratic group in the face of the common enemy of crimes, not only through the coordination of state agencies, but also with local communities through the mobilization techniques inherited from the "mass line."

However, survey results also show that the public is struggling with the side consequences of economic growth, which have been damaging the trust the state has established through intense policing techniques. For example, with regard to which type of social problem respondents cared about most, data from the journal *Insight China* indicate that from 2009 to 2013 public security concerns declined, with food security identified as the top social problem, followed by medical safety, road safety and environmental safety. In addition, according to online surveys taken every year before the Two Sessions,[69] though the ranking of concerns shifts every year, since 2002 safety has never been the public's top concern. What the general public is mostly worried about is corruption, social inequality and environmental protection, among others. The 2012 Pew report "Growing Concerns in China about Inequality, Corruption" presents similar findings that the Chinese "are grappling with the concerns of a modern, increasingly wealthy society." Concern about the safety of medicine has more than tripled from 9% in 2008 to 28% in 2012. The public also expresses concerns about the environment: with air pollution (36%) and water pollution (33%) as very big problems.[70]

Therefore, survey results do not contradict the pessimism on the internet. The fairly high sense of security coexists with anxiety about new social risks. "Common people have become the victims of such social phenomena, as environmental pollution, traffic accidents, and the production of hazardous products."[71] Cyber opinions are reflections of such anxieties. What the public fears are the emerging risks endangering daily life, such as food, medicine, traffic and environmental accidents and the possible intrusion of state power into basic human rights, all of which create support for criminal legislation. With the increase of such new risks, the public's sense of security drops, which damages the trust in the government, even though traditional crimes are harshly punished. Existing satisfaction with the living environment also promotes public demand for more safety based on trusts on public policing. In addition, the demographic structures of those who frequently use the internet and those who take surveys are also distinct from each other. Surveys are excellent for manifesting the preferences of the masses through their relatively accurate research methods, while direct expression on the internet clarifies public preferences and demands, especially in specific cases. It is also claimed that internet-active citizens are younger, wealthier, better educated and more likely to live in urban areas, and such people tend to be more apt to express opinions on the anonymous internet. Therefore, at present, a widespread rise in the number of critical citizens can still be expected, even though the rapid rate of economic development has produced high levels of satisfaction among the materialist public.

Finally, it should be noted that both surveys and internet opinions are not fixed. Inconsistencies in public opinion regarding criminal justice issues have been well documented all over the world.[72] They are subject to shifts in education, government propaganda, media reports, interactions with local officials, daily experience, etc. Survey design techniques and the sheer amount of information posted on the internet influence public perception. A sense of security is not always associated with changes in the crime rate. The public feel safer with a greater police presence, even when crimes increase. They will also become anxious for a short period after media coverage of serious crimes, even as the crime rate drops. News of traffic, food, drug and environmental accidents reduces their sense of security. For the public and the state, harsher criminal law is a win–win situation.

4.4 Conclusion

This chapter has argued that the development of the internet and increased public participation have led to the focusing events facilitating the amendment of Chinese criminal law. First of all, in parallel with the "unprecedented economy growth and significant rise in the standard of living,"[73] the Chinese public has started to recognize that the society is much less secure than in the era before economic reforms. But state strategies on crime fighting have succeeded in maintaining the sense of security at a relatively high level. Democracies do not appear to have an advantage in maintaining perceptions of public security. The current worries of the Chinese masses lie primarily in traffic offences, drug safety scandals and environmental accidents, which continue to add to feelings of vulnerability. News of accidents such as airplane crashes and train derailments also increases perceptions of the world's instability and vulnerability.

These anxieties are reflected in the widespread use of the internet, and they are also consistent with survey results. The active Chinese public promote the development of focusing events through the internet, demanding timely responses from decision makers. The social landscape, and the relationship between the public and the party-state are significantly different from what they were in the past. There are six models of agenda building in the Chinese social context, addressing variations in not only the origin of issues inside and outside government, but also the degree and direction of efforts to expand issues beyond the initiating groups[74] (see Table 4.2). Currently, ordinary people want to be involved in opinion-forming themselves, rather than allowing elites to do it for them.[75] What are emerging are the fourth, fifth and sixth models with increased public participation. The next initiative will be fostering an informed, rational public deliberation in such a relatively open arena.

Seen from another angle, the picture also sheds light on changes of governance. While keeping tight control of the internet over political issues, the party-state tolerates some social pluralism on non-political problems, as long as it maintains ultimate control over agendas and outcomes and "reflect[s] its problem-focused, issue and domain segmented nature."[76] Encouraging debate and discussion on specific topics while allowing a certain degree of critique will not only test new policy ideas, but also signify the development of a more open, participatory and accountable governance model in China. This model is also consistent with the "mass line" principle adopted in both lawmaking and implementation after the founding of the PRC.[77]

However, the picture of the future is becoming gloomier. Although Weifang He, a noted Chinese scholar, claims that "the Chinese have relied on the internet so much that no western Internets have showed such magnificent power for the freedom of express,"[78] according to the CNNIC's 33rd report in 2014, the enthusiasm for using social network services was fading, especially for those with high educational background.[79] Twenty percent of netizens were not as active on social networks as before; users of micro-blogs had declined by 9% and the number of netizens who participated in blogs was also declining. Thus, the long-term effect of the internet remains uncertain when people find it less and less appealing. If, in the long run, netizens find their participation fails to gain satisfying results, their devotion to the virtual world will decrease.

Table 4.2 Six models of agenda building

		People who propose agendas		
		Decision maker	*Brain trust*	*The public*
Level of participation of the public	**Low**	I Inside Model	III Inside Initiative Model	V Outside Initiative Model
	High	II Mobilization Model	IV Inside Model with expansion	VI Outside Initiative Model with pressure

Notes

1 Robert K. Yin, *Case Study Research: Designs and Methods (Applied Social Research Methods Series)* (Los Angeles, CA: Sage Publications, 2013) 88.
2 John W. Kingdon, *Agendas, Alternatives and Public Policies, Update Edition, with an Epilogue on Health Care*, 2nd ed. (New York: Pearson, 2010).
3 Murray Scot Tanner, *The Politics of Lawmaking in Post-Mao China: Institutions, Processes, and Democratic Prospects* (Oxford: Clarendon Press, 1998) 30.
4 John W. Kingdon, *Agendas, Alternatives and Public Policies, Update Edition, with an Epilogue on Health Care*, 2nd ed. (New York: Pearson, 2010) 114.
5 "Drunk Diver: Killing 9 in the Downtown of Nanjing", online: Sohu <http://news.sohu.com/s2009/nanjingcrash/>. This Chinese website covers the whole process of the accident, including words, photos and videos of the victims, the final judgment and legal explanations.
6 "Speeding in Hangzhou: Causing One Death", online: Sina <http://news.sina.com.cn/z/fjzbc/>.
7 John Pratt, *Penal Populism* (New York: Routledge, 2007) 5.
8 Huaxin Zhu, Xuegang Shan & Jiangchun Hu, "2009 Report on Cyber Opinions", online: Cyberspace Administration of China < http://www.cac.gov.cn/2014-08/01/c_1111902745.htm>.
9 John W. Kingdon, *Agendas, Alternatives and Public Policies, Update Edition, with an Epilogue on Health Care*, 2nd ed. (New York: Pearson, 2010) 73.
10 Loke-Khoon Tan, "Counterfeiting in the Pharmaceutical Industry: A Look at the Bitter Pill in China", online: Baker & McKenzie < http://www.bakermckenzie.com/de-DE/RRChinaCounterfeitingPharmaceuticalBitterPill/>.
11 Keqin Wang, "Shanxi Vaccine Scandal", *China Economic Times* (17 March 2010).
12 The 2008 Chinese milk scandal was a food safety incident in China, involving milk and infant formula, and other food materials and components, adulterated with melamine. The scandal broke on July 16, 2008 after 16 infants in Gansu province, who had been fed milk powder produced by Shijiazhuang-based Sanlu Group, were diagnosed with kidney stones. A number of criminal prosecutions occurred, with two people being executed, another given a suspended death penalty, three others receiving life imprisonment, two receiving 15-year jail terms, and seven local government officials, as well as the Director of the Administration of Quality Supervision, Inspection and Quarantine (AQSIQ) being fired or forced to resign.
13 Huaxin Zhu, Xuegang Shan & Jiangchun Hu, "2008 Report on Cyber Opinions", online: Cyberspace Administration of China < http://www.cac.gov.cn/2014-08/01/c_1111903561.htm>.
14 Huaxin Zhu, Xuegang Shan & Jiangchun Hu, "2008 Report on Cyber Opinions", online: Cyberspace Administration of China < http://www.cac.gov.cn/2014-08/01/c_1111903561.htm>.
15 "Water of Yancheng City in Jiangsu Province Seriously Polluted: Leaving the Whole City Out of Water", online: Sina < http://news.sina.com.cn/z/jsyczlswr/index.shtml>.
16 John W. Kingdon, *Agendas, Alternatives and Public Policies, Update Edition, with an Epilogue on Health Care*, 2nd ed. (New York: Pearson, 2010) 98.
17 Jianqiang Liu, "China's Environment Ministry an 'Utter Disappointment'", online: Chinadialogue <https://www.chinadialogue.net/article/show/single/en/5788-China-s-environment-ministry-an-utter-disappointment->.
18 "Focusing events" is a conception used by Kingdon in his book *Agendas, Alternatives, and Public Policies* to refer to crises or known cases in the problem stream. It plays an important part in agenda making, and it may individually lead to the final policy outcome.

19 John W. Kingdon, *Agendas, Alternatives and Public Policies, Update Edition, with an Epilogue on Health Care*, 2nd ed. (New York: Pearson, 2010) 111–114.
20 Modernity has been a period characterized by capitalist industrialization and imperialism, urbanization, secularization and constitutional government and welfare states. Gordon Hughes, *Understanding Crime Prevention* (Berkshire: Open University Press, 1998) 3–7.
21 John W. Kingdon, *Agendas, Alternatives and Public Policies, Update Edition, with an Epilogue on Health Care*, 2nd ed. (New York: Pearson, 2010) 114.
22 Guobin Yang, "Brokering Environment and Health in China: Issue Entrepreneurs of the Public Sphere Brokering News" (2010) 19 (63) *Journal of Contemporary China* 117.
23 Pierre Bourdieu, "The Force of Law: Toward a Sociology of the Juridical Field" (1987) 38 *Hastings Law Journal* 805–853.
24 In China, the laws include Constitutional Law, The Legislation Law, Administrative Procedure Law, Regulations on Letters and Visits, etc.
25 John Pratt, *Penal Populism* (New York: Routledge, 2007) 11.
26 Editors, "Criticizing the Black Jails" (2012) 5 *Legal Science* 114.
27 John Pratt, *Penal Populism* (New York: Routledge, 2007) 13.
28 "CNNIC Released the 33th Statistical Report on Internet Development in China", online: CNNIC <http://www.cnnic.cn/AU/MediaC/rdxw/hotnews/201401/t20140117_43849.htm>.
29 "The 45th China Statistical Report on Internet Development in China", online: CNNIC <http://www.cnnic.cn/hlwfzyj/hlwxzbg/hlwtjbg/202004/t20200428_70974.htm>.
30 "Livelihood Survey in Two Sessions 2011", online: China Economic Net <http://www.ce.cn/xwzx/gnsz/zg/201103/01/t20110301_22257907.shtml>.
31 Johan Lagerkvist, "The Rise of Online Public Opinion in the People's Republic of China" (2005) 3 *China: An International Journal* 123.
32 Johan Lagerkvist, "The Rise of Online Public Opinion in the People's Republic of China" (2005) 3 *China: An International Journal* 130.
33 "Is it Fair for Sun Weiming to Receive Life Imprisonment?", online: Tianya <http://bbs.tianya.cn/post-free-1682626-1.shtml>.
34 "Zhang Ming Bao Sentenced to Life Imprisonment, While Family of the Victim Asked for Capital Punishment", online: Tianya <http://bbs.tianya.cn/post-free-1769848-1.shtml>; "Is it Fair for Sun Weiming to Receive Life Imprisonment?", online: Tianya <http://bbs.tianya.cn/post-free-1682626-1.shtml>; "Debates with Those Who Claim for Harsh Penalties on Li Qiming", online: Tianya <http://bbs.tianya.cn/post-free-2026026-1.shtml>.
35 Juan Zhang & Pal Nylri, "'Walled' Activism: Transnational Social Movements and the Politics of Chinese Cyber-Public Space" (2014) 36 (1) *International Development Planning Review* 111–132.
36 Wenfang Tang, *Public Opinion and Political Change in China* (Stanford, CA: Stanford University Press, 2005) 192.
37 John Pratt, *Penal Populism* (New York: Routledge, 2007) 40. Even the elderly or people who live in rural areas who rarely use the internet in everyday life will resort to it for help in serious disputes, especially those concerning misbehavior of government agencies and civil servants like the police, the courts and urban management officers.
38 See John Pratt, *Penal Populism* (New York: Routledge, 2007).
39 J. V. Roberts, "Public Opinion and Mandatory Sentencing: A Review of International Findings" (2003) 4 *Criminal Justice and Behavior* 502.
40 John Pratt, *Penal Populism* (New York: Routledge, 2007) 52.
41 John Pratt, *Penal Populism* (New York: Routledge, 2007) 21.

42 John Pratt, *Penal Populism* (New York: Routledge, 2007) 4.
43 Cuiming Pang, "Self-Censorship and the Rise of Cyber Collectives: An Anthropological Study of a Chinese Online Community" (2008) 3 *Intercultural Communication Studies* 60.
44 John Pratt, *Penal Populism* (New York: Routledge, 2007) 84.
45 Yin Lu, "Reporting Public Opinion Polls in China" (Paper delivered at the 65th Annual Conference of World Association of Public Opinion Research of Hong Kong, 15 June 2012) [unpublished].
46 Randall Peerenboom, *China's Long March toward Rule of Law* (Cambridge: Cambridge University Press, 2002) 130.
47 The sample of this survey is 3785 people in 7 cities in eastern and central China. Horizon Research Consultancy Group, "2009 Report on National Opinions of Public Services", online: HorizonKey <http://www.horizonkey.com/c/cn/news/2012-08/01/news_2074.html>.
48 "The Public's Un-Confidence of the Government's Investigation of Contamination", online: Canton Public Opinion Research Center <http://www.c-por.org/index.php?c=news&a=baogaodetail&id=2369&pid=7>; "Citizens Un-satisfaction of Control of Water Pollution", online: Canton Public Opinion Research Center <http://www.c-por.org/index.php?c=news&a=baogaodetail&id=3270&pid=5>.
49 "Statistical Communiqué on National Public Sense of Security Survey in 2007", online: National Bureau of Statistics of China <http://www.stats.gov.cn/english/NewsEvents/200801/t20080109_25968.html>.
50 Haitao Cheng, "Rising Crime Rates in Parallel with High Sense of Security", online: Sina <http://news.sina.com.cn/c/2006-01-20/17218925755.shtml>. The news addresses the high level of satisfaction with public safety, as a contrast to the growing crime rates in China. Doubts of the scholars and the police are raised.
51 Xiaohu Zhang, "Chinese Crime Rates in the Era of Transformation" (2002) 1 *Journal of Ningxia University* 62–66.
52 The crime rate's ups and downs during the three strike-hard periods show that it is less than likely that the campaigns managed to reduce crime. Even official crime statistics quickly resumed their rapid upward trend almost immediately after the campaign ended. The anti-crime campaigns have also been notable for their brutal methods and their frequent use of the death penalty.
53 Michael S. Lewis-Beck, Wenfang Tang & Nicholas F. Martini, "A Chinese Popularity Function: Sources of Government Support" (2013) 67 (1) *Political Research Quarterly* 16.
54 "Xiao Kang Zhi Shu", online: Insight China <http://www.chinaxiaokang.com/zhongguoxiaokangzhishu/>. *Insight China* is a Chinese journal run by *Qiushi*, a bi-monthly political theory periodical published by the Central Party School and the Central Committee of the Communist Party of China.
55 Kam C. Wong, *Chinese Policing: History and Reform* (New York: Peter Lang, 2009) 6.
56 Yin Lu, "Reporting Public Opinion Polls in China" (Paper delivered at the 65th Annual Conference of World Association of Public Opinion Research of Hong Kong, 15 June 2012) [unpublished].
57 "Survey Topics on China", online: Pew Research Center <http://www.pewglobal.org/topics/china/>.
58 The 2008 Pew Global Attitudes Survey in China, "The Chinese Celebrate Their Roaring Economy, as They Struggle with Its Costs", online: Pew Research Center <http://www.pewglobal.org>.
59 Susan Trevaskes, "The Private/Public Security Nexus in China" (2007) 34 *Social Justice* 38.

60 The Chinese Ministry of Public Security has launched the project of establishing a safe China for a long time. "Establishment of a Safe China", online: Ministry of Public Security <http://www.mps.gov.cn/n16/n983040/n3695342/>.
61 "Conference Promoting the Establishment of a Safe China", online: People <http://legal.people.com.cn/GB/43027/364596/>. President Jinping Xi held the conference to promote the continuing establishment of a safer China in Jiangsu province in 2013.
62 "Crime and Corruption Top Problems in Emerging and Developing Countries", online: Pew Research Center <https://www.pewresearch.org/global/2014/11/06/crime-and-corruption-top-problems-in-emerging-and-developing-countries/>.
63 Terrorist actions like the 2014 Kunming attack, and a series of violent riots within Xinjiang Uyghur Autonomous Region in China.
64 Borge Bakken, "Punishment in China", in Liqun Cao, Ivan Y. Sun & Bill Hebenton, eds, *The Routledge Handbook of Chinese Criminology* (New York: Routledge, 2013) 45.
65 Borge Bakken, "China, a Punitive Society?" (2011) 6 *Asian Criminology* 44.
66 Borge Bakken, "China, a Punitive Society?" (2011) 6 *Asian Criminology* 42.
67 "Reports on the Public's Sense of Security Nationwide", online: National Bureau of Statistics of the People's Republic of China <http://www.stats.gov.cn/was5/web/search?channelid=288041&andsen=群众安全感调查公报>. The national surveys invited persons above the age of 16 from 104107 (Year 2005), 102448 (Year 2008) and 101029 (Year 2007) families all over the country as surveyees through questionnaires.
68 John Pratt, *Penal Populism* (New York: Routledge, 2007) 1–3.
69 "Investigations on Hot Topics of China's Two Sessions", online: People <http://npc.people.com.cn/GB/28320/374787/>. People's Daily holds this online survey of public opinions before the Two Sessions every year. People's Daily is an official newspaper of the Chinese government.
70 "Growing Concerns in China about Inequality, Corruption", online: Pew Research Center <http://www.pewglobal.org/2012/10/16/growing-concerns-in-china-about-inequality-corruption/>.
71 Jan Michiel Otto et al., *Law-Making in People's Republic of China* (The Hague: Kluwer Law International, 2000) 146.
72 Geraldine Mackenzie, "Sentencing and Public Confidence: Results from a National Australian Survey on Public Opinions towards Sentencing" (2012) 45 *Australian and New Zealand Journal of Criminology* 57.
73 Jianhong Liu, Lening Zhang & Steven F. Messnereds, eds, *Crime and Social Control in a Changing China* (Westport, CT: Greenwood Press, 2001) 1–10.
74 Roger Cobb, Jennie-Keith Ross & Marc Howard Ross, "Agenda Building as a Comparative Political Process" (1976) 70 *The American Political Science Review* 127; Shaoguang Wang, "Public Policy Agenda-Setting Patterns in China" (2006) 5 *Social Sciences in China* 86–99.
75 John Pratt, *Penal Populism* (New York: Routledge, 2007) 82.
76 Baogang He & Mark E. Warren, "Authoritarian Deliberation: The Deliberate Turn in Chinese Political Development" (2011) 9 (2) *Perspectives on Politics* 275.
77 Jan Michiel Otto et al., *Law-Making in People's Republic of China* (The Hague: Kluwer Law International, 2000) 142.
78 Weifang He, "The Chinese Reliance of the Websites", online: <http://past.nbweekly.com/Print/Article/1884_0.shtml>.
79 "The 33rd Statistical Report on Internet Development in China", online: CNNIC <http://www1.cnnic.cn/AU/MediaC/rdxw/hotnews/201401/t20140117_43849.htm>.

5 Policy stream for Chinese criminal lawmaking

The first section of this chapter investigates the key participants of policy making, known as the "policy entrepreneurs." Inclusiveness of the policy community promotes the amendment of Chinese criminal law. Besides the officials, certain groups such as non-communist parties, lawyers and NGOs, with the desire of enhancing power, have also increased the number of lawmaking proposals in their respective fields. After that, the second section claims that even though the policy entrepreneurs have addressed most of the theoretical issues, several concerns still require reconsideration. For instance, it is difficult to resist the expansion of criminal law using legal principles, if the state really intends to do so. Whether criminalization is effective and justified or not lacks cautious examination.

Chapter 4 sketched out the "problem stream" of Chinese criminal lawmaking. It argued that willingness of expression on the internet and anxiety over social safety create demands for rapid responses from the government. On the one hand, large portions of the Chinese population are satisfied with policing under CCP governance; fear of crime has decreased as a result of the war against crime. The sense of security is also enhanced by China's significant economic growth in the past 30 years, which has provided the Chinese with far more material goods, security and openness than before. On the other hand, challenges to the new socialist model—including political instability, corruption, the income gap, environmental deterioration and the transition from a centrally planned to a market-oriented economy—exaggerate social instability though the party-state's propaganda and suggest that the society is moving in a better economic, social and political direction. Uncertainty, dissatisfaction with government, a surging sense of individual rights and widespread internet use create demands to amend Chinese criminal law.

However, it is not guaranteed that intense public demand will bring about policy reforms. In China, there have been many issues about which the public have been concerned that still go unsolved. Becoming law requires the coexistence of several factors, of which an appropriate policy proposal is one that cannot be ignored. In the "policy stream" of Kingdon's MSA, many ideas are possible in principle and specialists try them out in a variety of ways—bill introductions, speeches, testimonies, papers and conversation.[1] Therefore, this chapter will examine the policy stream of Chinese criminal lawmaking. It argues that inclusiveness of the policy community provides opportunities for both the dominant and marginalized institutions to enhance their power. The engagements promote revisions of Chinese criminal law. However, policy changes are punctuated. Institutional restraints on criminal law expansion are also lacking.

Accordingly, the first section investigates the key participants of policy making, known as the "policy entrepreneur."[2] It suggests that the current Chinese political mechanism shapes the policy stream in two aspects. First of all, the inclusiveness of the policy community promotes the amendment of Chinese criminal law. "Inclusiveness" means that the community has incorporated more and more marginalized groups into policy-making procedures. Second, without political competition, the policy stream in China modifies Kingdon's model. The proposals usually will not stay for long; they also wait until serious problems emerge. After that, the second section analyzes the technical/legal rationales these proposals dealt with. The "policy entrepreneurs" who are able to present proposals directly to the NPC and its standing committee assess the effect of criminal law. The section claims that even though the policy entrepreneurs have addressed most of the theoretical issues, several concerns still require reconsideration. This chapter takes the drafting of the three amendments of Chinese criminal law as case studies. Data come from newspapers, government reports, journal articles, etc.

5.1 Roles of the specialists in the policy stream

The policy stream in Kingdon's model—as the process of specialists making and presenting policy proposals—has a clear boundary with the problem and political streams. The policy stream is simply involved with proposals. Concerns about national mood, bureaucratic bargaining (jurisdiction competition) and administrative changes all develop in the political stream. In China, setting the policy stream separate from the influence of public opinion and political turnover has both limits and strengths. The operation of the policy stream in the one-party Chinese environment lacks a clear boundary with the political stream. All the laws in China are policy-driven.[3] As a policy instrument, law in China is constantly subject to interpretation and intervention by central and local-level officials of the party/state. The CCP's power penetrates the whole society, imbuing the two streams of "problem" and "policy" with politics. Considering that the ministries are also involved in the making of agendas and alternatives, it is justified to address their activities and implications in the policy stream as well. However, examining the policy stream alone has its own advantages. Those who raise proposals are different from those who review and debate them. Classification of the participants and proceedings makes the process clearer. In addition, distinguishing the policy stream from the political stream could saddle proposal makers with technical issues. Therefore, this chapter still aims to follow Kingdon's model by analyzing specialists' roles, including government staff or think tanks, representatives of the National People's Congress and legal scholars, keeping in mind that the policy stream is not an entirely independent process. In contrast, bureaucratic and political manipulations will be discussed in the next chapter.

5.1.1 Proposal drafting specialists: The policy entrepreneurs

A variety of people were involved with making proposals of revisions to criminal law, including cyber activists, government staff, NPC representatives, members of the People's Political Consultative Conference, NGOs and legal scholars. The Ministry of Public Security, the China People's Political Consultative Conference (CPPCC) and the All-China Environment Federation (ACEF) are the three main institutions making proposals to amend Chinese criminal law with respect to drunk driving, fake medications and environmental pollution. The Ministry of Public Security is a government organ supervised by the State Council. The People's Political Consultative Conference is a political advisory body, established by the state with the intention of becoming more representative, with consultation with a broader range of people in government affairs. The All-China Environment Federation is a self-proclaimed non-profit national organization for environmental protection and sustainable development. It is an environmental NGO with deep government ties.[4] These three agencies have specialists in various policy areas such as criminal justice, health, economy, culture, resources and environmental protection. The specialists are composed of government staff, consultants, lawyers and researchers, among others.[5]

In China, since drunk driving has become a prominent social problem, a number of people and organizations online and offline have made proposals to criminalize it. Two that eventually submitted the proposal to the NPC during China's Two Sessions in 2010 were the Ministry of Public Security and a delegate of the Political Consultative Conference, Shi Jie, who was a criminal defense lawyer. In April 2010, a representative from the Ministry of Public Security made a report to the NPC standing committee during China's Two Sessions, arguing for a revision of criminal law on impaired driving to maintain road safety. At the same time, a delegate from the Political Consultative Conference who was also the defending lawyer on the nationally known drunk driving case involving Sun Weiming, drafted a proposal to create the offence of impaired driving.[6] Noting that the war on drunk driving was far from enough to deter such crime, both reports suggested replacing existing administrative or regulatory offences with criminal penalties. However, being a criminal defense lawyer provided Shi Jie a slightly different viewpoint from those of government agencies. His proposal originated from his opinions of the case he defended, in which the offender (Sun) was charged with the crime of endangering public security.[7] The lawyer claimed that the judgment was inappropriate, considering that the court intended to use harsher penalties on the offender. He insisted that there was a gap in criminal law between traffic crimes that are caused by accident, and crimes against public security, which are felonies and intentional. Inspired by this, he proposed amending criminal law, which would reduce penalties on similar behaviors in the future, after his further research and interviews with government officials.[8]

It was the Political Consultative Conference that made proposals to the NPC to revise criminal law in 2010 with respect to the crime of fake medications (NO. 000027 of the Third Session of 11th National Committee of CPPCC). The proposal was drafted by the Jiusan Society,[9] one of the eight legally recognized political parties in China, together with the China Food and Drug Administration and the Beijing Food and Drug Administration. Based on national research from May to October 2009, these institutions argued that fake drugs had caused significant social harm to Chinese society, but that existing criminal law failed to deter such offences, making it difficult to protect citizens against such risks.[10] The proposal, which the NPC finally accepted, became part of the changed criminal code in 2011.

The All-China Environment Federation submitted a proposal to the NPC through one of its representatives with regard to the crime of environmental pollution.[11] The federation drafted three proposals altogether, later summarized as one single proposal, to the second conference of the 11th NPC National Committee in 2009. The proposals were the collective advice of the participants in a national forum of "Criminal Law and Environmental Protection" organized by the federation.[12] The forum brought together government officials, lawyers and researchers, a majority of whom supported adopting severe penalties for environmental offences.

Overall, proposal makers are active in Chinese criminal lawmaking. The preventive shift of criminal law is the result of the collective effect of specialists, even if they don't have the specific intention of making criminal law more preventive per se. Although three changes cannot fully represent reforms of the eighth amendment of criminal law, this characteristic has been evident in Chinese lawmaking. Each proposal has evolved from the efforts of multiple actors, including government agencies, lawyers, political parties, NGOs and scholars. First, that the proposals are made in cooperation with government officials or raise similar issues as officials increases the chances of their being accepted by the NPC. The decentralization of power within the system, with the central party's gradual loosening of decision-making control over lawmaking, has been coupled with tremendous bureaucratic development by the State Council and NPC staff offices.[13] For instance, on proposals regarding the crime of fake medications, the Jiusan Society worked with the other two bureaucracies to obtain the data. On crimes of environmental pollution, the All-China Environment Federation held conferences inviting government staff, scholars and lawyers. Revisions on the crime of drunk driving have also obtained wide support not only from some lawyers and researchers, but also the ministries. The heated participation reveals the majority's reliance on criminal law as the most effective tool of social control. This consensus making made before the legislation addresses legal issues of revising criminal law. In contrast to the proposals that are based simply on a sense of natural justice, such agendas are more valued by the NPC and its standing committee due to the influential proponents and research-based evidence.

Second, the lawyers, NGOs and the Political Consultative Conference—which were marginalized in public policy making—are slowly starting to shape public affairs as well. The Political Consultative Conference, which is commonly ignored as a ceremonial and non-functional government body, has been consistently making proposals to the NPC to formalize its power, covering almost all areas of social life. The lawyer community has also become active in the last couple of years, not only in suing cases, but also in becoming policy entrepreneurs in public affairs.[14] Criminal law, criminal procedure law and environmental protection law are their main focus.[15] In general, the policy entrepreneurs themselves have to gain resources to have impact on the agenda making: e.g., expertise, such as technical and legal skills from officials, lawyers and researchers, and having a name or title that is recognized by legislation law, such as representatives of the People's Congress and the People's Consultative Conference.[16] The establishment of consultative democracy, the willingness to be involved in public affairs and most importantly, the institutions' desire to enhance power, all contribute to wide participation.

The inclusion of policy entrepreneurs in proposal drafting has a significant impact on the revisions to Chinese criminal law. The most explicit outcome is that the number of provisions in the amendment has greatly increased. The increase in provisions started from the sixth amendment of criminal law in 2006, and the eighth amendment has more revisions than seven amendments before it. The number of revisions in the ninth amendment in 2015 reached a peak of 52. Rather than covering a few areas of the law like before, current revisions of criminal law cover far more areas of the law, including those regarding cybercrime, terrorism and corruption.[17] Although wider participation from the legal community is not the only reason for the increase, proposal drafting and consultation with experts make for the incorporation of more opinions into the official policy-making process. This inclusiveness benefits Chinese criminal lawmaking: not only is broader participation a good sign of the establishment of democracy, but it also promotes the contribution of more discussion topics to improve criminal law.

5.1.2 Adaption and refinement of Kingdon's model

The policy stream in the Chinese context refines the multiple streams framework of Kingdon. In MSA, Kingdon argues that the policy stream develops independently of the other two streams in agenda making. In China, to resort to criminal law has always been an agenda to those who make proposals. For example, from the Two Sessions, it is evident that the representatives consistently refer to "criminalization" as the solution for a certain social problem. They point out that there are gaps in the current criminal law, so it is necessary to improve the law for better social governance. In that case, no matter if it is justified or not, revising criminal law, either by expanding the boundary, or increasing the penalties, exists as an idea routinely floating around in Kingdon's "policy primeval soup." It is continually brought out when serious problems come about, either to solve the problem, or to gain more support.

However, China's criminal lawmaking modifies MSA in one aspect. In China, in many cases, the policy stream operates more as a response to the problem stream. "One would observe in authoritarian regimes a highly punctuated policy process in which the policy making is too insulated to react until the built-up pressures can no longer be resisted."[18] In the West,

> Active and persistent policy advocacy and interest representation keep even the more idiosyncratic and marginal issues on the policy agenda, which has the effect of diversifying the contents of the agenda and the overall scope of issues being considered by the government.[19]

MSA proposed by Kingdon is based on such institutional design. In China, without such a mechanism of policy competition, it is usually hard for one proposal to stay too long in the "pool" of proposals. Compared with the West, there are more chances that the absence of political competition will leave the policy agenda unchanged until serious problems take place, when the government has no choice but to respond. Otherwise, without sustained support, ideas will be removed from agenda making. Even though the policy community has diversified topics of proposals, persistent debates on one topic, especially before crises happen, are really rare. For instance, specialists' preferences in choosing topics have a direct impact on the contents of criminal law, while these proposals have been heavily influenced by serious incidents of road, food, drug and environmental safety. The chosen topics reflect the specialists' criterion of choosing the right (most urgent) problem and drafting solutions that are most likely to be accepted by the legislator. One such example is that the Chinese government faces growing pressure from civil society as NGOs, internet activism and protests compel the government to proactively address environmental issues.[20] Among a number of issues requiring state action, only those that are able to attract national attention receive rapid treatment. Although criminal law is not the only law on which policy entrepreneurs concentrate, among the large number of laws that are made and revised every year, it is one that is closest to the public's perception of natural justice. Compared to other laws, criminal law proposals are good opportunities to enhance existing power, or to transform the power structure's poor public image as long as they look likely to meet public needs.

Furthermore, during discussions the deterring effect of criminal law is consistently stressed. Not only does the idea of deterrence prompt the revision of criminal law, but it also eliminates further discussions about the law's legitimacy. As one researcher has noted with regard to environmental protection, arguing with those in favor of criminalization in the conferences appears "weird, hostile, and inappropriate."[21] He even hesitated to ask such people to re-consider the proposals. Especially when the issue is justified by the goal of security or public safety, it is difficult to raise opposing ideas. Most often in cases of criminal law, scholars' theoretical arguments (which mostly serve as references) are rarely able to restrain the demands of ministry officials. Although it is suggested that, in general, "state elites and experts can control policy formation, downplaying or ignoring the public's emotional attachments and irrational impulses, leading to more rational, technical responses,"[22] such ability really depends on different circumstances, under the suppression of state power. In addition, these justifications all share the element of uncertainty identified in the concept of prevention. It is "law and order ideology"—most often associated with an emphasis, not on just desserts, but on deterrence and incapacitation—which gives rise to the harshest results.[23] The limits (negative effects) of these rationales for criminalization will be documented in the next section.

In all, hot topics (especially those related to public security) and strong support (particularly from bureaucrats) contribute to quick changes in the laws. The desire to maintain or expand power in policy making, the belief in criminal law's utilitarian effect, the unshakable desire for security and the lack of persistent debates of policies until serious incidents occur, make the current criminal lawmaking in China a bold project. Considering the ministries and even the courts (at times) have advocated being harsher on misbehavior to regain public order and safety, focusing events offer sound opportunities for such growth. Besides the officials, certain groups such as non-communist parties, lawyers and NGOs, with the desire of enhancing power, have also increased the number of lawmaking proposals in their respective fields. Criminal law is not the only part, but definitely an essential part, of their focus.

One direct result of resorting to criminal penalty as a tool of social management with such frequency is the expansion of criminal law. The next section will examine the legal implications of the proposals. In Kingdon's model, criteria for selecting the ideas include technical feasibility, congruence with the values of community members and the anticipation of future constraints, and politician's receptivity.[24] Though specialists have solved most of these technical issues connected to amending criminal law, there remain several legal problems that need to be considered.

5.2 Legal concerns of the proposals

As bureaucracies, the Ministry of Public Security, the Ministry of Environmental Protection and the Ministry of Food and Drug Administration generate monthly and yearly data, reports and plans. For the Political Consultative Conference and the NGOs, such data present numerous proposals for policy and lawmaking. There have also been many other proposals from specialists in other areas of law serving to either draft a new law or revise an existing one. The agendas, having been debated by specialists from multiple fields, have a greater chance of being accepted and confirmed as law for their technical feasibility. To revise criminal law, the specialists solve legal problems to make proposals acceptable in the light of criminal law values and the proper role of the state. The war on crime launched by the Ministry of Public Security's changes to administrative law, regulations made before revisions and existing scholarship on related misbehavior are all resources that policy entrepreneurs rely on in making proposals.

The first issue that needs to be addressed is whether there exists a legal problem. Is there really a legal gap in the system, or does a given issue simply require strict enforcement? In China, weak management techniques and practices in the administrative systems are one major reason for the development of new offences and changes to traditional offences. As a developing country undergoing modernization, its institutional arrangements often lag behind the rapidly growing economy. Most problems result from a lack of efficient, practical implementation rather than from a lack of rules. For instance, one of the most crucial reasons for the weak control of fake drugs and environmental pollution is local protectionism, which values greater local GDP development rather than justice and environmental protection.[25]In addition, Beijing's decentralized authoritarianism lacks the political processes and incentives needed to implement meaningful national reform and to encourage local governments and polluting factories to adhere to laws and regulations.[26] "The PRC has promulgated an increasingly comprehensive array of laws intended to speak to environmental concerns, but those laws suffer from the doctrinal infirmities and difficulties of enforcement that characterize contemporary Chinese law more generally."[27] Court data suggest that the number of environmental cases is very low.[28] Policy works better than law. What is more efficient is the CCP's five-year plan that creates guidelines for economic growth, economic structure, resources, environment and public services. Officials who fail to reach the goals must take responsibility for such failure.

After that, the justifications for criminalization are considered, particularly those of "just desserts" and the deterring (general prevention) effects of criminal law. Total elimination of harm is not possible. The seriousness of a criminal act is the focus for deciding whether to criminalize or not.

> There should be, in principle, an initial decision about whether the conduct constitutes a serious wrong that merits criminalization, with public censure and sentencing to follow, or whether the conduct is a minor wrong that can properly be dealt with in this non-stigmatic way by a financial penalty.[29]

Two conflicting forces of criminalization are the utilitarian effect of criminal law, which advocates criminalization by the state, and the principles of criminal law that act as a constraint on massive criminalization. "The use of state coercion stands as contrary to any basic respect for an individual's autonomy."[30] The state's power of punishment ought to be squared with the duty of providing a criminal justice system that respects individuals' autonomy as responsible moral agents. To justify criminal penalties there are also another three minor technical issues that need to be dealt with: the rationale of using criminal penalties to replace administrative penalties (that is, the necessity of using criminal law to solve problems), coherence of the criminal law system itself with regard to the proper balance of various sentences and the international trend of developing criminal law. Considering that the abolishment of the death penalty and less criminalization is the current world trend, criminalization in China requires justification.

During the legislation process of Chinese criminal law, specialists have presented answers for almost all the legal concerns above. However, has misbehavior caused enough harm that it ought to be considered a crime? Drunk driving, manufacturing fake medications and environmental pollution that have not resulted in injury, death or property loss has not generated social harm. They are criminalized based on the risk of harm. Justified through severe harm, insecurity and public anger, the definition of risk and the criteria for evaluating such risk are quite objective. Even though the data suggest that with the increasing ownership of automobiles drunk driving has become much more prevalent than before, there remains a lack of evidence pointing to any increase in the manufacturing of fake medications or polluting of the environment. The caseloads mostly depend on the willingness of local government and police efforts to crack down on related wrongdoings. It is also difficult to assess the effects of the law since the current "success" (decline in crime rate) after the promulgation of the law mainly results from intense police wars, which are far from normal, everyday practices. In history, the deterring effect of criminal law has raised numerous doubts. It remains unconvincing to justify criminal penalties with it. Therefore, rather than expanding the boundary of criminal law by arguing that administrative penalties are not effective, it makes more sense to strictly enforce existing criminal and administrative law. Instead of frequently making or changing the law, it is worth considering other strategies, such as community prevention, and situational crime control.

Furthermore, after the promulgation of the eighth amendment of criminal law, data suggest that a variety of minor cases, which were formerly simply considered misbehaviors, have been charged as well, including drunk driving and manufacturing fake medications. Some researchers argue that this model, which mixes criminal penalties and administrative penalties, is learned from the West.[31] Some minor offenders are given probation or released on parole, without increasing the burden on the judicial system.[32] The model maintains public respect for the law, since offenders who commit even minor offences receive criminal penalties instead of simple administrative sanctions.[33] Some also claim that it is better to treat the offences within the criminal justice system rather than leaving them to the discretion of the police so as to not circumvent the application of procedural safeguards in the criminal justice system. Criminal procedure law will provide better protection for suspects' and offenders' rights. However, even in the West, there is support for a more extensive regulatory field and less extensive criminal law. For instance, in its 2010 Consultation Paper, the English Law Commission proposed that the use of criminal law to reinforce regulatory systems in England and Wales should be reviewed.[34] Regulatory offences are generally denoted as "simple offences." Section 21(1)(c) of the Penal Code defines a simple offence as an offence "punishable with imprisonment for up to ten days or with fine of up to twenty-five thousand francs." However, this is not always so because a person convicted of an offence under section R. 370(7)–(10) is liable for more severe penalties.[35] Thus, what is the line between offences that merit criminalization and other minor infractions "that can properly be dealt with in this non-stigmatic way"? In China, those who receive criminal penalties will be faced with far more disadvantages in their future career and life. The distinction between administrative and criminal penalties still needs to be maintained, since "whereas the criminal law is a censuring institution, regulation has a less morally condemnatory tone."[36] "Harm done or risked should be regarded as serious enough to warrant criminalization."[37]

Indeed, some Western researchers have already recognized that "it seems that both the harm principle and the culpability principle require external supplements if they are to avoid collapsing into illiberal results."[38] They argue that the liberal criminal law theory lacks enough restraint on the criteria defining right and wrong. Instead, political theory may provide a more secure contemporary foundation for the objectivist limit.[39] For instance, in *Overcriminalization*, Husak suggests applying principles of political obligation, within the appropriate scope of an individual citizen's duties to the state, to the limits of the criminalization problem.[40] In "The Problem of Mistaken Self-Defense: Citizenship, Chiasmus, and Legal Form," Alan Norrie also insists that "what determines the matter in individual cases is a political understanding of the nature of citizenship in modern society."[41] Therefore, political consideration of the citizen–state relationship offers external criteria for dealing with theoretical legal problems. On one hand, when Chinese scholars apply Western liberal criminal law theory to Chinese practice, they face similar difficulties in carrying out deep legal analysis without political philosophy theories; on the other hand, it is difficult to resist the expansion of criminal law using legal principles, if the state really intends to do so. An interdisciplinary study with a political perspective may solve this problem, and that is the reason why socio-legal and sociological studies of criminal law are needed in Chinese research.

By reviewing the legal problems, this section investigated concerns about changes to criminal law. The community has made and reviewed specialists' proposals with legal reasoning, but the proposals stand more as a means to gain power and public support. Whether criminalization is effective or not lacks cautious examination.

Notes

1 John W. Kingdon, *Agendas, Alternatives and Public Policies, Update Edition, with an Epilogue on Health Care*, 2nd ed. (New York: Pearson, 2010) 19.
2 John W. Kingdon, *Agendas, Alternatives and Public Policies, Update Edition, with an Epilogue on Health Care*, 2nd ed. (New York: Pearson, 2010) 117.
3 See Pitman Potter, *China's Legal System* (Cambridge: Polity Press, 2013); Hualing Fu, "The Varieties of Law in China", online: Human Rights in China <http://www.hrichina.org/en/crf/article/5422>.
4 Rachel E. Stern, "The Political Logic of China's New Environment Courts" (2014) 72 *The China Journal* 58; "Introduction of All China Environment Federation", online: All China Environment Federation <http://www.acef.com.cn/en/aboutacef/2013/1216/1004.html>.
5 In the book, "specialists" refer to those who are directly involved in the process of raising and negotiating bills, rather than a layperson. Specialists include but are not limited to legal scholars.
6 Changyu Li, "Partner of Grandall Law Firm Shi Jie: A Protector as Well as a Builder", *People's Daily* (22 November 2014) A03.
7 "Bill Suggesting Criminalization of Impaired Driving", online: People <http://2010lianghui.people.com.cn/GB/180669/11050327.html>.
8 "Shi Jie, Promoter of the Criminalization of Drunk Driving", online: JCRB <http://www.jcrb.com/zhuanti/fzzt/2011nzch/mkp/67890/>.
9 "The No.000027 Bill to the Third Session of 11th National Committee of CPPCC", online: CPPCC <http://www.cppcc.gov.cn/2011/09/19/ARTI1316434127187911.shtml>.

10 "The No.000027 Bill to the Third Session of 11th National Committee of CPPCC", online: CPPCC <http://www.cppcc.gov.cn/2011/09/19/ARTI1316434127187911.shtml>.
11 "Bill of the ACEF on Criminal Law Revision Accepted by the NPC", online: CPPCC <http://www.acef.com.cn/envlaw/news/2009/0602/2217.html>.
12 "Suggestions of Scholars in the Conference of 'Criminal Law and Environmental Protection'", online: All-China Environment Federation <http://www.acef.com.cn/envlaw/news/2009/0602/2215.html>.
13 Murray Scot Tanner, "Organizations and Politics in China's Post-Mao Law-Making System", in Pitman B. Potter, ed, *Domestic Law Reforms in Post-Mao China* (New York: M.E. Sharpe, 1994) 87.
14 Cheng-Tong Lir Wang, Sida Liu & Terence C. Halliday, "Advocates, Experts and Suspects: Three Images of Lawyers in Chinese Media Reports" (2014) 21 (2) *International Journal of the Legal Profession* 195; Sida Liu & Terence C. Halliday, "Political Liberalism and Political Embeddedness: Understanding Politics in the Work of Chinese Criminal Defense Lawyers" (2011) 45 (4) *Law & Society Review* 832.
15 Sida Liu & Terence C. Halliday, "Political Liberalism and Political Embeddedness: Understanding Politics in the Work of Chinese Criminal Defense Lawyers" (2011) 45 (4) *Law & Society Rev* 833.
16 The identities are backed up by people who hold power, or have connections with power.
17 *Criminal Law of the People's Republic of China*, as amended by RS 2011.
18 Wai Fung Lam & Kwan Nok Chan, "How Authoritarianism Intensifies Punctuated Equilibrium: The Dynamics of Policy Attention in Hong Kong" (2014) 28 (4) *Governance* 552.
19 Wai Fung Lam & Kwan Nok Chan, "How Authoritarianism Intensifies Punctuated Equilibrium: The Dynamics of Policy Attention in Hong Kong" (2014) 28 (4) *Governance* 551.
20 Elizabeth Economy, "Environmental Governance in China: State Control to Crisis Management" (2014) 143 (2) *Daedalus* 184.
21 Jie Feng, "Background Information of the Interpretation of Crime of Environmental Pollution: Coming of the Era of Harsh Punishment?", online: Southern Weekly <http://www.infzm.com/content/93158>.
22 Vanessa Barker, *The Politics of Imprisonment: How the Democratic Process Shapes the Way America Punishes Offenders* (New York: Oxford University Press, 2009) 177.
23 Michael Cavadino & James Dignan, *Penal Systems: A Comparative Approach* (London: Sage Publications, 2006) 339.
24 John W. Kingdon, *Agendas, Alternatives and Public Policies, Update Edition, with an Epilogue on Health Care*, 2nd ed. (New York: Pearson, 2010) 200.
25 Xiaoping Qian, "Western Experience on Environmental Protection Legislation" (2014) 3 *Political Science and Law* 137.
26 Elizabeth Economy, "Environmental Governance in China: State Control to Crisis Management" (2014) 143 (2) *Daedalus* 184.
27 Willam P. Alford & Yuanyuan Shen, "Limits of the Law in Addressing China's Environmental Dilemma" (1997) 16 *Stanford Environmental Law Journal* 127.
28 Chunxiang Yuan, "Analysis of Cases of Environmental Pollution from 2002–2011: Based on Data from Courts Nationwide" (2012) 12 *Legal Information* 19–23.
29 Andrew Ashworth & Lucia Zedner, *Preventive Justice* (Oxford: Oxford University Press, 2014) 117.
30 Andrew Ashworth & Lucia Zedner, *Preventive Justice* (Oxford: Oxford University Press, 2014) 6.

31 Mingkai Zhang, "Criminal Law in the Cyber Age: On the Principle of Necessity" (2014) 9 *People's Procuratorate Semi-Monthly* 9–12.
32 Some researchers have argued that the judges strive to moderate the severity of laws. Rachel E. Stern, "The Political Logic of China's New Environment Courts" (2014) 72 *The China Journal* 70; Benjamin L. Liebman, "Leniency in Chinese Criminal Law? Everyday Justice in Henan" (2015) 33 (1) *Berkeley Journal of International Law* 153–222.
33 Xingliang Chen, "Critical Doctrinal Analysis of Risk Theory Society" (2014) 1 *Peking University Law Review* 125.
34 Andrew Ashworth & Lucia Zedner, *Preventive Justice* (Oxford: Oxford University Press, 2014) 117.
35 Part four of the Penal Code lists many simple offences. The provisions under this part are designated as "section R…" The "R" stands for "regulation." The offences grouped under part four invite a number of preliminary observations. Furthermore, all simple offences are sub-categorized into what the Code calls "classes." There are altogether four classes of simple offences, namely, simple offences of the first, second, third and fourth class. Carlson Anyangwe, *Criminal Law in Cameroon: Specific Offences* (CMR: Langaa RPCIG, 2011).
36 Andrew Ashworth & Lucia Zedner, *Preventive Justice* (Oxford: Oxford University Press, 2014) 116.
37 Andrew Ashworth & Lucia Zedner, *Preventive Justice* (Oxford: Oxford University Press, 2014) 117.
38 Peter Ramsay, "Preparation Offences, Security Interests, Political Freedom", in R. A. Duff et al., *The Structures of the Criminal Law* (Oxford: Oxford University Press, 2011) 227.
39 Peter Ramsay, "Preparation Offences, Security Interests, Political Freedom", in R. A. Duff et al., *The Structures of the Criminal Law* (Oxford: Oxford University Press, 2011) 228.
40 See Douglas Husak, *Overcriminalization* (Oxford: Oxford University Press, 2008).
41 Alan Norrie, "The Problem of Mistaken Self-Defense: Citizenship, Chiasmus, and Legal Form" (2010) 13 (2) *New Criminal Law Review: An International and Interdisciplinary Journal* 357.

6 Political stream for Chinese criminal lawmaking

Role of the CCP and the bureaucracy

This chapter examines other key influential institutions of the legislation, including the National People's Congress (NPC), the administration, the media and scholars. That criminal lawmaking is used frequently to solve social crises manifests as an active and responsive legislation. Bureaucratic reports and claims shape the law to the greatest extent through the inter-agency review process, with advice from think tanks/scholars taking an assistive role through expert argumentation meetings.

"Law making constitutes one of the fundamental functions of any society and touches up such important issues such as the trias politica and the relationship between politics and law as well as between policy and law."[1] In Kingdon's model of policy making, compared to the concept of "political" in political science research, the political stream is a narrow concept that includes electoral, partisan or pressure group factors.[2] The political stream is imposed of diversified variables like swings of national mood, organized interests, election repercussions, changes of administration and the orientations of elected officials.[3] "Although Kingdon's original application referred only to agenda setting in a single national setting, the scope of the framework is clearly broader than that."[4] For instance, it is claimed that, "the most important variable in the political stream in parliamentary systems is party politics and (where they occur) coalitions."[5] In the Chinese context, the Chinese political stream consists of CCP influence and bureaucratic negotiations on existing legal proposals. Accordingly, the first section will examine the impact of the CCP on Chinese criminal lawmaking. In China, on the one hand, although the public, the media and the specialists have played a crucial role in bringing about drafts of criminal law, the proceedings nonetheless operate within the party-state framework. Developments of national incidences and proposal bundles are essentially permitted by the party-state; otherwise, the state will intervene when needed. On the other hand, "typical analyses of Chinese law making still tend to portray a top-down law-making process, highly centralized and integrated,"[6] "but observations illustrate that party leadership over law making is far less centralized and unified than has often been supposed."[7]

The second section examines other key influential institutions of the legislation, including the National People's Congress (NPC), the administration, the media and scholars. That criminal lawmaking is used frequently to solve social crises manifests in an active and responsive legislation. It is these institutions that are eventually evolved in the process. The dynamic of lawmaking sheds light on how key institutions in China are engaged in the fundamental questions of social governance and their existence within an evolving system.[8] Police involvement plays an essential role in the proceedings.

The third section summarizes the chapter with the hierarchy of Chinese lawmaking and the law's instrumental use imbued in the legislative process. It identifies which element plays an essential role within legislative practices, and to what degree public opinions are valued in the process.

This chapter is based on a mix of data including official documents, cyber discourses, foreign surveys, foreign literature and my own observations. In contrast to most Western reports on China that focus on political suppression, this section suggests both positive and negative changes are taking place in Chinese rule of law. However, I am well aware of the limitations of the lack of data on the legislative process, and the risk of over-relying on open documents that are usually not privy to behind-the-scene activities. The chapter is a speculation on the picture of the Chinese landscape with an all-sided view of all the information that the author could obtain.

6.1 The role of the CCP in Chinese criminal lawmaking

The CCP's influence on Chinese society remains immense. Through both formal and informal mechanisms, it maintains "Foucault's panopticon" in the midst of the rapidly transforming society.[9] Drawing on Western experience, since 1978 China has established an almost entirely new legal system from nothing. This system plays an enormous role in regulating social activities. The party-state claims that, as any civilized society, China respects the rule of law, honoring equality and freedom. However, this is only true in mostly non-sensitive or non-political cases. Sometimes, "the grand theory of law in a book seldom, if ever, explains the behavior of law on the streets of China."[10] Although not announced, the law is inevitably influenced or, more precisely, directed by the party:[11] "in principle there should be no law that could be in conflict with the Party's interest and/or inconsistent with the Party's policy."[12] As an important decision maker in its own right, the party has immunized itself from legal challenges to its decisions.[13] "If somebody uses law to threaten the party's ruling status, the party may not tolerate it."[14] The CCP, which stays above the law itself, is not ready for a genuine rule of law. Of late in particular, to call the current system "a legal system with the characteristics of a communist China" justifies a departure from the modern or Westernized understanding of legal rules. The party's supervision of the legislation can be reflected in the aspects described below. Rather than "an actor in the affairs of the state," it is "an organization integrated within the state apparatus."[15] At present, the basic structure remains unchanged. The "Decision" of the 4th Plenum of the 18th Central Committee in October 2014[16] emphasized that the socialist legal system would remain bound by the Constitution and thus by the principle of party leadership. The priority of party leadership remains.

First, control is realized through organizational penetration of the NPC's leadership and control over key NPC appointments through the NPC Party Group. The ruling CCP maintains effective control over the composition of People's Congresses at various levels through this system.[17] Since legislation is the most important function of the NPC, the law, either made or revised, reflects the will of the party. However, according to the Constitution, the NPC, which is voted for by the people, is the supreme power entity in mainland China, representing the will of the Chinese public. In China, "rather than solely relying on what is written on the norms, examining the role of the congress has to analyze its true condition in the political life."[18] In both official documents and news reports, the party's name is commonly put before the People's Congress. The number of party members account for more than 60% of the NPC's representatives.[19] They are required to participate in CCP activities before the legislation to become familiar with the CCP's principles and guidelines. The NPC's central and provincial groups, whose presidents are mostly CCP leaders, are always subject to the supervision of the CCP's leading group in the legislation-making process as well.

Second, the CCP's influence on the NPC is also maintained through the initiation, approval and oversight of meeting agendas. Legislative reports commonly cite CCP demands as the most crucial drivers of legislation in China. For instance, in the *Explanations of the Draft of the Eighth Amendment of Criminal Law*, the NPC Commission of Legislative Affairs noted that the CCP's suggestion of deepening judicial reform required changes to criminal law.[20] It is also compulsory for the laws of great economic, administrative and political importance to be reviewed by the CCP before NPC meetings so that the CCP's Central Committee can approve the legislative thoughts and principles beforehand. Furthermore, presidents of central and provincial NPC groups monitor the lawmaking process, making it relatively harder for other representatives to voice objections. Therefore, even though the NPC's autonomy has increased over the years, the CCP still dominates the NPC in multiple aspects. It remains the CCP that monitors and legitimates the institutional arrangements in China. The NPC and other public mechanisms still lack the ability to restrain the power of the CCP.

However, in concrete lawmaking processes, the CCP's role is much more blurred. Although revisions of criminal law are taken within the framework of CCP dominance (which is the same as in the making of other laws), the law is not intended for political suppression. The process is carried out in a manner less concerned with "revolutionary fervor," and more on addressing urgent problems (driven by social crises), applying international rules (to reduce death penalties), increasing rationality (to improve the integrity of the legal system) and becoming more accountable to public demands (growing safety anxieties). Whether the laws eventually reach such goals is another issue. The CCP only monitors the process on a macro level of policy guidance, leaving the career bureaucrats and scholars to take the technical legislative jobs. Party discipline in concrete lawmaking is weak: "Power resources within the system are fragmented among the various leaders and bureaucracies involved in the law making."[21] The CCP's decentralization of power is consistent with Tanner's findings in his book *The Politics of Law Making in Post-Mao China*, where he contends that "centralized top-level Communist Party control over lawmaking has eroded greatly since 1978, and seems very unlikely to be significantly recentralized in the foreseeable future."[22] Even though the book was published years ago, the phenomenon has not changed. There has been a high degree of continuity in many areas.[23] The actual retreat of the CCP from lawmaking may be due to a lack of training and interest in the details of the draft bill among party officials. It makes no difference if the current model is labeled "rule of law" or "rule by law," and as long as it keeps monitoring legislative structure and proceedings, the authoritarian regime can pursue an advanced legal system without facing challenges to its leadership.

The benefits of the law that the CCP experiences are not limited to the economic needs of the market economy. It is also a requirement of the state to ensure certainty and predictability in governance, something that is not unique to China. Criminal law is a sound tool to enhance the country's leadership through increased mass support. The CCP understands that risks of both "instability" and "insecurity" from internal and external pressures keep challenging its legitimacy, especially when the economy slows down and the side effects of the fast-growing economy are increasingly serious. These side effects include corruption, social inequality and environmental deterioration, as well as problems of lack of management in food and medication production. During the Hu–Wen era, the slogan emphasized maintaining social stability and constructing a "harmonious society."[24] At present, the slogan of establishing the "Chinese dream of great rejuvenation of the Chinese nation" also makes stability and security the basis of the party-state policy. Pursuing stability relies on support from the people. Thus, appeals to populism[25] often mix with party efforts to assert oversight over the society. In particular, when fear of crime is triggered by moral panic,[26] resorting to criminal law by creating new legal rules and institutions satisfies the demands of the punitive Chinese public. Given that environmental protection and food and medication manufacturing are problems requiring systematic treatment, it is far more practical to simply increase criminal penalties. Furthermore, through the congress, the CCP's principles and policies are stressed again in lawmaking. The policies shape not only policing but also the harshness of criminal sentences to a great extent. "Policies are now to be translated into laws in accordance with proper procedures for law-making."[27] For instance, in July 1983, the CCP's Central Committee initiated the "strike hard" policy. Then, in September, the NPC standing committee followed up with a "Decision on punishing criminal offenders of serious crimes" and a "Decision on speeding up the trial of criminal offenders of serious crimes."[28] The current criminal policy of "combining leniency with severity"[29] was also first written in by the CCP, and legalized by the Supreme Procuratorate the following year in judicial announcements. This balance reflects the policy of establishing a harmonious society.[30] It is a positive change, since introducing the concept of leniency into criminal justice can not only reduce international criticism (e.g., minimizing the number of death penalties), but also save judicial resources, while being harsh on serious crimes is effective in maintaining social order. Compared to the most criticized policy of "strike hard,"[31] "combining leniency with severity" is problem-driven, and less politically inspired. First adopted in 2005 and implemented in 2007, it has already impacted both criminal lawmaking and adjudications.

Overall, the CCP's guidance in Chinese lawmaking is a mix of intense political suppression, formal composition control and loose practical restraints. It shows much flexibility in certain non-sensitive areas, even in the field of criminal lawmaking. As a matter of survival instinct,[32] the CCP understands that "it is imperative to improve the governing capacity of the party in the increasingly affluent yet divided Chinese society."[33] With the decline of the Confucius and Marxist–Leninist ideology, the law is a governance tool for the CCP that has transformed it from a revolutionary party to a ruling party.

> If China is to cope with the many problems that are by-products of economic reform, including a decline in social order, spreading corruption and a general crisis of values, it will need strong legal institutions and a legal culture that promotes the rule of law.[34]

The CCP relies on the law to advance its leadership, and to boost economic and social reforms without damaging its authority. Criminalizing certain crimes most concerning to an anxious public is a reflection of such politics.

6.2 The role of other participants in the legislative process

This section will analyze the players in the process of legislation. It identifies the importance of each participant that has separate power and interests, as well as the way each is important in lawmaking. The participants include the National People's Congress (NPC), the judiciary, the administration and the media, among others. In reality, most people have mixed identities. For instance, the "public" is a general term that can comprise all the participants. A great number of government officials in China are CCP members. Some legal scholars not only serve in government positions, but also act as consultants in legal affairs. The categories are a rough way to organize the discussion.

6.2.1 The NPC

The NPC is the highest-ranking organ in the Chinese state system. Outside of plenary meetings, the NPC functions through its committees. The most important of these is its standing committee, which consists of 150–200 members and meets every 2 months.[35] However, as it has been claimed, though the congress is the supreme power entity in China, in reality it lacks enough authority. The NPC can neither decide on its own organization, nor independently determine state affairs. With gloomy prospects for political reform into a pluralistic liberal system in the near future, the NPC will continue to be under the party's censorship.

At the same time, both the NPC and the CCP have to adapt to the increasingly open society. Without challenges to its leadership, the CCP allows the NPC a certain autonomy. At present there are two phenomena evident in the legislation which manifest in "a high degree of experimentalism with consultation, deliberation, and limited forms of democracy."[36] The first phenomenon consists of more effort from the Legislative Affairs Commission[37] to incorporate popular views into legislative drafting. Before the final draft of the eighth amendment of criminal law, the commission posted drafts on the website for public review; before the Two Sessions, the CCP's official website (www.people.com.cn) conducted online surveys to gauge public concerns.[38] Cyber consultation has become routine in lawmaking in China. There have also been more press broadcasts of the proposals that are closely related to public livelihood from both the NPC and the People's Political Consultative Conference representatives, such as drunk driving and food scandals. "NPC deputies primarily influence policy through the introduction of opinions and motions."[39] An explanation of the eighth amendment's draft made by the legislative office also cited these proposals as crucial reasons for making the amendments. If the proposals are followed by focusing events and match proposals from government agencies, they will have a better chance of being seriously considered. Otherwise, the proposals will fade away with an uncertain future. Whether public opinion counts depends on the magnitude of national attention, consistency with bureaucratic needs and the preferences of CCP leaders, among others. The above activities can be reactions to former criticisms of the NPC's useless representation and the lack of public expression in the democratic dictatorship regime. Some foreign observers identify the expanding public participation in legislation as "deliberative authoritarian," "consultative authoritarian" or "a combination of command and consultative authoritarianism."[40] The press, such as *Southern Weekly*, has suggested that though the media shows that the representatives are much more active in presenting proposals, few proposals result in actual drafts of law.[41] Scholars also point out that the ultimate result is still controlled by the party. The final enacted amendments of criminal law have shown a trend of being more responsive to public demand in selected cases (such as drunk driving).

Besides efforts to gain more justification from the bottom-up approach, the NPC's second explicit change is to raise the level of legislative expertise by combining information from, among others, bureaucratic considerations and academic concerns. The amendment drafting process inspired heated arguments from influential institutional actors like the Supreme Court, the Supreme Procuratorate, the Ministry of Public Security and the Ministry of State Security. While some committee staff were legal researchers themselves, they consistently held meetings with other legal scholars for professional advice. Both news reports and official documents show that by negotiating different viewpoints, arranging for consultations and briefing materials, staff of the Commission of Legislative Affairs "borrowed ideas from such sources as academic studies, executive branch reports and proposals, interest group materials, and members' opinions."[42]

> Now, quite routinely, when such laws come before the NPC or its standing committee, even though they already bear the endorsement "in principle" of the highest Party offices, they are subjected to extended, repeated subcommittee review and serious floor debate.[43]

The draft was "a blend of the substantive and the political, the academic and the pressure group information, the bureaucracy and the constituency."[44] However, at the same time, though the NPC is exposed to "an impressive variety of information—studies, administration arguments, leaks, interest group pressures, complaints from the districts, concerns of constituents, experiences of Western countries and international rules,"[45] what needs to be better understood is that fighting risk through criminalization is a primary claim of the representatives. Most members of the NPC and its standing committee still deliberate draft bills through a control perspective for more effective social management than the "rule of law" which restricts state power. It seems that NPC members have a lack of restraining power against the rhetoric of problem solving and the desire to create new offences.

In all, without the party's leadership, one cannot correctly understand the NPC's role in China. Due to the CCP's overwhelming number of seats in the NPC, the NPC still lacks authority, even though non-Communist Party members have been on the rise. At the same time, there has been an incrementally more transparent and participatory legislative process (involving advice from academics and other experts), discretionary use of public hearings, less formal public workshops and the publishing of draft laws and administrative rules and regulations for input from the general public.[46] On the one hand, "China's legislatures are more important than they were thirty years ago, reflecting both the increased complexity of law and the increased professionalism and legal knowledge within people's congresses." On the other hand, to balance populism and professionalism in the making of the law, "The NPC has begun to exercise something more than a rubber stamp function though it is still a weak legislator."[47] One of the reforms the CCP is undertaking in order to change its authoritarian image is to open up drafts to public consultation, rather than actually seeking democracy in the Western sense. Though public demand is consistently criticized as populist, media-driven and having a "supposed three-minute attention span", it cannot be excluded from policy and lawmaking.[48] Unlike adjudication that pursues independence and fairness, legislation on a democratic foundation should seek as much public opinion as possible. A promising option is to guide and encourage informed and reasoned public debates for high-quality participation.

6.2.2 The judicial system

The supremacy of the party was expressed through the continued role of party committees across the judicial system and in particular the role of party secretaries in chairing the Adjudication Committees in the People's Courts that review and approve judicial appointments and decisions. As it is with the other institutions, the party monitors both the Supreme People's Court and the Supreme People's Procuratorate. In their annual reports to the NPC, "correct guidance of the CCP" is routinely placed before "effective supervision of the NPC"; policies and duties that are defined by the CCP have priorities over the pursuit of justice and equality; "to keep state security and social stability" has always been the goal in deciding criminal cases.[49] Reports from the Supreme Procuratorate are closely attached to CCP policy.[50] The same is the case with Supreme Court reports ("to adhere to the leadership of the CCP"), except that the contents reflect the characteristics and duties of the courts. For instance, in the beginning of the 2009 "Report on the Work of the Supreme People's Court," the goal was highlighted "to implement the spirit of the Seventeenth Meeting of the CCP (the Party) and the first meeting of the eleventh NPC (the People's Congress)," "to prioritize the interest of the Party, the interest of the People, the Constitution and the law." In 2010, the report started with "to work for the CCP's strategy of ensuring economic growth, people's livelihood and social stability." In 2011 and 2012, it stressed "the establishment of the socialist legal system," as well as the policy of "resolving social conflicts, innovating on social management skills, and maintaining equality and integrity."[51]

It is usually believed that the Chinese court could not maintain independence in authoritarian China. Compared to those in democratic countries, "they (the judges) are responsible for ensuring that national goals, including the preservation of social stability, are met."[52] In addition, "evaluations of judges in many Chinese courts include evaluation of the social effect of their work, not just whether decisions are legally correct."[53] The judiciary's relationship with party and government agencies in China continued to be organized in such a way as to maximize the successful outcomes of state objectives and to accommodate the smooth implementation of party policy.[54] It is difficult for the courts to maintain independence at all times, especially before the interests of powerful parties. This applies to not only criminal cases, but also civil and administrative cases. However, most of the cases the courts deal with are not politically sensitive or widely known. Courts have been making reforms such as "improving education and training of judges, raising qualifications of new judges, fighting corruption, and taking modest steps to reduce the political emphasis in court work."[55] Besides, remaining "at the same level as other bureaucratic hierarchies of the state and lack[ing] authority over them,"[56] the court has been acting differently from its weak standing in the metaphor of the public security bureau cooking, the procuratorate serving and the court eating.

For instance, under party leadership, the Supreme People's Court and the Supreme People's Procuratorate, as the supreme judicial bodies in China, take part in the making of criminal law, enact judicial interpretations of the law and manage nationwide trials and prosecutions. Indeed, they are main participants in the making of criminal law. Even though the two are not legislative bodies, during legislation the NPC's Commission of Legislative Affairs (the entity that drafts the law) frequently consults with them for legal advice. Due to limited information, it is difficult for outsiders to become privy to their arguments and debates with the other institutions on the agenda. However, one week after the enactment of the eighth amendment, the vice president of the Supreme People's Court suggested that the courts ought to be cautious with the crime of drunk driving. In contrast to the assertions of the Ministry of Public Security and the Supreme Procuratorate, the argument that "not all offences of drunk driving are crimes" raised controversy around too much leniency and possible unfairness in enforcement. Though the argument was not a direct response to the other two bodies, it manifested the court's attempts to expand its autonomy and authority. This was an effort to maintain the Supreme People's Court's jurisdiction in competition with administrative agencies and congressional committees. Though in cases of criminal lawmaking, court pursuits of leniency are difficult given the predominant police system and populist demands, in actual practice, studies suggest that both supreme and local courts have been exercising leniency in criminal cases through suspended sentences, mediations or reduced penalties.[57] Thus, a complex relationship is developing between the court and the other entities where they are both allies and at odds, depending on the nature of the cases.

The Supreme People's Court and the Supreme People's Procuratorate making official interpretations of and commentaries on law has become common practice in China, something that has been consistently opposed by legal researchers.[58]

> The Supreme People's Court is engaged in a creative law-making process, despite Constitutional prohibitions against it, by issuing interpretations of national legislation that are binding on the lower courts and circulating judicial decisions chosen to provide 'guidance' to the courts.[59]

Caught in the dilemma of the NPC's heavy lawmaking workload and limited time at its conferences, the Supreme Court is the most valued alternative institution to make such interpretations. The interpretations are sometimes more valued by local judges in the adjudications due to their preciseness, practical use and guidance of the upper courts on the lower courts. For instance, on the crime of drunk driving, since the eighth amendment there have been requests for judicial interpretation since similar criminals have received sentences that were largely different in local courts, which challenges the equality of criminal law. For the crime of environmental pollution, after the eighth amendment the Supreme People's Court and the Supreme People's Procuratorate also passed the "Interpretations on criminal cases of environmental pollution" to match with changes to criminal law. Furthermore, the Supreme People's Court publishes certain cases as "precedents" from local courts. China does not have case law tradition, but those "guiding cases" function like precedents to maintain similar and predictable outcomes in trials. The crimes of drunk driving and environmental pollution both have guiding cases.

In all, within the current framework of the party-state, the judicial bodies still maintain a cooperative relationship with other agencies. What can be expected is a growth of independence, influenced by how the CCP defines the role of the judicial system, how the courts and procuratorate themselves resist internal and external pressures, and how litigants as well as lawyers perform in lawsuits. With the exception of trials, the court currently impacts lawmaking through inter-agency reviews and the drafting of judicial interpretations, without oversight powers over other entities. Its legitimacy is still rooted in meeting popular demand, protecting public interests and maintaining social stability. The future role of the court depends on which model—"rule of law" or "rule by law"—is applied in China. Western researchers debate about whether current changes in the Chinese legal system are signs of "rule of law" or "rule by law."[60] The answer largely relies on how to define the two concepts. As long as the CCP remains the ruling party without election, China will not become a "rule of law" regime like in Western democratic countries.[61] China lies in the middle between typical models of the instrumental use of the law, and valuing the law as an all-binding rule of society. The efforts of the court itself to expand power do indeed matter, but considering "the imperative of maintaining political supremacy for the party-state remains a salient feature in this process,"[62] the ultimate determinant lies in the role of the Communist Party in the running of the legal system. Rome was not built in a day: "Whether state leaders will allow law to become sufficiently powerful to impose significant restraints on state power, and whether the CCP will ever allow legal and political reforms to threaten its own privileged position, remains to be seen."[63]

6.2.3 The administration

According to Weber, in a modern state the ruler is necessarily and unavoidably the bureaucracy, since power is exercised neither through parliamentary speeches nor monarchial enunciations, but through the routines of administration.[64] Kingdon refers to the administration as group pressure: "Bureaucratic agencies and congressional committees battle for their share of the policy turf, affecting agendas in the process."[65] In this book, "the administration" refers to the Chinese State Council comprised of the Ministry of Public Security (the police), the Ministry of Food and Drug Administration and the Ministry of Environmental Protection, among others. This section will mainly document the role of the police since suggestions from the police have more impact on legislation than others. Other government departments led simultaneously by the party, including the Ministry of Public Security, the Ministry of Food and Drug Administration and the Ministry of Environmental Protection, will not be emphasized to the same degree as the police.

"Police is a centrally organized, bureaucratically administered, functionally specialized, professionally trained agency in China."[66] It has been one of China's major forces in the fight on crime and the maintenance of the CCP regime. "The Chinese political system places a special reliance on them: they often become an important force in the maintenance of the CCP's monopoly on state power and in the suppression of any resistance to this system."[67] "Over the past two decades, the Chinese domestic security apparatus has expanded dramatically. 'Stability maintenance' operations have become a priority for local Chinese authorities."[68] Chinese police involvement is focused on campaign-like actions against law violations and police reports remain the major initiators for amendments to criminal law. In China, Western policing—under the guise of bureaucratic, scientific, technocratic and legalistic policing—began to take root and spread after 1979.[69] Based on demands from both central and provincial bureaus for fast, mobile and effective policing, the Ministry of Public Security and provincial public security departments have launched wars against certain misbehavior every year since then. Besides serious crimes that police target all the time, it has become routine for the ministry to lead the crack-down on crime by investing huge amounts into the police force before big events. For instance, from 2009 to 2013 (except the year 2012), the number of special actions and strikes against crime from the central government went from four to six.[70] "Special struggles" have almost become a constant state of affairs in China.[71] Though high-ranking police officials have recognized the limits of campaigns, they prefer the short-term effects of deterring crimes to decrease the pressure on them.

More resources will generate more problems that need to be addressed, all of which lead to proposals to amend criminal law and criminal procedure law. Evidenced by the power gained from the fight against crime, the police indeed have a say in China's lawmaking. Suggestions from police to expand criminal law and restrict procedural protection of suspects account for a large number of proposals. For instance, proposals on the above three discussed proposals were more or less impacted by police suggestions. Even though faced with resistance from some scholars and other institutions, they still have more influence on final legislative outcomes than others. When it comes to policy and lawmaking, bureaucratic considerations take precedence. In the West, the police have considerable power and exercise great influence on decisions regarding what types of conduct are to be subjected to the criminal process.[72] The current Chinese institutional structure, in which legislators and courts are incrementally gaining power, still favors the police. The police remains a department of huge power, and not just in lawmaking and enforcement.

According to the Legislation Law, the Ministry of Public Security itself is also entitled to make regulations. In 2009, the ministry drafted a regulation to amend laws on drunk driving, which generated controversy over punishing even passengers riding with drunk drivers.[73] In 2013, the ministry also worked with the Supreme People's Court and the Supreme People's Procuratorate to publish the "Regulation on legal issues of criminal cases of drunk driving" which aimed to severely punish offences of drunk driving.[74] In addition, from 2009 to 2010, the Ministry of Public Security was frequently invited to participate in the making of the eighth amendment of criminal law. Therefore, the police, empowered by Chinese law with a wide range of functions and discretion that their Western counterparts do not enjoy, have great power within the current institutional framework. The police definitely influence the making and enforcement of laws in China.

In addition, the Chinese police also shape lawmaking based on their close connections to everyday life by undertaking both judicial and administrative work. A comprehensive cooperative system with multiple government agencies for potential crises exists in the Chinese context. Traditionally

> the police mode of operation calls for following the mass line and for taking part in a comprehensive approach—an approach that calls for the police to work closely with government, factories, enterprises, schools, neighborhoods, and other institutions in order to maintain public order and prevent, reduce and forestall crime through ideological, political, economic, educational administrative and legal work.[75]

Public security work is also guided by the general policy of "comprehensive management of social order," which encourages mobilizing all possible forces from the party, military and public to maintain social order. The Ministry of Public Security develops partnerships with other state departments in fields that are not directly within the police scope—which is similar to the multi-agency partnerships in Western policing strategies—with varied power at different stages or arenas involving partnerships against crime.[76] Due to the nature of the cases, the degree of police participation varies. For instance, drunk driving is solely managed by the police, fake medications are apprehended mainly by the Ministry of Health and the police, while environmental protection is overseen by both the Ministry of Environmental protection and the police. Such centrally driven multi-agency crime prevention projects further empower the police, both in administration and in the creating of norms. With the exception of revising criminal law, the institutions work out "interpretations, decisions or notice" collectively. They even have more impact on society than abstract laws. In 2009, the Ministry of Public Security cooperated with the Ministry of Public Health in creating the Agenda to Maintain Drug Safety. In 2013, the ministry issued "Opinions on strengthening the work of environmental protection through coordination with the public security departments" jointly with the Ministry of Environmental Protection.

Besides the police, other government agencies also provide professional advice to law drafters as policy entrepreneurs. Though it is insisted that changes to the eighth amendment were made out of the will of the CCP and the public, when it comes to issues of technique it remains expert suggestions that count the most. The draft bill presented to the NPC's standing committee represents a primary consensus among the agencies. Deliberation among delegates and consultations with the public only take place within the framework of such agreements.

> This happened because new economic forces presented bureaucrats with increasingly complex problems that could not be resolved by traditional methods relying on consensus, compromise and the internalization of disputes. The rationalization of work styles also occurred because of the bureaucracies' specialization and professionalization and their adoption of Western methods.[77]

However, practices of these state institutions reflect more of a practical requirement of control than a pursuit of rule of law. In China, both cases of fake medication and environmental pollution have illustrated the inefficiencies of joint strategies and the coordinated approach. The rise of fake drugs and environmental pollution also partly results from deficits in local enforcement—the police and municipal or provincial bureaus. Failed multi-agency cooperation calls for revisions to criminal law to enhance public security and social stability. These claims also gain more public support, since in China the old but resurging approach of punitive retribution continues to be a central basis of law-and-order politics. There is still a clear preference for strong punishments for crime.[78]

6.2.4 The media

After the economic reform, media on the mainland (subject to the limits of party oversight and primarily by the involvement of party-state actors)[79] aims for a balance between the CCP's censorship, grass-roots demands and their own interests. As media commercialization and increased editorial discretion have combined with growing attention to social and legal problems, the media has gained incentives to expand its traditional mouthpiece roles in new directions.[80]

The media also has a crucial effect on the agenda of lawmaking. First, the media (including newspapers, TV and the internet) creates "focusing events" as long as "the media remain within certain boundaries and do not directly challenge fundamental norms."[81] "The mere fear of crime may be perceived as a greater threat to quality of life than actual criminal incidents."[82] Like in the West, criminal stories from the media commonly focus more on the crudeness of the suspects and the harm suffered by the victims. By listing similar events together (e.g., drunk driving, fake medications, environmental protection), media coverage of criminal cases and public perspectives has raised national awareness of certain problems in a relatively short time period. In China, "the redlines that journalists cannot cross still exist, but changes are taking place."[83] The media, especially the internet, encourages political activism rather than political alienation by generating virtual "interest groups."[84] These groups have started to "challenge traditional media" by both reflecting and creating public opinion beyond "direct" party control.[85] The wide scope of public discussion leads officials to intervene in cases,[86] facilitating changes either in future lawmaking or enforcement.

The media also acts as a channel for lawmakers to gauge public attitude in the process of lawmaking. In the legislation of the eighth amendment, both official and commercial websites employed online surveys to assess popular preference. Through this strategy, websites controlled by the authority (such as www.people.com.cn and www.npc.gov.cn) seek to promote the legitimacy of the CCP and the government. This strategy is consistent with the change of "respecting public opinion," which is mentioned more and more in official reports. The effects of official surveys are improving; whereas before, the Legislative Affairs Commission only showed the amount of feedback, it has started to categorize and post the replies for the public's further reference.[87] Commercial websites enjoy more autonomy in survey design and outcomes. Based on the intended audience, most such surveys only focus on controversial issues, like punishing drunk driving with criminal penalties. The surveys are also inclined to raise easy and casual moral questions, such as: have you recognized the legal changes? Will you support them or not? What efforts should we make to prohibit such behavior?[88]

At the same time, the media, which is the main facilitator of state propaganda, maintains the image of the CCP and the government in their rule of law. Besides personal experience, what the public view as an authority is shaped by information provided by the media and, as such, the media structures the public's understanding of their environment to a large degree. Serving both as the mouthpiece and as the "eyes and ears" of the party,[89] the media covers breakthroughs in legislative proceedings of the Chinese law. As directed by the CCP, most of what is covered is about improvements and praise, rather than criticisms or worries. It is risky for the media to set its own agenda. For instance, the *Southern Metropolis Daily*'s report on the Sun Zhigang case in Guangzhou city promoted reforms of Chinese administrative law. However, at the same time, repealing the "custody and repatriation" regulation failed to win support from local residents since they prefer a sense of security rather than rights for the homeless, and the public assumes that public security is challenged because of media reports.[90]

Compared to traditional media, the internet is a much more open arena. However, intense internet censorship at the hands of the Chinese government significantly reduces the internet's effectiveness in the pursuit of democracy. It is suggested that the government acts as external pressure to either end or interrupt this pursuit by blocking related news coverage and online discussion, particularly in the reporting of foreign affairs and domestic dissent.[91] In addition, fear of punishment from the government also leads to retreat in the Chinese online community and, as such, China remains an authoritative regime with the coexistence of technological censorship and media control.[92] While it is evident that there is a tight, strict and centralized internet control system (through the hierarchical Communist Party, an extensive police system and a highly penetrating local organizational network based on community policing),[93] as has been argued, this book still holds a positive view of the internet's role in China. Nonetheless, "It is more likely that a spirit of citizenship and the will to mobilize, were it to appear, are more important than the censoring technology itself."[94]

However, online public discourse is also open to criticism on the basis that it is subject to irrational, emotional and intolerant mass politics known as "cyber populism."[95] For example, in one study of cyber discourse, "expressions of negative sentiments were more common than expressions of positive sentiments. In fact, not a single comment was coded as expressing even a moderately positive attitude toward the current health system."[96] It is even contended that "many messages on BBS sites in China are the online equivalent of the big character posters of the Cultural Revolution."[97] "The style of comments in web blogs ranges from emotional outburst to cynical rebuke to enthusiastic support to rational discussion."[98] Researchers argue that there are three elements of informed public opinion: information, deliberation and taking responsibility.[99] Giving an opinion is different from official action when participants must weigh competing goals, sensitivities and constraints to have a rational debate. The former provides a suitable platform for expressive opinion, and the latter for sober judgment.[100] Most of the time, the anonymous internet is the former and facilitates a populist regime of collective irresponsibility. Particularly when it is related to criminal justice where the public knows little about the actual structure of the sentencing process or sentencing trends,[101] the populist debate on crime and punishment revolves more around emotion than rational judgment.[102] There are also underground, hired people who make comments for profit by pretending to be commoners (known as "Wumao Dang," they earn around ten cents for posting one comment).

This book argues that despite the populist emotion-oriented characteristic of cyber opinions, the positive effects of the internet on facilitating public expression cannot be overlooked. The internet works as a pioneer to discover issues demanding to be addressed by the bureaucracy. It has increased the impact of public opinions on the Chinese lawmaking. For instance, the 11th amendment, which has been enacted at the end of 2020, criminalizes the behavior of intentionally throwing objects from high-rise buildings. It is regarded as a response to public demands to protect the "safety above the head."[103] Those demands would not have attracted so much attention without the help of the internet.

Besides, whether cyber opinions are rational or not is not the key problem. First, offline comments can have similar characteristics as cyber voices. Especially when faced with crime, the public attempts to protect the well-being and security of law-abiding "ordinary people" by punishing those whose crimes jeopardize them. This is the same for both online and offline expression. Second, populism partly results from a lack of legitimate procedures of voting and decision making. In the Chinese context, the internet's growth as an essential arena for public involvement, the rise in the public's consciousness of rights and the increasing gap of social inequality together boost the desire for mass expression. When opinions explode in the cyber world, what is needed is to channel opinions by establishing responsive mechanisms, rather than dismissing them as purely populist like some scholars do. Besides, it is unfair to claim that all comments are irrational, since there are many arguments that are reasonable and inspiring, such as those of opinion leaders. The public, most of whom have a common sense of right and wrong, will gradually develop the consciousness that full information should be gathered before making sober judgments. Third, there is still a benefit for the public to highlight problems before making possible improvements, such as in focusing events. Most of the public are not experts on specific fields (e.g., lawmaking), so it is much more efficient to leave technical problems to the experts. Perhaps one of the most meaningful aspects of the rise of cyber arenas and discourse in China is to know, to observe and to voice.

Overall, the party-state still exercises extensive control over the media through government outlet ownership and censorship. It is able to intervene in media coverage at any time. In Chinese lawmaking, the media acts positively for the authority by highlighting their goal of valuing public attitudes, evaluating popular preferences and enhancing the government's good image. For the public, the media serves as a restrained forum of communication. Even though the internet may contribute to the increase of populism, it stands as one of the most essential channels of public sentiment in China. The internet in China is a domain to express, as well as to censor.

6.2.5 The legal experts

Drafts of policy proposals constitute a portion of bureaucratic activities, but they come without open information on those who originally proposed or drafted them. Compared to those within the government, legal experts are part of a more open and flexible community that is able to accommodate different opinions. Legal scholars are also playing an important part in contemporary Chinese rule of law. This section will examine the role of legal experts in Chinese criminal lawmaking.

As mentioned, legal scholars have been very active in the legislation of criminal law. Acting as rule makers themselves, some scholars/intellectuals are directly involved in the agenda-forming and reviewing process. A number of legal researchers serve in multiple positions in the NPC, judicial institutions, government agencies and business organizations at different levels. For instance, in the Legislative Affairs Commission and the NPC's law committee, there are members who have pursued academic careers before or simultaneously with their work in the NPC, such as Xianming Xu, Chunying Xin and Guangquan Zhou. Zhou is a well-known professor of criminal law at Tsinghua University. He was also a member of the Constitution and Law Committee of the NPC.[104] The influence of legal doctrine obtained in university early in life on their legislative and administrative work is mostly distinct from that of officials who complete degrees later in life simply for job promotions. However, since there is no empirical research on the dynamic and influence of the shifting identities of scholars, it remains difficult to assess how their attitudes are shaped by their diverse roles in making and reviewing proposals.

Besides being directly involved as lawmakers themselves, scholars and think tanks are frequently invited to participate in making agendas at both local and central levels.[105] On revising the crime of environmental pollution, legal researchers were invited to the conference held by the All-China Environment Federation to debate and draft proposals. The legislative affairs committee also sought guidance from legal researchers for opinions on the first draft of the amendment. The legislative reports of the eighth amendment mentioned expert suggestions as references. In other laws, such as contract law and property law, the committee even granted scholars the opportunity to draft the laws. The final enacted laws were basically the same as the primary drafts. In 2014, the "Decision on Major Issues Concerning Comprehensively Deepening Reforms of the CCP" finally institutionalized legal consultancy of governmental affairs introducing researchers and lawyers as government consultants. In addition, not only in criminal justice but also in other areas of law, another common practice among scholars is to assist in the design of the legal system based on existing claims from bureaus, ministries, departments and commissions; for example, to provide documents of Western practices on similar problems. It remains difficult for the scholars to turn down a proposal of criminalization that has already become a consensus among bureaucracies.

Furthermore, scholars hold conferences and seminars, and publish papers before and after legislation to point out problems, examine details and propose improvements. There is much scholarship on the three amendments of drunk driving, fake medications and environmental pollution.

> By reaffirming her links with the civil law tradition, China is rejoining a great community of legal thought which unites half the world and which owes its chief debt, as has been pointed out already, to the Romans rather than to Marx.[106]

"That education is beginning to show the influence of intellectual forces other than the dogma of the Communist Party, suggesting the possibility of the gradual development of legal science as an autonomous branch of reasoning about government and society."[107] Dicks made these statements 30 years ago, but they remain unchanged at present. Though most of these academic activities serve more as internal discussions within the legal community rather than affecting legislation, they do help specialists form their perceptions of the law and its enforcement through focused research and debate.

Increasing legislative professionalism is a requirement of modern society. With rapid social development, lawmaking activities "have become so specialized and sophisticated that common people without special training can only deliver amateur opinions."[108] Both Eastern and Western practices reveal that "politicians turn to that [researcher-analyst] community for proposals that would be relevant to their concerns and that might constitute solutions to their problems."[109] If it is lay citizen discussions on the internet that contribute to focusing events, it is elite debates that determine the proper solution to a crisis. Academic proposals directly related to problems will be given more attention. However, "intellectuals remain critical of their government."[110] In China, "they (scholars) also have more contact with the West and thus more understanding of the basic elements of a democratic system, such as free elections and checks and balances."[111] A number of them embrace the dream "to modernize and civilize China's legal system, which has lagged behind the rising standards of legality, rationality and humanism that have been achieved in the West since the advent of modernity."[112] It is obvious that in both drafting and reviewing revisions of criminal law, scholars (especially criminal law scholars who are more conscious of principles of equality and human rights) mostly demonstrate an adherence to the model of rule of law in their speeches and publications. For instance, for the crimes of drunk driving and environmental pollution, several researchers indicate their opposition as a reflection of their concerns regarding the over-expansion of criminal law. They consistently argue that the criminal justice system has to stick to fundamental principles of criminal law, such as the principle of legality and proportionality. Thus, there remains tension between crime control agendas of state development and legitimacy agendas upon which modern institutions are based. This tension could be beneficial since it exerts pressure on the government to improve.

Contrary to their close relationship with the government, criminal law scholars keep a certain distance from the public. They rarely take the lead in focusing events. Except for a few that appear on traditional media or post on the internet, most criminal law scholars focus on research within the academy and interactions with courts and agencies. Apart from explanations concerning technique, it is difficult to witness any communication between criminal law specialists and the public. The conflict between popular demands for public security and academic claims against extending criminal law is intensifying. That "expert rationality and public preferences often fail to coincide"[113] is one reason for the tension. Requirements protecting criminal rights are consistently attacked by the populist masses. Most importantly, in China today, this tension between professionalism and populism is also a result of the lack of trust between the public and scholars. Scholars are assumed to be part of a group whose interests lie with the advantaged rather than the masses. The belief in selective law enforcement compromises the professionalism of legal experts, while the scholars who hold themselves as elite criticize public demands as populist, disorganized and irrational. Working with the party elite is probably the most practical way of not only promoting reform but also of getting funding for their projects. Thus, society has witnessed both suspicion of legal expertise and the academy's spontaneous removal from the public. This does not mean that scholars ignore social affairs; scholars who view the rule of law both as their career and their collective pursuit commonly come up with proposals after issues rise to popular attention.

Overall, scholars have positive long-term effects on lawmaking,[114] especially when their role is supported by the policy of the CCP, which promotes scientific and democratic legislation. However, even though the intellectual issues they face are more or less the same as their counterparts in Japan, Germany and even common-law countries, the influence of Chinese scholars on the rule of law remains within non-political terrain. Party officials control and approve agenda topics, consultant procedures and the extent to which elite and public opinion will be "taken into account" in the final result.[115] A great many scholars have shown a collective retreat from sensitive political issues in an effort to protect themselves. Since the 1990s, they view themselves more as professional or academic elites than as voices of the public conscience.[116] Instead of criticizing the CCP through socio-legal studies, criminal justice scholars (criminal law, criminal procedural law, etc.) are more interested in solving technical issues within the legal system. The methodology of doctrinal analysis is not only a civil law system tradition inherited from continental Europe (like Germany), but also a shelter against political risk, since there is a dilemma of maintaining academic integrity without highlighting the exact role of the CCP in China. Scholars also receive funding from the government as a primary way of earning a living, making it impossible for them to challenge the dominance of the party-state. Therefore, scholar involvement enhances the rule of law in China by providing professional legal advice. Their input is a positive change, even when they are unable to bring about direct political reform. "More consultations with elite groups, and increased possibilities for ordinary people to influence decision making at the lowest local level"[117] could contribute to a more deliberate and consultative democracy in the long run.

6.3 Conclusion

This chapter analyzes the participants of Chinese criminal lawmaking, including the CCP, the NPC, the judiciary system, the administrative agencies, the media and scholars. It is an examination of the law–politics nexus with regard to the crime control model upon which the system is based.[118] All of the participants are directly involved in the creation, review and revision of draft bills, with varied influence on the proceedings and final results.

First, while it is commonly assumed that in authoritarian China it is the CCP that has dominated the law and decides the function and content of the rules, this book finds that the CCP's leadership on specific legislation has actually become more ambiguous, mostly exercised through personnel selection, thought work, policy development and agenda/outcome review. In non-political affairs such as social governance, although Chinese political reforms are often seen in the West as lagging behind the country's sweeping economic changes, the CCP has actually shown a remarkable degree of political flexibility and adaptability over the last three decades.[119] Although there remains a lack of autonomous citizen organizations since the party fears potential political risks resulting from collaboration of the citizens, the CCP allows space for think tanks and the public to propose agendas under its supervision. This increased power allotted to such entities is more a result of practical daily needs than of any upright intentions of the party. Given that contemporary China is a more modern, diverse and conflicted country, the CCP has become unable to manage all the aspects of running the huge state machine. Indeed, "most of the concrete reform initiatives arise from below in response to the practical concerns of those on the front lines."[120] Bureaucratic interests and public demand have prompted the party to be more inclusive, open and transparent. Therefore, the CCP's retreat is a reactive adaptation of the social environment. It is a balance between "governing at a distance" and "governing with no distance." That is, broad discretion in social regulation with strict censorship on political issues; incremental (or slow) steps for problem solving with rapid treatment of high-profile cases, and growing consultative participation with ultimate control over laws and policies. Western researchers have focused on the wide-ranging control mechanisms for what are considered highly sensitive social and political issues, arguing that the CCP is the major impediment to the realization of rule of law and political reform in China.[121] Fewer are concerned with regular domestic issues that constitute the routines of everyday life for the Chinese. A smaller role of the party could raise the hope of reform.

Second, in revisions to Chinese criminal law, the hierarchy of impact on lawmaking is shown in the following illustration: instead of a tightly hierarchical, unitary, top-down lawmaking process, the Chinese system should be seen as a "multi-actor" process with numerous conferences, consultations and workshops among the state organs. Bureaucratic reports and claims shape the law to the greatest extent through the inter-agency review process, with advice from think tanks/scholars taking an assistive role through expert argumentation meetings (see Figure 6.1). "Advocacy is largely contained in a system of elite co-optation, and the exclusiveness of political leadership preserves the integrity of control at the top of the hierarchy."[122] Online consultation[123] is frequently used to gain feedback on draft bills, which can "promote the notions that government can be responsive to public needs and that citizens can voice their views in a context of equality and mutual respect."[124] However, it remains unclear how the NPC and the government actually deal with public opinion after focusing events, especially those events that are unable to assert pressure through collective action.

> Because comments submitted during the consultation period were not made public unless the person or organization making the submission published it elsewhere, it is impossible to do a thorough analysis of the questions collected by the NPC or to assess how those comments might have been taken into consideration in the legislative drafting process.[125]

That opinions of draft bills are mostly sent in an anonymous fashion raises the difficulty of assessing state responsiveness to such comments. It is also unlikely that one comment can generate significant change.

This pyramid (see Figure 6.1) is similar to the model of decision making in modern countries which balances bureaucratic practical needs, academic expertise and popular support. The ideal structure would be one in which the participants are not only governed by the rule of law, but also one where they see the rule of law as the ultimate goal. However, in reality, and apart from varied understanding of justice and law, the pursuit of self-interest raises the importance of power restraint. In the West, interest seeking is subject to legal and electoral constraints. The Chinese problem lies in the party's superior role, the imbalance

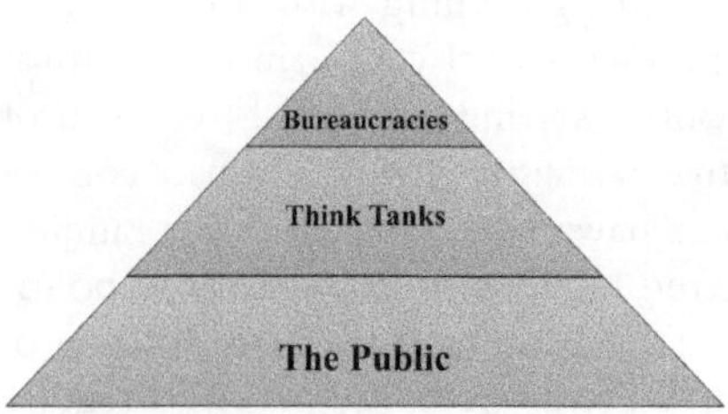

Figure 6.1 Roles of the participants in Chinese lawmaking.

in the separation of power (the weak court) and the lack of the public's restrictive power to the party-state, leaving little space for external legal and legitimacy review. While most of the attention in existing literature is on the CCP as a main impediment to the rule of law project, the power of the ministries in both lawmaking and administration requires special caution as well. "The key here consists not in ideological/theoretical choices, but rather in the grasp of operative realities and how they might be changed,"[126] particularly in criminal justice where the Ministry of Public Security and State Security has been gaining power in dealing with affairs related to public security.

Furthermore, the current legislative framework also manifests in an instrumental use of the rule of law rather than considering it a primary aim. A noted scholar in China used to call it the "functionalization of law," or a constant search for practical solutions by resorting to law.[127] Other Chinese specialists call it "laws for emergencies," "legal pragmatism" or the "piecemeal approach" which keeps challenging the stability of the legal system.[128] In criminal law revisions, the participants are more focused on its problem-solving function than on fighting abuses of power from the ruling state. It looks that the public prefer to surrender their rights when faced with risks to their security, as shown not only in serious crimes like terrorist acts, but also food, drug and environmental offences. Drafting laws sometimes takes years, but making these amendments in China happened quickly. For social problems in China, such as the three rural issues (migrant workers, compulsory education and social security), it usually takes three to five years for proposals to turn into government policy. However, it has taken a minimum of two years to make amendments to criminal law, from drafting the legislative plan to the promulgation of the revisions. As previously stated, it was not until 2008–2009 that drunk driving, manufacturing and selling fake medications and environmental pollution commanded special attention from state agencies. Meanwhile, in December 2009, the standing committee of the National People's Congress wrote amending criminal law into the legislative plan for 2010, even though the seventh amendment had just been passed in February 2009. The authoritarian state structure authorizes the government to act quickly. Despite the fact that the real effects of the legislation are yet to be determined, they save the government from crises (focusing events), showing the public that efforts have been made to solve the problems. With a large variety of other concerns like corruption and income distribution taking turns in the media spotlight, current criticisms of lenient penalties gradually fade out of sight. As a matter of fact, criminal law and other areas of law have also been under frequent revision since 2000. In the modernization process, the Chinese state is not only faced with new challenges, but also suffers from side effects of former reforms, including a weak legal system, a deteriorating environment, slow political reform and an unjust social structure, all of which are difficult to change. The party-state, which "wades across the stream by feeling the way," has to cope with emergencies every day, resulting in the frequent changes of criminal law.

Indeed, the practical vision of criminal law is not unique in China. The punitive turn of Western criminal justice over the last decade partly results from public demands to regain "law and order" at the tipping point of transitioning into a late-modern society. Increased concerns about risk cannot be separated from the neoliberal policy of the Reagan government in the US and the Thatcher government in the UK to boost the market economy.[129] However, in Western democratic countries, such policies and laws are subject to judicial review by the courts. The court's supreme power, a most crucial sign of law, maintains the legality of laws. Hence, even though the laws are made to meet functional needs, the court is still able to rely on a basic structure that works against bad laws. For instance, in the UK, a number of preventive laws—including the stop-and-search powers under Section 44 of the Terrorism Act of 2000, and the Anti-Terrorism, Crime and Security Act of 2001—were either ruled as illegal, or repealed. Meanwhile, in China, both the NPC and the courts lack such power. Even though it is suggested that "Increasingly, delegates [of the NPC] are willing to vote against or abstain on draft laws, decrees and even high-level personnel appointments which Party and state bodies submit to the NPC for approval,"[130] such cases are rare. "The instrumentalist approach to law continues to dominate,"[131] but "Law has gained more importance than it has ever possessed in Chinese history."[132] Hopefully, in the long run, legal reforms will impose more and more limits on the power of the party-state.

Notes

1 Jan Michiel Otto et al., *Law-Making in People's Republic of China* (The Hague: Kluwer Law International, 2000), Introduction.
2 John W. Kingdon, *Agendas, Alternatives and Public Policies, Update Edition, with an Epilogue on Health Care*, 2nd ed. (New York: Pearson, 2010) 145.
3 John W. Kingdon, *Agendas, Alternatives and Public Policies, Update Edition, with an Epilogue on Health Care*, 2nd ed. (New York: Pearson, 2010) 163.
4 Sabatier Paul A. & Weible Christopher M., eds, *Theories of the Policy Process*, 3rd ed. (Boulder, CO: Westview Press, 2014) 30.
5 Nicole Herweg, Christian Huß & Reimut Zohlnhofer, "Straightening the Three Streams: Theorizing Extensions of the Multiple Streams Framework" (2015) 54 (3) *European Journal of Political Research* 435–449.
6 Murray Scot Tanner, "Organizations and Politics in China's Post-Mao Law-Making System", in Pitman B. Potter, ed, *Domestic Law Reforms in Post-Mao China* (New York: M.E. Sharpe, 1994) 57.
7 Murray Scot Tanner, "Organizations and Politics in China's Post-Mao Law-Making System", in Pitman B. Potter, ed, *Domestic Law Reforms in Post-Mao China* (New York: M.E. Sharpe, 1994) 65.
8 See Laura Paler, "China's Legislation Law and the Making of a More Orderly and Representative Legislative System" (2005) 182 *The China Quarterly* 301–318.
9 In *Discipline and Punish*, Michel Foucault elaborates upon the function of disciplinary mechanisms and illustrates the function of discipline as an apparatus of power. This panoptic design can be used for any "population" that needs to be kept under observation or control, such as prisoners, school children, medical patients or workers. See Michel Foucault, *Discipline and Punishment* (New York: Vintage Books, 1995).
10 Kam C. Wong, *Chinese Policing: History and Reform* (New York: Peter Lang, 2009) 3.

11 Keyuan Zou, "The Party and the Law", in Kjeld Erik Brodsgaard & Yongnian Zheng, eds, *The Chinese Communist Party in Reform* (London: Routledge, 2006) 78.
12 Keyuan Zou, "The Party and the Law", in Kjeld Erik Brodsgaard & Yongnian Zheng, eds, *The Chinese Communist Party in Reform* (London: Routledge, 2006) 82.
13 Edward J. Epstein, "Law and Legitimation in Post-Mao China", in Pitman B. Potter, ed, *Domestic Law Reforms in Post-Mao China* (New York: M.E. Sharpe, 1994) 24.
14 Keyuan Zou, "The Party and The Law", in Kjeld Erik Brodsgaard & Yongnian Zheng, eds, *The Chinese Communist Party in Reform* (London: Routledge, 2006) 83.
15 Susan Trevaskes, "Political Ideology, the Party, and Politicking: Justice System Reform in China" (2011) 37 *Modern China* 333.
16 *Communique of the 4th Plenary Session of the 18th Central Committee of CCP*, 2014.
17 Jianmin Zhao & Rongwei Lai, "Principle of the CCP's Leadership in NPC" (2000) 2 *Mainland China Studies* 3–10.
18 Jianmin Zhao & Rongwei Lai, "Principle of the CCP's Leadership in NPC" (2000) 2 *Mainland China Studies* 2.
19 Jianmin Zhao & Rongwei Lai, "Principle of the CCP's Leadership in NPC" (2000) 2 *Mainland China Studies* 11.
20 "Explanation to the Draft of the Eighth Amendment of Criminal Law", online: NPC <http://www.npc.gov.cn/huiyi/lfzt/xfxza8/2011-05/10/content_1666058.htm>.
21 Murray Scot Tanner, "Organizations and Politics in China's Post-Mao Law-Making System", in Pitman B. Potter, ed, *Domestic Law Reforms in Post-Mao China* (New York: M.E. Sharpe, 1994) 57.
22 Murray Scot Tanner, "How a Bill Becomes a Law in China: Stages and Processes in Lawmaking", (1995) 141 *The China Quarterly* 45; Murray Scot Tanner, "The Erosion of Communist Party Control over Lawmaking in China" (1994) 138 *The China Quarterly* 381–403.
23 Donald C. Clarke, ed, *China's Legal System: New Developments, New Challenges* (Cambridge: Cambridge University Press, 2008) 12.
24 Benjamin L. Liebman, "Legal Reform: China's Law-Stability Paradox" (2014) 143 (2) *The Journal of the American Academy of Arts & Sciences* 98.
25 "Populism" in the Chinese legal system refers to a range of forms of public expression, from public opinion created by the state-run media, to opinions in internet forums, to collective action and individual protests by persons seeking redress of grievances. Populism also refers to efforts by legal institutions to seek public support by aligning outcomes with perceived dominant social norms or conceptions of popular morality, or by making legal institutions more accessible. See Benjamin L. Liebman, "A Return to Populist Legality? Historical Legacies and Legal Reform", in Elizabeth Perry & Sebastian Heilmann, eds, *Mao's Invisible Hand* (Cambridge: Harvard University Asia Center Press, 2011) 166.
26 Borge Bakken, "China, a Punitive Society?" (2011) 6 *Asian Criminology* 42.
27 Randall Peerenboom, *China's Long March toward Rule of Law* (Cambridge: Cambridge University Press, 2002) 169.
28 The strike hard or campaign-style policing generally involved a sudden increase of police law enforcement over a short period of time that targeted particular types of crime.
29 The "balancing leniency and strictness" policy encourages procurators and courts to treat serious crimes harshly, but also encourages them to be lenient toward

minor crimes, in particular those not reflecting malice or posing significant risk of harm to society. In the courts, the emphasis on leniency primarily manifests in reduced sentences for those who confess and on the use of suspended sentences in minor criminal cases for those who agree to pay restitution or compensation to their victims. See Benjamin L. Liebman, "Leniency in Chinese Criminal Law? Everyday Justice in Henan" (2015) 33 (1) *Berkeley Journal of International Law* 153–222.

30 Susan Trevaskes, "Political Ideology, the Party, and Politicking: Justice System Reform in China" (2011) 37 *Modern China* 320.

31 See Susan Trevaskes, *Policing Serious Crime in China: From 'Strike Hard' to 'Kill Fewer'* (Oxon: Routledge, 2010).

32 Wenfang Tang, *Public Opinion and Political Change in China* (Stanford, CA: Stanford University Press, 2005) 26.

33 This involves upgrading the quality of the cadre corps and producing outstanding leadership. Political leadership determines the fate of a political regime or its path of reform and change. See Kjeld Erik Brodsgaard & Yongnian Zheng, "Whither the Chinese Communist Party", in Kjeld Erik Brodsgaard & Yongnian Zheng, eds, *The Chinese Communist Party in Reform* (Oxon: Routledge, 2006) 4.

34 Stanley Lubman, "Introduction: The Future of Chinese Law" (1995) 1 *The China Quarterly* 1.

35 Jan Michiel Otto et al., *Law-Making in People's Republic of China* (The Hague: Kluwer Law International, 2000) 1–2.

36 The institutional capacity of the People's Congresses has been enhanced steadily through a variety of measures, including rapid expansion of personnel, the development of subcommittees responsible for specific technical tasks and efforts to raise delegates' educational level.

37 The Legislative Affairs Commission is the legislative body of the Standing Committee of the NPC. The main responsibility of the commission is making drafts and revising drafts of the law.

38 "Investigations on Hot Topics of the Two Sessions", online: People <http://npc.people.com.cn/GB/28320/374787/>.

39 Rory Truex, "Consultative Authoritarianism and Its Limits" (2014) 6 *Comparative Political Studies* 7.

40 See Baogang He & Mark E. Warren, "Authoritarian Deliberation: The Deliberate Turn in Chinese Political Development" (2011) 9 (02) *Perspectives on Politics* 269–289. Indeed, they are sometimes justified as an alternative to "Western" adversarial, multiparty democracy. In democracies, decisions are typically the consequence of voting or vote-based authorization of representatives, not deliberation. Even in cases of consensus, voting still stands as an implicit part of the process—the moment in which the work of deliberation is transformed, unanimously, into a collectively binding decision.

41 Zhongzhou He, "Why Bills to the NPC Have Decreased?", online: Southern Weekly <http://www.infzm.com/content/42431>. According to this news, there are also a number of representatives who have no proposals at all. Meaningful representation can and does arise in an authoritarian setting. It arises not from electoral accountability, but from top-down accountability to a regime with informational needs.

42 John W. Kingdon, *Agendas, Alternatives and Public Policies, Update Edition, with an Epilogue on Health Care*, 2nd ed. (New York: Pearson, 2010) 41.

43 Murray Scot Tanner, *The Politics of Lawmaking in Post-Mao China: Institutions, Processes, and Democratic Prospects* (Oxford: Clarendon Press, 1998) 5.

44 John W. Kingdon, *Agendas, Alternatives and Public Policies, Update Edition, with an Epilogue on Health Care*, 2nd ed. (New York: Pearson, 2010) 37.

45 David P. Auerswald & Colton C. Campbell, eds, *Congress and the Politics of National Security* (Cambridge: Cambridge University Press, 2011) 86.

46 Jamie P. Horsley, "Public Participation in the People's Republic: Developing a More Participatory Governance Model in China", online: Yale Law School <http://www.law.yale.edu/documents/pdf/Intellectual_Life/CL-PP-PP_in_the__PRC_FINAL_91609.pdf>.

47 Stanley Lubman, "Introduction: The Future of Chinese Law" (1995) 1 *The China Quarterly* 4.

48 Michael Cavadino & James Dignan, *Penal Systems, a Comparative Approach* (London: Sage Publications, 2005) 342.

49 This conclusion is drawn from summaries of the Work Reports of the Supreme People's Court to the NPC from 2008 to 2014.

50 This conclusion is drawn from summaries of the Work Reports of the Supreme People's Procuratorate to the NPC from 2008 to 2014.

51 This conclusion is drawn from summaries of the Reports of the Supreme People's Court to the NPC from 2008 to 2014.

52 Benjamin L. Liebman, "Assessing China's Legal Reforms" (2009) 23 *Columbia Journal of Asian Law* 27.

53 Benjamin L. Liebman, "Assessing China's Legal Reforms" (2009) 23 *Columbia Journal of Asian Law* 27.

54 Susasn Trevaskes, "Courts on the Campaign Path in China: Criminal Court Work in the 'Yanda 2001' Anti-Crime Campaign" (2002) 42 *Asian Survey* 674.

55 Benjamin L. Liebman, "China's Courts: Restrained Reforms" (2007) 21 *Columbia Journal of Asian Law* 86. Most participants in the debate readily admit that there is no judicial independence in China, but they argue that gradual improvements are taking place.

56 Stanley B. Lubman, *Bird in a Cage: Legal Reform in Post-Mao China* (Stanford, CA: Stanford University Press, 2002) 2.

57 See Benjamin L. Liebman, "Leniency in Chinese Criminal Law? Everyday Justice in Henan" (2015) 33 (1) *Berkeley Journal of International Law* 153–222.

58 Mengya Jiang & Shimei Gai, "Analysis on the Chinese Judicial Interpretation" (2004) 4 *Journal of Nanjing Party Institute of CCP* 45–50; Ziping Li, "Legitimacy of Judicial Interpretation of Chinese Criminal Law" (2009) 5 *Legal Forum* 74–79; Jianwei Zhang, "Scope and Boundary of Judicial Interpretation of Chinese Criminal Procedure Law" (2013) 7 *Tsinghua Law Review* 24–35.

59 Stanley B. Lubman, *Bird in a Cage: Legal Reform in Post-Mao China* (Stanford, CA: Stanford University Press, 2002) 8.

60 The Chinese criminal process continues to reflect overt links between law and policy. To say that the courts, at best, only coordinate with other bureaucracies is simply another way of expressing how far away China is from establishing a notion of the supremacy of law, at least as that concept is conceived in the West. In various ways, then, the articles echo the familiar idea that law is still frequently conceived as William Alford has observed elsewhere: as a tool of state administration, and always within close reach of the CCP.

61 To be sure, single-party socialism is not compatible with a liberal democratic rule of law or even communitarian rule of law, as both advocate genuine democracy defined by multiparty elections at all levels of government.

62 Pitman Potter, "The Chinese Legal System: Continuing Commitment to the Primacy of State Power" (1999) 159 *The China Quarterly* 673.

63 Randall Peerenboom, *China's Long March toward Rule of Law* (Cambridge: Cambridge University Press, 2002) 153.

64 Edward J. Epstein, "Law and Legitimation in Post-Mao China", in Pitman B. Potter, ed, *Domestic Law Reforms in Post-Mao China* (New York: M.E. Sharpe, 1994) 25.

65 John W. Kingdon, *Agendas, Alternatives and Public Policies, Update Edition, with an Epilogue on Health Care*, 2nd ed. (New York: Pearson, 2010) 153.
66 Kam C. Wong, *Chinese Policing: History and Reform* (New York: Peter Lang, 2009) 32–37.
67 Weifang He, "The Police and the Rule of Law: Commentary on Principals and Secret Agents" (2007) 191 *The China Quarterly* 117.
68 Yuhua Wang & Carl F. Minzner, "Rise of the Security State" (2015) 222 *The China Quarterly* 339.
69 Kam C. Wong, *Chinese Policing: History and Reform* (New York: Peter Lang, 2009) 32.
70 The bureaucratic system sets impersonalized goals and standards, with a system of inspections and of incentives to control and motivate local officials.
71 On environmental issues, China also relies on large-scale campaigns to meet targets. "The leadership uses mass campaigns to tackle macro-level environmental threats, including land degradation, water pollution, and water scarcity." Elizabeth Economy, "Environmental Governance in China: State Control to Crisis Management" (2014) 143 (2) *Daedalus* 184.
72 Frank J. Remington & Victor G. Rosenblum, "The Criminal Law and the Legislative Process" (1960) 481 *Current Problems in Criminal Law* 496.
73 "Passengers of Drunk Driving May Get Punished", *Guangzhou Daily* (11 October 2009) A2.
74 *Regulation on Legal Issues of Criminal Cases of Drunk Driving of the People's Republic of China*, 2013.
75 Dorothy H. Bracey, "Policing the People's Republic", in Ronald J. Troyer, John P. Clark & Dean G. Rojek, eds, *Social Control in the People's Republic of China* (New York: Praeger, 1989) 133.
76 Gordon Hughes, *Understanding Crime Prevention: Social Control, Risk and Late Modernity* (Berkshire: Open University Press, 1998) 77.
77 Edward J. Epstein, "Law and Legitimation in Post-Mao China", in Pitman B. Potter, ed, *Domestic Law Reforms in Post-Mao China* (New York: M.E. Sharpe, 1994) 26.
78 Borge Bakken, ed, *Crime, Punishment, and Policing in China* (Lanham, MD: Rowman & Littlefield Publishers, 1992) 13.
79 Benjamin L. Liebman, "China's Courts: Restrained Reforms" (2007) 21 *Colum Journal of Asian Law* 40.
80 Benjamin L. Liebman, "Watch Dog or Demagogue? The Media in the Chinese Legal System" (2005) 105 (1) *Columbia Law Review* 1.
81 Benjamin L. Liebman, "Watch Dog or Demagogue? The Media in the Chinese Legal System" (2005) 105 (1) *Columbia Law Review* 154.
82 Borge Bakken, ed, *Crime, Punishment, and Policing in China* (Lanham, MD: Rowman & Littlefield Publishers, 1992) 13–15.
83 John L. Thornton, "Long Time Coming, The Prospects for Democracy in China" (2008) 87 (1) *Foreign Affairs* 15.
84 See Wenfang Tang, *Public Opinion and Political Change in China* (Stanford, CA: Stanford University Press, 2005).
85 Benjamin L. Liebman, "Watch Dog or Demagogue? The Media in the Chinese Legal System" (2005) 105 (1) *Columbia Law Review* 154.
86 Benjamin L. Liebman, "China's Courts: Restrained Reforms" (2007) 21 *Columbia Journal of Asian Law* 22.
87 "Summary of Opinions Nationwide on the Draft of Employment Promotion Law of China", online: NPC <http://www.npc.gov.cn/npc/flcazqyj/2007-04/26/content_1464893.htm>.
88 One example is: "What is Your Opinion on Drunk Driving?", online: CNWest <http://news.cnwest.com/content/2011-05/13/content_4581039.htm>.

89 Benjamin L. Liebman, "China's Courts: Restrained Reforms" (2007) 21 *Columbia Journal of Asian Law* 21.
90 See Wenfang Tang, *Public Opinion and Political Change in China* (Stanford, CA: Stanford University Press, 2005).
91 Yuqiong Zhou & Patricia Moy, "Parsing Framing Processes: The Interplay between Online Public Opinion and Media Coverage" (2007) 57 *Journal of Communication* 84.
92 Johan Lagerkvist, "The Rise of Online Public Opinion in the People's Republic of China" (2005) 3 *China: An International Journal* 119.
93 Xiaoming Chen, "Community and Policing Strategies: A Chinese Approach to Crime Control" (2002) 12 *Policing and Society* 10.
94 Johan Lagerkvist, "The Rise of Online Public Opinion in the People's Republic of China" (2005) 3 *China: An International Journal* 129.
95 Zixue Tai, "Networked Resistance: Digital Populism, Online Activism, and Mass Dissent in China" (2015) 13 (2) *Popular Communication* 120–121.
96 Steven J. Balla, "Health System Reform and Political Participation on the Chinese Internet" (2014) 7 *China Information* 219.
97 Yongming Zhou, *Historicizing Online Politics: Telegraphy, the Internet, and Political Participation in China* (Stanford, CA: Stanford University Press, 2006) 235.
98 Kam C. Wong, *Chinese Policing: History and Reform* (New York: Peter Lang, 2009) 13.
99 David Indermaur, "A Matter of Judgment: The Effect of Information and Deliberation on Public Attitudes to Punishment" (2012) 14 *Punishment & Society* 149.
100 David Indermaur, "A Matter of Judgment: The Effect of Information and Deliberation on Public Attitudes to Punishment" (2012) 14 *Punishment & Society* 150.
101 Roberts J. V., "New Media Influences on Public View of Sentencing" (1990) 14 *Law and Human Behavior* 453.
102 John Pratt, *Penal Populism* (New York: Routledge, 2007) 16.
103 "An Explanation on the 11th Draft Amendment to the PRC's Criminal Law by the Legislative Affairs Commission of the Standing Committee of the National People's Congress", online: pkulaw.cn <https://www.pkulaw.com/protocol/51e78abb3a002802aa4c64e7a954f2edbdfb.html>.
104 Constitution and Law Committee of the NPC, online: <http://www.npc.gov.cn/npc/c34375/xffl.shtml>.
105 Jan Michiel Otto et al., *Law-Making in People's Republic of China* (The Hague: Kluwer Law International, 2000) 141.
106 Anthony Dicks, "The Chinese Legal System: Reforms in the Balance" (1989) 119 *The China Quarterly* 571.
107 Anthony Dicks, "The Chinese Legal System: Reforms in the Balance" (1989) 119 *The China Quarterly* 570.
108 Jan Michiel Otto et al., *Law-Making in People's Republic of China* (The Hague: Kluwer Law International, 2000) 145.
109 John W. Kingdon, *Agendas, Alternatives and Public Policies, Update Edition, with an Epilogue on Health Care*, 2nd ed. (New York: Pearson, 2010) 55.
110 Wenfang Tang, *Public Opinion and Political Change in China* (Stanford, CA: Stanford University Press, 2005) 185.
111 Wenfang Tang, *Public Opinion and Political Change in China* (Stanford, CA: Stanford University Press, 2005) 172.
112 Jan Michiel Otto et al., *Law-Making in People's Republic of China* (The Hague: Kluwer Law International, 2000) 70.
113 David Garland, "The Rise of Risk", in Richard V. Ericson & Aaron Doyle, *Risk and Morality* (Toronto, ON: University of Toronto Press, 2003) 58.

114 "The increase in the number of legislative bureaus and lawyers in the government should in the long term have a favorable impact on legal certainty." Jan Michiel Otto et al., *Law-Making in People's Republic of China* (The Hague: Kluwer Law International, 2000) 17.
115 Baogang He & Mark E. Warren, "Authoritarian Deliberation: The Deliberate Turn in Chinese Political Development" (2011) 9 (02) *Perspectives on Politics* 269–289.
116 Liu Kang, "Searching for a New Cultural Identity: China's Soft Power and Media Culture Today" (2012) 21 (78) *Journal of Contemporary China* 921.
117 Baogang He & Stig Thogersen, "Giving the People a Voice? Experiments with Consultative Authoritarian Institutions in China" (2010) 19 (66) *Journal of Contemporary China* 677.
118 Michael McConville et al., *Criminal Justice in China: An Empirical Enquiry* (Cheltenham: Edward Elgar, 2011).
119 Baogang He & Stig Thogersen, "Giving the People a Voice? Experiments with Consultative Authoritarian Institutions in China" (2010) 19 (66) *Journal of Contemporary China* 676.
120 Randall Peerenboom, *China's Long March toward Rule of Law* (Cambridge: Cambridge University Press, 2002) 156.
121 See Jane Duckett & Ana Inés Langer, "Populism versus Neoliberalism: Diversity and Ideology in the Chinese Media's Narratives of Health Care Reform" (2013) 6 *Modern China* 653–680.
122 Wai Fung Lam & Kwan Nok Chan, "How Authoritarianism Intensifies Punctuated Equilibrium: The Dynamics of Policy Attention in Hong Kong" (2014) 28 (4) *Governance* 553.
123 Online consultation is "a process through which government officials provide citizens with opportunities to offer feedback on draft laws and regulations." Steven J. Balla, "Health System Reform and Political Participation on the Chinese Internet" (2014) 7 *China Information* 227.
124 James S. Fishkin et al., "Deliberative Democracy in an Unlikely Place: Deliberative Polling in China" (2010) 40 (02) *British Journal of Political Science* 447.
125 Joshua Rosenzweig, "Disappearing Justice: Public Opinion, Secret Arrest and Criminal Procedure Reform in China" (2013) *The China Journal* 73–97.
126 Philip C. Huang, "Introduction to 'Constitutionalism, Reform, and the Nature of the Chinese State: Dialogues among Western and Chinese Scholars, III'" (2010) 36 (1) *Modern China* 10.
127 Zhiping Liang, *Rule of Law in China: Institutions, Discourse, and Practice* (Beijing: China University of Political Science and Law Press, 2002) 140.
128 Wei Liu, "Trend of the Amendment of Criminal Law and Its Principles" (2011) 5 *Political Science and Law* 95–101. Legal pragmatism again became a means to an end, to stabilize society and to initiate and/or consolidate change which would save party rule from the threat of massive popular discontent. Edward J. Epstein, "Law and Legitimation in Post-Mao China", in Pitman B. Potter, ed, *Domestic Law Reforms in Post-Mao China* (New York: M.E. Sharpe, 1994) 21; Jan Michiel Otto et al., *Law-Making in People's Republic of China* (The Hague: Kluwer Law International, 2000) 12.
129 See Emma Bell, *Criminal Justice and Neoliberalism* (Basingstoke: Palgrave Macmillan, 2011).
130 Murray Scot Tanner, *The Politics of Lawmaking in Post-Mao China: Institutions, Processes, and Democratic Prospects* (Oxford: Clarendon Press, 1998) 73.
131 Benjamin L. Liebman, "A Return to Populist Legality? Historical Legacies and Legal Reform", in Elizabeth Perry & Sebastian Heilmann, eds, *Mao's Invisible Hand* (Cambridge: Harvard University Asia Center Press, 2011) 167.
132 Stanley B. Lubman, *Bird in a Cage: Legal Reform in Post-Mao China* (Stanford, CA: Stanford University Press, 2002) 2.

7 The role of the state in the criminal justice system

Through a comparative perspective

In China, crime prevention, with the trend towards enhanced risk control, is a product of the collective "it works" beliefs on fighting crime. It is one approach within the Chinese mixed problem-solving approaches of security governance. Faced with crises, the authoritarian party-state regime demonstrates advantages in mobilizing required resources in a short time period, during which police from different levels are devoted to intense battles. This plays a crucial role in decreasing the public's fear of crime. With the massive support of the punitive law, the CCP also strengthen its power, and the authoritarian system continues to demonstrate its resilience. It is the reason China has been able to remain united despite dramatic upheaval, and it is why the party-state has been able to maintain its authority.

The three streams discussed in previous chapters reflect the role of the state in the system of crime control. This chapter aims to make a comparison between that of the West and China. In the first section, it argues that in a number of Western countries, risk management, as a governing technique of the state, manifests a distributive network of security governance as well as solidified state power in certain areas. It is a transformation of power relationships in response to the pessimism about declining social order. After that, the second section focuses on the politics of the Chinese dynamic of crime prevention. In China, crime prevention, with the trend towards enhanced risk control, is a product of the collective "it works" beliefs on fighting crime. It is one approach within the Chinese mixed problem-solving approaches of security governance. With the massive support of the punitive law, the CCP also strengthen its power, and the authoritarian system continues to demonstrate its resilience.

This chapter locates the Chinese experience within the world context. It suggests that the social environments and the interactions between the individuals and the state in the West and in China are distinct from each other. To examine the orthodoxy of crime prevention with this paradigm shed lights on the Chinese characteristics, which other theories like the risk society theory are unable to accomplish.

7.1 Risk control in the Western criminal justice system

7.1.1 Conceptualizing risk in the Western criminal justice system

The paradigm of risk in the preventive shift of Western criminal justice can be analyzed from multiple angles. Risk is an approach through which more and more objects, techniques and logic are viewed and managed. The way that risk discourses shape the penal field originates from reforms in society and public policies. First, risk, as an object, needs to be identified and controlled through actuarial methods.[1] It exists more as logic rather than a practice, shaped by the circumstances in which it is set. In criminal law, that crimes are considered everyday risks introduces a new perspective of classification and surveillance mechanism against crimes. Accidents, danger to public security generated by inchoate crimes of violent offences and risky personalities of recidivist sexual offenders have been challenging human societies for centuries. The offenders have not changed; the significance lies in the way in which they are viewed and treated. Unlike the moral agent that should be blamed for his/her own evils and the sick who need to be corrected through clinical techniques, offenders are now considered normal risks that should be managed.[2] Accordingly, the duty of the state is partly shifted to information monitoring and exchange on a macro level.

Second, risk is a technology of the government. It is more about the statistical prediction of the sanction of free will through actuarial reasoning. With the use of probabilistic techniques, in criminal lawmaking the boundary of public interest that criminal law protects is expanding. A case in point is in the anti-terrorism laws of the US, the UK and Australia where the supposed preparatory acts of terrorism, which are far away from actual harm, are increasingly criminalized.[3] Fault is replaced with the prediction of dangerousness and requirement of social management, rationalized by utilitarian purposes. In practice, "a particular manifestation of this is the spread of actuarialism (the mathematical calculation of levels of risk) and a consequent focus upon aggregate risk groups rather than individuals."[4] Considering that the pursuit of security is a never-ending project, it invites worry that without concrete harm, aggregate risk prediction may give rise to power abuse and the exclusion of disadvantaged groups. For example, the ascendance of preventive justice in the UK—characterized as coercive methods dealing with risk before harm has been done—and preparatory offences of serious crimes raise concerns due to the ambiguity of the criteria of criminalization, which cause concerns over the overexpansion of the boundary of criminal law.[5] The state's use of penalties and out-of-court penalties, which bypass the normal procedures of criminal law, have been consistently problematized and criticized. Thus, risk, as a technology of the state, ought to be under the restriction of legal principles against state power.

Third, growing concerns of risk in the West reflect changes in the Western social context and governance dynamic. As Pat O'Malley insists, there is a shift from the pessimist ("nothing works") to the optimist ("what works") stances favoring evidence-led intervention.[6] Since the 1970s when it was widely believed that penal modernism was failing to deliver its promises of rehabilitation and social inclusion, the state has adopted the acting-out strategy (such as Megan's Law and "three strikes") mainly for incapacitation. At the same time, it also attempts to seek "what works" by establishing a collective crime-prevention system, for example, fostering the preventive capacity of individuals and communities, developing situational crime control methods and enacting proactive sanctions. The citizens are both active agents of their own security and coerced objects of state penal power. Compared to the era before, it is a re-arrangement of the power structure in which the state is shifting to fields that it is more capable of dealing with. However, this does not mean that state power is declining. Instead, its power is increasing in certain areas such as fighting serious crime with harsher penalties or preventive techniques, monitoring private security, identifying and classifying risk and social discipline on a macro level. The risk-based preventive shift in criminal penalties, ancillary orders and policing reflects the new logic of crime prevention based on the conservative role of the state. It sheds light on not only "how authorities come to understand and manage their relations to the problematized field, and the forms of power, knowledge and technology necessary to their activities,"[7] but also how the governing practices of authorities shape and are shaped simultaneously by the power of the autonomous subjects' engagements.

7.1.2 State's role of risk control in the Western social context

The current Western criminal justice system is a myriad of actions that are both inclusive and exclusive, private and public, neoliberal and conservative. A most prevalent feature lies on the chain of coordinated actions of crime control between individuals and communities, like the "responsibilization strategy" with the government governing at a distance. This shift is mainly facilitated by the transformation from welfarist to neoliberal politics led by politicians and their followers such as Thatcher in the UK and Reagan in the US, seeking market-driven individualized responsibility for the management of uncertainty. "The status and economic well-being of citizens tend to be much more heavily dependent on the market in this type of society."[8] The USA is the archetypal example of a neoliberal society. The other historically Anglo-American nations (the UK, Australia and New Zealand) also feature in this group.[9] Under the influences of the neoliberal theory and policy, in Western criminal justice there coexists a contract-out pattern of policing and an emphasis on the self-governing capacity of individuals and communities for their own risk management. This partnership, which reduces the state's accountability for security provision, fosters a mechanism of mixed governance between public and private spheres. The neoliberal theory is highly influenced by the Foucauldian governmentality theory,[10] which addresses organized practices, including rationalities and technologies, through which the society is rendered governable by its government. The "government" that Foucault and his followers use is not confined to the traditional sovereign government; rather, it is about a range of actors including state agencies, families, schools, churches and individuals. "What is to be governed is itself self-governing, and thus any act of governance must take account of the self-regulating order of things."[11] The self-governance capacity of individuals is stressed by the risk society theory as well, though its analytical framework is quite distinct from the others with regard to the focus, hypothesis, analytical approach and conclusions. Risk society theory is mainly based on the reflexive thinking of the side effects of modernity that have emerged since the last decade of the past century. Beck argues that, "science and technology are now being challenged at the grassroots level by a politics born out of the recognition of modernist experts' inability to govern the monsters they created."[12] In the risk society, every individual has to be cautious of the risks by themselves. Therefore, risk control is privatized, dispersed and segmented for "responsibilized" autonomy.

However, though the impact that diffused power has on political programs and individual subjectivities is examined by a number of analytical frameworks, it does not suggest that the state has completely retreated or the social is "dead." In parallel with the collaboration for crime prevention among individuals, communities and state authorities, when the state rolls backward it has actively increased the use of proactive techniques and longer detentions, manifesting in an intensified concern for security and surveillance at the macro level. A free economy requires a strong state. After 9/11, this is increasingly justified for the prevention of terrorist acts, an essential problem of the state for the deterrence of national deviances. Besides the enhanced "technologies of the self through which individuals work on themselves to shape their own subjectivity,"[13] the state still takes a strong position as a sovereign authority to facilitate market competition, safeguard the rule of law, intervene when conflicts arise and exclude offenders who fail to be rehabilitated. The state still serves as the main provider of basic public security and guide of the private security market, characterized by the prevention of serious crime, increased use of surveillance technology, civil detention of persons with mental illness and the introduction of preventive orders on risky offenders. The sovereign command remains one key tactic from multiple centers of self-government and government. For instance, Foucault argues that "the rise and continuation of discipline relied on the continuation of sovereign power, and that both sovereignty and discipline (rather than disappearing) are essential to the complex form of government that has emerged more recently."[14] Thus the government should govern to an appropriate degree without disrupting the self-governing capability of those it governs.

The combination of private self-governance and public surveillance is consistent with the arguments of Garland and Rose on the two extremes (or two poles) of governance due to the allied relationship between neoliberalism and conservatism.[15] The combination also resonates with the claims of a great many researchers that the penal system in the West is "a mixed and contradictory picture,"[16] that there is no abrupt change,[17] that the shift to a postmodern penalty system may be evolutionary rather than radical in nature and that its exact contours are still somewhat vague and ill defined.[18] Preventive methods are typical examples of this "state-based" approach of viewing the current role of authorities in crime control and security governance. They exist as a balance between the conservative and neoliberal ideologies of criminal justice. In the UK, the US and some Commonwealth countries like Australia, a large number of preparatory crimes and preventive detention are used for the deterrence of serious offences and their associated crimes or misbehaviors, reflecting the old penology of being harsher on crime. Other changes in the same period such as "rising levels of punishment, the apparent decline of human rights discourse in the penal realm and the resurgence of interest in 'pre-modern' modes of punishment," or the neo-feudalization of punishment which involves new forms of humiliation and degradation as well as public displays of remorse,[19] also reflect the conservative ideology of the state's role and criminal justice. Preventive lawmaking and postmodern penology both show that there are certain responsibilities monopolized by state authorities such as lawmaking, law enforcement and policing, even though both social forces and economic elements have been gradually introduced into the programs. The power, which is dispersed in pluralist social institutions, is eventually centralized in the state, which remains as a key nodal point of governance with the other actors. However, distinctive from Keynesian welfare modernism, in the post-social politic, "the language of probability and risk increasingly replaces earlier discourses of clinical diagnosis and retributive judgment."[20] The preventive shift is concerned with techniques to identify, classify and manage groupings sorted by dangerousness, rather than individualized correction and rehabilitation based on moral concerns, illustrating this systematic transformation to an aggregate classification system for purposes of surveillance, confinement and control.[21] This shift is driven by a mix of factors, comprised of the collapse of penal welfarism, the war against terrorism and the development of statistical technology, among others.

In all, Western liberal societies have witnessed a shift from penal welfarism to restructured criminal justice that relies on cost control, risk management and public surveillance, with a favoritism for governmentality technology that may reduce uncertainty, foster self-regulation and prevent loss.[22] "Risk thinking has become central to the management of exclusion in post-welfare strategies of control."[23] At the same time, it should be noted that it is a picture that is still forming, without a clear-cut boundary with the past. There is certainly solid empirical evidence to support that postmodern changes are taking place. For instance, research suggests that in the control of sexual and violent offenders, new forms of partnership and accountability dispersal have been driven by the logic of risk.[24] However, the picture is much less clear on some other points. The transition itself is not an overall and sudden change. Neither is risk thinking completely novel, nor rehabilitation entirely declined. "There are numerous aspects of culture and practice which reflect the continuing strength of the modernist project, for example, interest in the individual case, and the use of professional judgment to overrule actuarial assessments."[25] Both lawmaking and enforcement are hybrids of new and traditional methods with diverse pursuits like retribution, deterrence, rehabilitation and risk control. American penal sanctioning itself is fragmented, multidimensional and often contradictory among different states.[26] In addition, the transition does not apply to all Western countries, like Canada and Japan, which have shown a certain resistance due to their political and cultural arrangements.

7.2 Risk control in the Chinese criminal justice system

7.2.1 The "it works" belief in criminal justice in China

The development of Western criminal justice inspires an examination of Chinese practices based on a state-centered approach. Unlike the mechanisms of the US and the UK which are shaped by neoliberal policy, the Chinese field of crime control is primarily monopolized by the coercive power of the central and local governments. Governance theory can only explain part of the picture on mass line policy, private security and other policing practices. In general, since the 1980s, the Chinese criminal justice system has been a model of "it works," searching for "what works better," rather than "nothing works." In the UK, the public expressed pessimism about the crime rate in the 2000 British Crime Survey, which suggested that two-thirds of the respondents believed that crime at the national level had increased over the previous two years, even though that is contrary to the actual rates.[27] Meanwhile, Chinese legislation and policing have made progress with the help of public support. China is shifting to be more in line with the Western pattern of rule of law with a top-down approach, providing the overall social background for legal analysis. However, this shift is based on the law's utilitarian value in solving problems and earning public support, rather than the intention of upholding legal principles. The shift will consolidate state power with a more stable society.

Resorting to the law, as Western democracies do, is a necessity for the survival of China and the CCP. After the launch of economic reforms and the opening-up policy in the late 1970s, the Chinese state has started to use the law as a key tool of social governance. The significance of the law for China is rising, primarily to meet the needs of economic development, as well as for more efficient social control. Max Weber argues that governments can derive their authority from three sources: tradition, the qualities and charisma of a given leader and constitutional and legal norms.[28] In China, after Mao and Deng, neither tradition nor a leader's fine qualities can sustain a stable governance over the increasingly pluralist and open society. Accordingly, "the reliance on the ideology of mass line and class struggle was toned down, and the importance of the rule of law was repeatedly emphasized."[29] There has been an unprecedented increase in state-initiated laws across almost all fields. The first Chinese criminal law came out in 1979. Then, the 1997 Criminal Law replaced the 1979 Criminal law with many more advances. Not only did it abandon the revolutionary tone of the former law, but it was also drafted using the latest models from Germany and Japan. After that, the state has made 11 amendments to criminal law to date. Revising the law with amendments was also learned from the West (e.g., the US). Compared to before, the laws are more complete and professionally created. Law enforcement has improved as well. The "strike hard" policy has been criticized for its violation of human rights since the 1980s. After the early 2000s, it was replaced by the new criminal policy of "balancing leniency with severity." Similar to other laws and policies, the decision makers wrote it with reference to Western policies that demonstrated two extremes in the criminal justice field, that of being harsh on serious crimes and being lenient on minor deviances. This new criminal policy is both more compatible with the trend of international development of criminal law, and with Chinese crime rates during that time (which have been rising at a slower pace than in the 1980s). The leniency policy also goes deeper; research shows that its local implementation has significantly reduced the crudeness of Chinese criminal law in daily adjudications.[30] In Chinese criminal procedure law, incremental progress has also been made to restrict police power, though it remains difficult to change the imbalance of power. Therefore, the history of criminal lawmaking progress, enforcement and policing does show development toward a Chinese model of rule of law. The process is basically monitored by the state, though it may be not what the top authorities originally expect or intend.

Such progress runs parallel to the support of Chinese citizens who still hold high expectations of the government's capacity to fight crime, underlined with the impression of "it works." As Chapter 4 noted, with strict policing Chinese citizens are more or less satisfied with the Chinese government's security function. They tend to believe that although the future is uncertain, progress will be made step by step. However, the Chinese population favors stability and fears political disorder. Most of those who have been through the mess and trauma of either the Sino-Japanese wars, internal wars or the cultural revolutions are relatively tolerant of the CCP, which has not only brought China out of such wars, but also brought in remarkable material advancements in recent decades.[31] The CCP's media censorship also helps to maintain the image of the party-state by blocking unwanted information and showing the negative aspects of other countries. Therefore, unlike Western crime governance, the Chinese scenario is more "it works" than "nothing works." Interactions between the public and the state continue to boost increased lawmaking and stricter surveillance with solid public support. One case in point is the expansion of criminal law which has received little public resistance. A secure social environment enhances the legitimacy of the authoritarian regime, and a centralized, strong government proves to be effective in crime fighting. The authoritarian structure sustains national unity through power and authority. Western democratic countries do not have obvious advantages in security provision over China.

Overall, criminal law expands hand in hand with the overwhelming belief of "it works" with regard to the Chinese criminal justice system. With public demand (as shown in focusing events) and bureaucratic considerations, each of these various organizations now has its own unique package of power resources that allows it to influence lawmaking at different stages of the process. As has been documented, first, the legislative body is amenable to the social and political impact of focusing events. "Populist pressure has become a key characteristic of the legal system over the past decade."[32] Legislative history show that external pressures from the public serve as one of the boosters of criminal lawmaking in China. The reason that driving accidents, fake drug scandals and environmental pollution become prominent issues lies more in their national awareness than their seriousness. Authorities failed to react earlier due to lack of awareness, or due to the problems' complexities requiring systematic solutions, until emergencies arise and they have to act quickly. Even though drunk driving is supposed to be less harmful than fake drugs and environmental pollution, it receives equal or even more attention from both the public and legislators than the other two. Whether the problems—which actually have existed for a long time—could enter the legislative stream largely depends on how much attention they garner nationwide. How much attention the issues are able to raise relies on the magnitude of the problems themselves, the discretion of the media, the open spaces allowed by local or central governments, the results of the power struggle among the participants and the extent of public activism. "Impact of populist views of law is particularly strong in China."[33] It is officially claimed that responsiveness in lawmaking manifests that the state "serves the people" or tends to meet public demand, through which the CCP's legitimacy is justified. However, from another angle, the government's rapid response to crises is also a result of intense fear of potential social instability and bankrupt public confidence. In almost all cases, compared to municipal and provincial governments, the central government succeeded in maintaining its reputation by urging quick feedback from locals, holding lower-level authorities accountable or enacting new laws to fill gaps in the legal system. "China's rulers now try to resolve, rather than crush, conflicts among competing interests, suppressing such conflicts only when they perceive them to be especially big threats."[34] Thus, even though evidence from both quantitative and qualitative studies has suggested widespread expression of dissatisfaction among locals, the Chinese regime as a whole continues to enjoy a relatively high level of acceptance from the public.

Second, if external public pressures get more chances of triggering of criminal legislation, results of criminal lawmaking are mainly decided through bureaucratic negotiations of social control. Bureaucratic concerns and relationships between these agencies go hand in hand with the CCP's decentralization of power. As has been argued, the CCP's actual power has been dispersing into departmental bureaucracies, levels of government and judicial bodies: "Government ministries, have enormous influence over the detailed content of legislation and its implementation,"[35] where the police (the Ministry of Public Security) maintains supreme power over the other agencies. Most of the bargaining process is hidden from public view, with limited information available to the public. There has also been little study on domestic policy issues where actors within the government take different positions.[36] However, the separation of responsibilities and spheres of authority—which Max Weber saw as definitive characteristics of the modern state—has gradually increased. "The professionalization of legal actors and institutions is perhaps the single most significant accomplishment of China's legal reforms."[37] At most times, the agencies cooperate with each other in both lawmaking and enforcement. This collective national social control strategy is rooted in "reformulated mass-line ideology in response to the changing socioeconomic reality in the post-reform era,"[38] where the courts may coordinate with other bureaucracies to maintain social order. However, it seems that the court has started to shift away from the police and prosecutors, who appear to act differently from those in the West and in authoritarian countries, in order to expand its own authority, defending legal principles from a professional perspective or addressing technical issues of sentencing that the other entities are not familiar with.

Regime theory holds that authoritarian systems are inherently fragile because of weak legitimacy, over-reliance on coercion, over-centralization of decision making and the predominance of personal power over institutional norms.[39] Scholars have also debated whether totalitarian regimes can adapt to modernity. China offers a different model of authoritarianism with efficient provision of economic and public security. Through increased consultation, dispersed leadership and enhanced legitimacy generated by the collective efforts of the CCP, the bureaucrats and the citizens, the regime has actually reconsolidated itself. "Alternative political regimes may appear increasingly unlikely and unappealing."[40] The era of transformation requires a strong government to reduce public anxiety. The Chinese authoritarianism not only provides highly placed leaders with the power to launch reform, but also does well in selectively meeting public demand. For instance, faced with crises, the authoritarian party-state regime demonstrates advantages in mobilizing required resources in a short time period, during which police from different levels are devoted to intense battles. This plays a crucial role in decreasing the public's fear of crime. It is the reason China has been able to remain united despite dramatic upheaval,[41] and it is why the party-state has been able to maintain its authority.

However, though the current framework is practical in deterring crime, as it has been suggested, the institutional arrangements lack restraining power on the use of criminal law. They focus more on the law's utilitarian value rather than upholding its fundamental spirit of restricting state power. This is consistent with research that finds that "the emphasis that courts, procuratorate, and the police place on settling cases reflects trends in the Chinese legal system away from formal adjudication in favor of mediated outcomes."[42] This is even referred to as "return to populist legality."[43] As to the elites, both the court and scholars are unable to defy the expansion of the law within the current state structure, given the coexistence of the weak incentives of top-down political reforms, the absence of a constitutional spirit of limiting state power,[44] court intentions to defend itself from criticism, the influence of traditional patriarchy, the rationale of improving the lagging legal system and the pursuit of public security. Pursuit of public security is the crucial driving element among these factors, which unavoidably leads to concerns of law and order, as well as to a preventive shift in criminal law. As to the masses, the mix of populist punitiveness and the lack of respect for legal principles and procedures suggest that the establishment of legal culture will no doubt be a long process in China. "Legal discourses do not exist above society or simply to control citizens, but instead are embedded in how people interact as legal conventions or cultures."[45] Public insistences on the zero-tolerance approach are not unique to China. For instance, in the West, "although the new penology speaks the language of managerialism and systems theory, populist punitiveness remains rooted in normative judgments about aberrational evil."[46] One study of US sex offenders argues that the new sex offender laws "must merge appeals of this populist response while enabling state bureaucracies themselves, ever more technocratic in orientation, to actually implement the policies" [47]. But compared to the West, Chinese society traditionally lacks respect for the law. In China, laws were traditionally transplanted rather than growing automatically from the needs of society. As such, some of the principles, like everyone should be treated equal or that criminals ought to be protected from state power, diverge from traditional Chinese values. Popular demand for security promotes risk consciousness, while weak respect for the law fails to restrain popular preference toward adequately severe sanctions. In such a political and social environment, more and more laws will be generated within the legal system.

7.2.2 The Chinese mixed problem-solving approach

In Western criminal justice, policy changes are primarily made based on the pessimistic belief that the formal penal modernism failed to reduce crime rates, which creates skepticism over the government's ability to provide security. The state not only abandons some of its responsibilities to the citizens themselves, but also transforms criminal policy from individualized clinical rehabilitation to systematic risk prevention and control, with little moral sense. By contrast, in Chinese criminal lawmaking, that criminal law is expanding in a preventive sense is highly influenced by the public's anxiety about dangers (which has become a pervasive feature of contemporary life), as well as positive belief in the current criminal justice system, which remains rationalized through criminal law's moralized retribution and deterring effect. "The law in general broadens the legal foundation of surveillance practices."[48] In China, anti-terrorism laws continue to create preparatory offences. However, the shift from "result-based" punishment to "behavior-based" prevention blurs the boundary between criminal penalties and administrative penalties.[49] The Chinese style of management through criminal law reveals a coexistence of theories and practices at different stages: self-generated or borrowed from abroad; pre-modern, modern or post-modern; retribution, deterrence, rehabilitation or risk management. During the transition period, neither the Chinese people nor their leaders appear at ease with the current situation.[50] China, as a developing country, offers the chance to experiment with the various models as long as the joint problem-solving approach proves to be effective. The pursuit of utilitarian effects is the top concern. It used to be claimed that, "China's legal reform experience is unique in its ability to mix foreign imports with Chinese tradition, and to recast many imported ideas to be in line with the ideological goals of the party."[51] The proactive expansion of criminal law goes hand in hand with concerns of risk in criminal trials and policing. Besides the legislation that has manifested a preventive shift, in adjudication, the judges carry out risk assessments of the suspect's personality and threats to society in sentencing. The assessment is mixed with moral components and policy concerns. The area that most resembles Western penology is policing, where the police monitor the society through statistic assessment and widely used surveillance technology, judging and minimizing the risks that various situations and individuals pose. In general, crime is normalized as a by-product of modern societies and organized in terms of a risk profile. Tools such as target hardening, statistical profiling, opportunity minimization and loss prevention that are prevalent in Western policing have also been gradually put in place in China.

In addition, the development of managerialism is also evident in Chinese criminal justice. In governance theory, the aim of government is shifted toward regarding the central issue as the optimal harnessing of these self-governing capacities—the "conduct of conduct" in Foucault's words.[52] In Chinese criminal justice there have been practices resembling Western neoliberal practices, such as the growth of private security, the progress of community policing, contracting out of police services and a series of money-based bonus systems. "The desire to replace the Maoist-induced collective dependence upon the state with a notion of rationally calculable individual obligation was central to Deng's reform program."[53] The free market mechanism, the essential element of a capitalist economy, has been gradually introduced into spheres of Chinese public service. For instance, parts of security provision—once managed exclusively by the government—have been subject to privatization and market forces.[54] This shift undoubtedly aims to reduce the government's spending and commitment of resources. However, unlike the West, the legality of some such privatization remains uncertain since there have been no laws to approve it. A number of practices are therefore taken underground. However, considering even private security companies are managed by the Chinese police, it is impossible for the Chinese government to contend, as Western neoliberal countries do, that "the most effective protection would result where individuals partnered or cooperated with the state and police while acting on their own behalf." The balance of market forces and authoritarian governance sheds light on the features of the current Chinese society.

7.3 Conclusion

This section documented differences and similarities of the development of Chinese criminal justice with those of Western neoliberal countries. Both China and the West are at political and economic crossroads, leading to different models of criminal justice. The Western model is shaped by the shift from welfare to neoliberal policies, reflecting an economic reconstruction of criminal justice, while the Chinese one is based on the transforming faces of the party-state's authoritarian governance with the aim of resolving contentious social issues through mixed theories and approaches. In both China and the West, the central government remains strong in crime prevention, but the underlying rationales are quite distinct from each other, including an understanding of the role of authorities in relation to crime, the power structure, governing rationalities and technologies. It appears as though the Chinese government has successfully used the criminal justice system, including criminal law, to steer and guide. It is equally, or even more, attentive to public requirements, since they are the criteria through which Chinese citizens evaluate the socialist democracy and government legitimacy.

Bellin's findings suggest that China's experience may be typical of state-led late development, which breeds dependence on the state from capital and labor.[55] This is the same with crime fighting, through which citizens become more reliant on the state. In this aspect, China stands in contrast with Western rulers in the early capitalist development when social, economic and legal advances empowered citizens to challenge the political system. The Chinese authoritarian regime is becoming more stable. The worry still lies on future of the rule of law within this utilitarian framework. Hopefully in the future, the public, who may become more legal-conscious, will bring about true legal and political reform from the bottom-up approach. There is currently no such opportunity.

Notes

1 Bernard E. Harcourt, *Against Prediction: Profiling, Policing, and Punishing in an Actuarial Age* (Chicago, IL: University of Chicago Press, 2006).

2 Karen Harrison, *Dangerousness, Risk and the Governance of Serious Sexual and Violent Offenders* (London: Routledge, 2011).

3 Andrew Ashworth & Lucia Zedner, *Preventive Justice* (Oxford: Oxford University Press, 2014).

4 Nicola S. Gray, Judith M. Laing & Lesley Noaks, *Criminal Justice, Mental Health and the Politics of Risk* (London: Cavendish, 2001) 177. The state also guides citizens to employ preventive technologies for their personal security.

5 Andrew Ashworth & Lucia Zedner, *Preventive Justice* (Oxford: Oxford University Press, 2014).

6 Pat O'Malley, "Governmentality and Risk", in J. Zinn, ed, *Social Theories of Risk and Uncertainties* (Oxford: Oxford University Press, 2008) 52–75.

7 David Garland, "'Governmentality' and Problem of Crime: Foucault, Criminology and Sociology" (1997) 1 (2) *Theoretical Criminology* 173–208.

8 Michael Cavadino & James Dignan, *Penal Systems: A Comparative Approach* (London: Sage Publications, 2006) 16.

9 Michael Cavadino & James Dignan, *Penal Systems: A Comparative Approach* (London: Sage Publications, 2006) 17. It is argued that with the introduction of the free-market economic policies, the countries have witnessed growing inequality in material distribution.

10 Trent H. Hamann, "Neoliberalism, Governmentality, and Ethics" (2009) 6 *Foucault Studies* 38.

11 Pat O'Malley, "Governmentality and Risk", Sydney Law School Research Paper No. 09/98, P3, in J. Zinn, ed, *Social Theories of Risk and Uncertainties* (Oxford: Oxford University Press, 2008) 52–75.

12 Pat O'Malley, "'Uncertainty Makes Us Free': Risk, Insurance and Freedom", in Limor Samimian-Darash & Paul Rabinow, eds, *Modes of Uncertainty: Anthropological Cases* (Chicago, IL: University of Chicago Press, 2015) 13–28.

13 David Garland, "'Governmentality' and Problem of Crime: Foucault, Criminology and Sociology" (1997) 1 (2) *Theoretical Criminology* 173.

14 Pat O'Malley, "Governmentality and Risk", Sydney Law School Research Paper No. 09/98, P1, in J. Zinn, ed, *Social Theories of Risk and Uncertainties* (Oxford: Oxford University Press, 2008) 52–75.

15 Nikolas Rose, "Government and Control" (2000) 40 *British Journal of Criminology* 321–339; David Garland, "'Governmentality' and Problem of Crime: Foucault, Criminology and Sociology" (1997) 1 (2) *Theoretical Criminology* 173.

16 Hazel Kemshall & Mike Maguire, "Public Protection, Partnership and Risk Penalty: The Multi-Agency Risk Management of Sexual and Violent Offenders" (2001) 3 *Punishment & Society* 237–264.
17 Simon Hallsworth, "Rethinking the Punitive Turn Economies of Excess and the Criminology of the Other" (2000) *Punishment and Society* 145–160.
18 Hazel Kemshall & Mike Maguire, "Public Protection, Partnership and Risk Penalty: The Multi-Agency Risk Management of Sexual and Violent Offenders" (2001) 3 *Punishment & Society* 260.
19 Michael Cavadino & James Dignan, "Introducing Comparative Penology", in Michael Cavadino & James Dignan, *Penal System: A Comparative Approach* (Sage Publications Ltd; 1st edition, 2005) 8; Vanessa Barker, *The Politics of Imprisonment: How the Democratic Process Shapes the Way America Punishes Offenders* (New York: Oxford University Press, 2009) 45.
20 Malcolm M. Feeley & Jonathan Simon, "The New Penology, Notes on the Emerging Strategy of Corrections and Its Implications" (1992) 30 *Criminology* 450.
21 Malcolm M. Feeley & Jonathan Simon, "The New Penology, Notes on the Emerging Strategy of Corrections and Its Implications" (1992) 30 *Criminology* 452.
22 Richard V. Ericson & Kevin D. Haggerty, *Policing the Risk Society* (Toronto, ON: University of Toronto Press, Scholarly Publishing Division, 1997) 52.
23 N. Rose, "Government and Control", in David Garland & Richard Sparks, eds, *Criminology and Social Theory* (Oxford: Oxford University Press, 2000) 198.
24 Hazel Kemshall & Mike Maguire, "Public Protection, Partnership and Risk Penalty: The Multi-Agency Risk Management of Sexual and Violent Offenders" (2001) 3 *Punishment & Society* 237–264.
25 Hazel Kemshall & Mike Maguire, "Public Protection, Partnership and Risk Penalty: The Multi-Agency Risk Management of Sexual and Violent Offenders" (2001) 3 *Punishment & Society* 254.
26 Vanessa Barker, *The Politics of Imprisonment: How the Democratic Process Shapes the Way America Punishes Offenders* (New York: Oxford University Press, 2009) 6.
27 Roger Matthews & Jock Young, *The New Politics of Crime and Punishment* (Devon: Willan, 2013) 41; C. Kershaw et al., *The 2000 British Crime Survey: England and Wales, Home Office Statistical Bulletin 18/00* (London: Home Office, 2000) 59.
28 David M. Lampton, "How China is Ruled: Why It Is Getting Harder for Beijing to Govern", in Gideon Rose, ed, *Tiananmen and After* (Foreign Affairs, 2014) 119.
29 Ivan Y. Sun & Yuning Wu, "Chinese Policing in a Time of Transition, 1978–2008" (2010) 26 *Journal of Contemporary Criminal Justice* 25; A. Lepp, "Note, The Death Penalty in Late Imperial, Modern, and Post-Tiananmen China" (1990) 11 *Michigan Journal of International Law* 987–1038.
30 See Benjamin L. Liebman, "Leniency in Chinese Criminal Law? Everyday Justice in Henan" (2015) 33 (1) *Berkeley Journal of International Law* 153–222.
31 Coercive repression—in 1989 and after—may itself have generated legitimacy by persuading the public that the regime's grip on power is unshakeable.
32 Benjamin L. Liebman, "A Return to Populist Legality? Historical Legacies and Legal Reform", in Elizabeth Perry & Sebastian Heilmann, eds, *Mao's Invisible Hand* (Cambridge: Harvard University Asia Center Press, 2011) 178.
33 Benjamin L. Liebman, "A Return to Populist Legality? Historical Legacies and Legal Reform", in Elizabeth Perry & Sebastian Heilman, eds, *Mao's Invisible Hand* (Cambridge: Harvard University Asia Center, 2011) 177.

34 David M. Lampton, "How China is Ruled: Why It Is Getting Harder for Beijing to Govern", in Gideon Rose, ed, *Tiananmen and After* (Foreign Affairs, 2014) 122.
35 Murray Scot Tanner, *The Politics of Lawmaking in Post-Mao China: Institutions, Processes, and Democratic Prospects* (Oxford: Clarendon Press, 1998) 132.
36 Jane Duckett & Ana Inés Langer, "Populism versus Neoliberalism: Diversity and Ideology in the Chinese Media's Narratives of Health Care Reform" (2013) 39 *Modern China* 654.
37 Taisu Zhang, "The Pragmatic Court: Reinterpreting the Supreme People's Court of China" (2011) 25 *Columbia Journal of Asian Law* 4.
38 Linda Shuo Zhao, "Anomie Theory and Crime in a Transitional China (1978–)" (2008) 18 *International Criminal Justice Review* 151.
39 Andrew J. Nathan, "China's Changing of the Guard, Authoritarian Resilience" (2003) 14 (1) *Journal of Democracy* 6.
40 Teresa Wright, "State-Society Relations in Reform-Era China: A Unique Case of Post-Socialist State-Led Late Development?" (2008) 40 (3) *Comparative Politics* 369.
41 Zhenjie Yang, "'Fragmented Authoritarianism' – The Facilitator Behind the Chinese Reform Miracle: A Case Study in Central China" (2013) 6 (1) *China Journal of Social Work* 12.
42 Benjamin L. Liebman, "Leniency in Chinese Criminal Law? Everyday Justice in Henan" (2015) 33 (1) *Berkeley Journal of International Law* 157.
43 Carl Minzner, "China's Turn against Law" (2011) 59 *American Journal of Comparative Law* 935; Benjamin Liebman, "A Return to Populist Legality: Historical Legacies and Legal Reform", in Elizabeth Perry & Sebastian Heilmann, eds, *Mao's Invisible Hand* (Cambridge: Harvard University Asia Center Press, 2011) 165–200.
44 Kam C. Wong, "Legalism and Constitutionalism in the People's Republic of China" (2006) 1 (2) *International Journal of Criminal Justice Sciences* 1–26.
45 Neil J. Diamant, Stanley B. Lubman & Kevin J., "Law and Society in the People's Republic of China", in Neil J. Diamant, Stanley B. Lubman & Kevin J., eds, *Engaging the Law in China: State, Society, and Possibilities for Justice* (Stanford, CA: Stanford University Press, 2005) 15.
46 Jonathan Simon, "Managing the Monstrous: Sex Offenders and the New Penology" (1998) 4 *Psychology, Public Policy and Law* 452.
47 Jonathan Simon, "Managing the Monstrous: Sex Offenders and the New Penology" (1998) 4 *Psychology, Public Policy and Law* 456.
48 Richard V. Ericson & Kevin D. Haggerty, *Policing the Risk Society* (Toronto, ON: University of Toronto Press, Scholarly Publishing Division, 1997) 65.
49 This boundary was set to not only save judicial resources but also to restrain the over-extension of the scope of criminal law. To replace administrative penalties that are managed by the police with criminal penalties provides more procedure protections to the offenders, but the deprivation of general liberty requires much more concern.
50 Elizabeth J. Perry, "Growing Pains: Challenges for a Rising China" (2014) 143 (2) *Daedalus* 5–13.
51 Benjamin L. Liebman, "A Return to Populist Legality? Historical Legacies and Legal Reform", in Elizabeth Perry & Sebastian Heilmann, eds, *Mao's Invisible Hand* (Cambridge: Harvard University Asia Center Press, 2011) 187–188.
52 Pat O'Malley, "Governmentality and Risk", Sydney Law School Research Paper No. 09/98, P12, in J. Zinn, ed, *Social Theories of Risk and Uncertainties* (Oxford: Oxford University Press, 2008) 52–75.

53 Michael Dutton, "Toward a Government of the Contract: Policing in the Era of Reform", in Borge Bakken, ed, *Crime, Punishment and Policing in China* (New York: Rowman and Littlefield, 2005) 190.

54 Deborah S. Davis, ed, *The Consumer Revolution in Urban China* (Berkeley and Los Angeles, CA: University of California Press, 2000); Anthony J. Spires, "Contingent Symbiosis and Civil Society in an Authoritarian State: Understanding the Survival of China's Grassroots NGOs" (2011) 117 (1) *American Journal of Sociology* 1–45.

55 Teresa Wright, "State-Society Relations in Reform-Era China: A Unique Case of Post-Socialist State-Led Late Development?" (2008) 40 (3) *Comparative Politics* 369.

8 Policy window of Chinese criminal lawmaking and conclusion

At last, the book argues that the preventive shift remains evident in revisions of Chinese criminal law after the enactment of the eighth amendment in 2011. The number of endangerment crimes, inchoate crimes and pre-inchoate crimes keeps increasing. It is hoped that the government could give equal consideration to restraining criminal law. Otherwise, the Chinese society will become more and more exclusive.

Previous chapters of the book have examined the problem stream, policy stream and political stream in Chinese criminal lawmaking. The interplay of public demands, legal culture, bureaucratic politics and political influences is evident in legislative activities, reflecting a controlled participation with selective use of consultation and jurisdiction competition. Kingdon's MSA explains in detail what the "policy windows" are, why they open and how the coupling of the streams takes place. The policy window is an opportunity for advocates of proposals to push their pet solutions, or to push attention to their special problems. It opens when the three streams are all available, through which government agendas turn into the final decisions. At this policy window, "a problem is recognized, a solution is developed and available in the policy community, a political change makes it the right time for policy change and potential constraints are not severe."[1]

As to Chinese criminal lawmaking, law reform is a routinized opportunity to change the law. The legislation is consistently up for renewal, and several factors come together at this given point just in time. It is a window that opens quite frequently and predictably. This chapter not only summarizes previous chapters through the factors contributing to the opening of the policy window, but also predicts future developments of the Chinese criminal justice system. The first section of this chapter examines law renewal as a window for revising criminal law. It also argues that, compared with the policy stream, the problem and political streams have played the most important parts in opening the policy window. It can be risky since the policy stream fails to restrain the expansion of the law, as long as the political institutions tend to meet public demands with criminal law.

Then the second section concludes with analysis of two concerns of future development of Chinese criminal justice: will the authoritarian state structure lead only to harsh penalties, and is China an exclusive or inclusive society? It suggests that the future is not dark since the current institutional arrangements do not necessarily refer to an entirely disciplined society.

The last section examines legislative changes after the eighth amendment to Chinese criminal law. After the enactment of the eighth amendment in 2011, China has promulgated three more amendments. A number of clauses in these new amendments, including but not limited to terrorism-related crimes, crimes against public security and crimes related to fake or poor-quality medications, manifest a similar proactive shift for the pursuit of security. The discourse of crime control is increasingly structured around the symbolic and politically useful notion of prevention. It is therefore wise to remain cautious of the expanding concept of prevention and security.

8.1 Legal renewal: Easily opened windows for law reforms

8.1.1 Frequent coupling of the streams

In Kingdon's model, "policy entrepreneurs" use national events and themes to push new ideas to the fore. In lawmaking, the subjects rise and fall on the agenda according to the renewal cycle.[2]

> The renewal becomes a window giving policy entrepreneurs of various descriptions an opportunity to advance their ideas, raise their problems, and push their proposals. When the three streams are all available, they simply need to be ready when the time for renewal comes.[3]

The Chinese criminal legal renewal takes the form of making amendments, rather than redrafting of all existing criminal statutes. This model, which is learned from the West,[4] is the traditional method of revision in criminal law.[5] In China, plans to revise the law, as policy windows, open quite frequently. Since it is believed that "China's growing legal system, is relied on both by the CCP for its governance and by Chinese citizens as a safeguard for their increasing individual rights," in the last decade, "the legislative program is so extensive and ambitious that it probably knows no equal in the legal history of the world."[6] For instance, criminal law has been revised several times since 1997. Changes made by the eighth amendment in 2011 and the ninth amendment in 2015 were also much more numerous than the previous amendments. These easily opened windows encourage the specialists from the ministries, intellectual community, law firms, members of the Two Sessions and NGOs to draft proposals for amending criminal law. And vice versa, increased proposals will lead to more chances of the opening of the "revision windows." Compared with former amendments that made piecemeal changes to the criminal law, the eighth amendment has started to make broader changes, including the general section and the special section of the law. It increases and decreases the boundary of criminal law at the same time. The present-day "legalization" program echoes a long-standing tradition in late developers (Confucian and otherwise), which accorded the state a key, proactive role in political, economic and social development.[7] Wider consultation, which brings in combined factors such as public expressions, bureaucratic considerations and intellectual arguments, prompts such changes. What is needed is the development of institutional methods, for broad discretion to be exercised in ways that are visible, subject to critical review and to methods of insuring that the discretion is not abused.[8] Unfortunately in China there remains a lack of restraining institutional arrangements and power on the expansion of criminal law.

As a matter of fact, not only China but some other countries also amend criminal law at a fast speed. For instance, the Criminal Code of Germany has been under frequent revisions since 1969. In 1998, a new criminal code was passed because the old one had been amended for too many times. After 1998, the revision is still going on.[9] It is common for criminal law to be revised to meet the needs of social development, to deal with emerging problems and to match with shifts of dominant theories.[10] The Chinese case is fused more with supervision of the party, public support for the government and enthusiasm of the establishment of rule of law. As in the West, in China, criminal law, as an aspect of the institutional structure of the state, "much will still depend on the disposition of the decision making body, on evidence adduced on crucial issues of security,"[11] and on the ways in which a state should deal with and relate to its citizens. "Revision must be justified on the basis of real need, upon a determination that there is something basically wrong with present criminal statutes and that revision will result in significant improvement in administration."[12] What China lacks is universal respect for the principles of criminal law, and a judicial review system that could ultimately sustain the legality of the law.

8.1.2 Two important streams for legal renewals

The problem stream and the political stream are the two main streams that facilitate renewals of Chinese criminal law. According to Kingdon, the agenda, in a general sense, is affected more by the policy stream and political stream, and the alternatives are affected more by the policy stream. Three components that set governmental agendas are problems, politics and visible participants like the president, members of Congress, the media and so on.[13] The combined impact of the problem stream and the politics stream applies to the Chinese political structure and social environment as well. The approval of policies, including proposals of the law, and other criminal policies, is based on the coexistence of public supports and political confirmation. Since there is a variety of social issues to be addressed, those with the most risk of generating social unrest will be prioritized. That is the reason why social protests will commonly get settled at an early stage, or be absorbed beforehand, which inspires potential protesters to make efforts at boosting attention. Considering there have always been solutions to emerging social problems as long as they have gained enough attention from the Chinese authorities, when they fit with the guidelines or plans set by the CCP, the problem, policy and political streams will be grouped together, through which changes of the law come about.

8.1.2.1 Public influences: Public mood and public participation

Public opinions do have influence on the procedures of the legislation and content of the law. In China, the problem stream consists of national incidents that reflect public mood, serving as external pressure for public administration. In the political stream, the CCP and bureaucracy claim to enhance public participation in the final decision-making. While both (public mood and public participation) are related to the public, their implications and influences are distinct from each other. Public mood affects the social affairs in an indirect and un-institutionalized way, while public participation may directly determine the process of how the proposals are negotiated and the result of such negotiations through legislative proceedings.

In criminal justice, penal populism discusses influences of public mood, and democratic involvement of law making considers institutional designs of public participation in criminal and penal policy making. Public mood and public participation sometimes are not distinguished from each other, but from a narrow perspective, public or national mood is a vague presence that the state notices; it is subject to manipulation from the government and the media. On the other hand, public participation relates to the seats of the parliament, components of the party and institutional arrangements of decision-making. As has been noted, in the US and the UK, penal populism is one crucial reason for the increasingly punitive penal system.[14] National mood has important policy consequences. "It has an impact on election results, on party fortunes, and on the receptivity of governmental decision makers to interest group lobbying."[15] To seek votes, the political parties compete to be tough on crimes to meet with public demands for retribution and deterrence, rather than to enhance justice or reduce crime rates. Thus, it seems that public false perception, such as fears of crime, of strangers and of the young, is the origin of the problematic criminal justice system, and ought to keep a certain distance away from criminal law. However, in the book *The Politics of Imprisonment*, Vanessa Barker suggests that the way Americans engage in the democratic process significantly shapes the way they punish offenders.[16] Barker compares the civic engagement in California, New York and Washington. She finds that the inclusive decision making in Washington facilitates social cohesion and trust, reducing state coercion against the disadvantaged group. On the contrary, in California, with few people participating in local affairs, officials tend to pursue a more retributive penal regime. Therefore, she contends that:

> High levels of civic engagement and social trust can constrain the intensity of penal sanctioning, enabling inclusionary but normalizing conditions of citizenship. Under-democratized polities with lower levels of social capital

> can amplify state coercion, creating restrictive and exclusionary conditions of citizenship, often in the name of public good.[17]

Compared with criminological scholars that solely examine the exemplary impacts of the punitive penal system of the US, this idea traces political reasons for the diversity of imprisonment among the US states. Citizenship has three elements—rights, responsibilities and a voice in the country's and the local community's decision-making processes. As Barker has suggested, wide participation in elections, through facilitating social cohesion and trust, may lead to mild treatment of crimes or misbehaviors in Washington, but at the same time, the inclusion may also be due to open discussions among people with different social status and backgrounds that contribute to more reasonable results. Rather than a certain group dominating the process, broader public participation enhances the legality and legitimacy of the law. It is also the symbol of contemporary democracy.

The distinction between public mood and public participation applies to the Chinese context as well. In brief, the problem stream mainly demonstrates public mood, and the political stream addresses the degree and impacts of public participation. Previous chapters examining public mood claim that the CCP pays great attention to the management of public mood to maintain social stability and enhance its own legitimacy. Overall, the public is generally satisfied with the security conditions of Chinese society due to intense policing from the state. This satisfaction is also mixed with media censorship that keeps sending positive messages of police work, and gratitude for the CCP's leadership that has brought huge social and economic progress to China in the past 60 years. But at the same time, the citizens are anxious of a variety of risks that keep decreasing their sense of security. Although many of them have been developing a sense as rights-holders, their rights are focused on rights to safety, fairness and equality rather than rights against state power. The Chinese conception of "rights" distinctly privileges socioeconomic security and collective livelihood, in contrast to the Anglo-American tradition that emphasizes political liberty and individual freedom. Hence most people still prefer a retributive and deterrent criminal justice mechanism to maintain "law and order" in the era of transition. In Western penal philosophy, it is commonly suggested that a reasoned and informed public debate is needed to combat penal populism (with the domination of the tabloid media and the contemporary citizen's supposed three-minute attention span).[18] Public outrage with criminal law, whether or not misguided, will eventually find its way to change. While in China, changes also depend on the long-term legal education of the citizens and reduced control of the media that has already enjoyed much more freedom.

As to public participation, in the legislative proceedings, the CCP and NPC have absorbed diversified groups to make proposals and pass laws. Though the votes are still taken within the CCP's authoritarian framework, on non-sensitive affairs the CCP's supervision has more political rather than practical implications. The process is also similar to Western democratic participation, which is a good sign for the development of a rational criminal justice system. What are problematic are the supreme power of the police and the collective misconceptions of the social control effects of criminal law. Wider participation will definitely have positive influences on the making of criminal law, such as rescuing the declining moral cohesion, fighting against the monopoly of bureaucratic power and restricting biased opinions, but since numerous representatives still favor the utilitarian belief in penal sanctions, there remains a lack of efficient restraining agents and institutions against state power expansion.

In all, public mood and public participation reflect the role of the public in the Chinese criminal lawmaking. The examination of public impacts on lawmaking suggests that the Chinese legislation has become more and more inclusive. The public influences criminal legislation in a diversified way, depending on the ways that the opinions are formed, represented and controlled. Impacts of the public on criminal law can be both positive and negative. On one hand, if decision makers are able to view public mood in a rational way, that is, being responsive and keeping away from an instrumental use of the law, the legitimacy of the law will be better maintained. On the other hand, much still depends on the efforts of the government to introduce more social forces against the dominant power in the legislative proceedings. It enhances the legitimacy of the law.

8.1.2.2 Political influences: Focusing on social stability and public security

As has been claimed, in the Chinese party-state, both the public and political streams demonstrate prevalent influences of the party's preference and supervision. It is the CCP that holds the deciding power of lawmaking. In Kingdon's model, the political stream consists of the public mood, shift of administration and judiciary competition. According to him, in the US the mood–election combination plays the most important part in consensus building. In China, primary changes of administration of the CCP are the elections of the National Congress of the CCP, which generate the new general secretary and central committee every five years, bringing in policy changes. From Jiang's "Three Represents" theory,[19] to Hu's "Harmonious Society,"[20] and subsequently to Xi's "Chinese Dream," the goals of the CCP have undergone transformations. The policies, with the shifting focuses of the presidents, shaped the development of Chinese criminal law. Two policies during President Hu Jintao's administrative period that had impacts on the eighth amendment of criminal law were "Harmonious Society" and "promotion of public security." "Harmonious Society," as the key feature of President Hu Jintao's signature ideology of the "Scientific Development Concept" developed in the mid-2000s, was focused on the fights against social injustice and inequality. First raised in 2004, it was composed of a number of strategies to improve the livelihood of the public and enhance equality. Compared with former policies that were mainly targeted at economic progress, "Harmonious Society" shifted the attention to political, social and cultural growth to avoid social conflicts.

However, it gradually developed into "stability at all costs," which consistently justified surveillance and repression against the public. The concept of the "promotion of public security" was originally noted in the 17th National Congress of the CCP in 2007. After that, "security provides a lens through which more and more problems are viewed, a hazardous phenomenon neatly captured by the tag securitization."[21] In contrast with the reports before, the 2007 report of the National Congress of the CCP especially elaborated techniques of "security protection" in the section on "enhancing social management and maintaining social stability" under the theme of "accelerating social development with the focus on improving people's livelihood," rather than the traditional sections of "national defense" or "international relations." The shift suggests that the CCP considers current public security as the main concern of the series of Chinese security problems. In 2014, President Xi Jinping emphasized the need to take a holistic view of national security and explore a "national security path with Chinese characteristics."[22] The conception of security is continuously expanded into a national strategy that covers almost every aspect of the society.

Accordingly, the eighth amendment of criminal law, with the largest number of changes, was promulgated with this background, emphasizing the pursuits of public security and social stability. Lucia Zedner describes security as "a slippery and contested term."[23] Actually both "stability" and "security" can mean different things under different circumstances. When the social problems are categorized as these "law-and-order" policy priorities, they will have more of a chance of being solved or repressed by the officials. Hence, why do agendas rise and become prominent in China? Demands from the bureaucrats matter; still, that the problems, which have been floating around in Chinese society, are coupled with special policy focuses of the authorities also determines the speed at which they are able to bring about legal changes. This is the underlying logic of why the Chinese criminal law is expanding with a preventive tone. However, while recognizing the necessity and desirability of administrative discretion, how to channel and control such discretion to ensure a proper degree of responsibility remains a tough issue. The identity of who makes the final decision remains unknown. The current realities of the legislative process are such that efforts at legislative revision and recodification are likely to produce only changes of degree, and the necessity for the responsible exercise of discretion of the authorities will continue to be of vital importance.

Fortunately, although power relations take time to change, since 2008, the Standing Committee of the NPC has been trying to make legislative plans every year.[24] The plans, set by the Legislative Affairs Commission of the Standing Committee under the supervision of the CCP, outline the workload of the Standing Committee in lawmaking for the next year.[25] Observations of those plans shed light on some positive characteristics of the Chinese legislation. For instance, to enhance "democratic participation" and "professionalism legislation," goals of legislative plans, has gradually been institutionalized in practice. On democratic participation, compared with before, Chinese lawmaking has absorbed more opinions from the public and those marginalized groups. The process reflects characteristics of "consultative authoritarianism": the CCP has displayed increased concerns for feedback from the public and intellectuals on non-sensitive affairs to enhance its legitimacy. Since justice and equality are often regarded as being of more relevance to criminal procedure than to the substantive criminal law, criminal law legislation involves more and more participation with fewer political and bureaucratic restraints, which is quite similar to Western democratic negotiations. On "professional legislation," the legislation itself is an elite-led intra-bureaucratic debate. The criminal justice system is a creature of its professionals, and their satisfaction appears to be critical.[26] There remains no post-revision evaluation of the eighth amendment of criminal law since its enactment. A detailed assessment needs to be worked out, including not only the deterrent effect of the revisions, but also the compatibility with the administrative penalty system, judicial costs, implementation status, trend of the international development of criminal law, etc. Besides, "it also seems reasonable to suggest the potential utility of informing the public about some of the more important issues, their temporary resolution in law change, and the resultant impact."[27]

Overall, this section examines legal renewal as a policy window for changes of Chinese criminal law. Public involvement and political guidelines play the most important roles in the making of Chinese criminal law. The legitimacy of the law is promoted through being responsive to public needs, expansion of participation and emphasizing public security issues. Besides the judicial review system, step-by-step legislative plans and post-assessments of the laws are needed to maintain the legitimacy of the law.

8.2 Reflections on Chinese criminal justice

8.2.1 Will an authoritarian regime necessarily lead to harsh penalties?

A comparative study of criminal policies of transitional states helps to gain more insights into the Chinese criminal justice system. The current Chinese criminal justice regime somewhat resembles that of Turkey, which is transforming into a democratic society with remaining authoritarian impacts.[28] The experiences of the two countries promote one essential question: will authoritarian regimes inevitably result in harsh penalties? Or will democratic process necessarily lead to lenient penalties? It is commonly believed that "democratization is generally suggestive of more liberal, humane and consensual criminal justice practices, especially when contrasted with the arbitrary terror and human right abuses characteristic of authoritarian regimes."[29] Research also shows that democratic institutions also matter to the penal practices of various states of the US, including California, Washington and New York.[30] But the answer is not that simple. First, democracy helps to enhance legitimacy but not the legality of the decision. For instance, in the US and UK, since the late 1970s, given the rise of neoliberalism and decline of the welfare state ideal, the criminal justice systems have witnessed a punitive turn, leaving criminological scholars quite pessimistic about the future. The US has a higher crime rate than many other countries all over the world. In the UK, "the state (modern Britain), or rather the political administration of the day, becomes increasingly powerful, centralized and remote."[31] Research on Turkey's experiences also suggests that "the imposition upon democratizing countries of Western models of criminal justice policy, without contextual appreciation, many have unforeseen repressive outcomes."[32] It is the reactive rather than preventive criminal Turkish criminal justice itself that retains the humane results for the offenders. Thus, democracy does not have a direct relationship with the severity of criminal penalties. The policy transitions rely on the changes of social contexts and discretion of the decision makers at that specific time period. Democracy also does not guarantee lenient sanctions. The institutions have to be under constitutional check like the judicial review system for legality. But for authoritarian countries that would like to survive and transform in the contemporary era, becoming democratic is also important since it will not only fight against power abuse but also contribute to more reasoned decisions.

Second, it is hard to compare the harshness of criminal penalties considering the variations of the systems. Comparisons of the boundary of criminal law or gravity of criminal sanctions have to be limited to particular circumstances with fully consideration of social and cultural origins. For example, China does not have preventive orders. In addition, China, as a developing country, has broad spaces for new laws, making it hard to compare the progress of legalization between the East and the West. Even within the Western countries themselves, apart from the main trend, the crime control landscape also demonstrates mixed and contradictory pictures with differentiated responses to crime.

Third, under some circumstances the authoritarian regime does have a positive correlation with the expansion or harshness of criminal justice. The pragmatic state seeks to use criminal law as a policy response. In China, the statist orientation was apparent throughout the dynastic era and only intensified when the Leninist conception of a vanguard party was grafted onto an already authoritarian political tradition.[33] The authoritarian regime itself lacks a systematic check and restraint of the dominant power. Under the governance of the CCP it is quite possible that police force and criminal law will continue to be expanded. However, at the same time, it has to be noted that the democratic transition of China is more difficult, since the CCP currently is seeking a new authoritarian model distinct from the Western liberal democratic countries, characterized as social and economic prosperity under the strict political control of the CCP. Though the government still maintains control over the scope and content of the discussion, as has been illustrated, public participation has been boosted in Chinese policy and lawmaking. Furthermore, the Standing Committee of the NPC consults with intellectuals and government officials in the legislative process. "Intellectuals deliberated both behind closed doors, by attending government-sponsored meetings, and in the public sphere, at academic conferences or during debates organized by the media."[34] They constitute counter-forces to the authoritarian regime, though it is the CCP that ultimately determines when and how to intervene in the dynamic.

Hence the regime (Party-state) is strong, increasingly self-confident, and without organized opposition in the foreseeable future, but we don't have to be too pessimistic about it. On the one hand, wide participation in actual policy making has added increased democratic elements to the authoritarian country. Compared with before when the CCP held monopolized power, the decisions will become more rational and humane. On the other hand, attention needs to be paid to other aspects as well, such as systematic protection of the citizens' constitutional rights, respect for the principles of criminal law, etc.

8.2.2 Is China an exclusive or inclusive society?

Combinations of political manipulations and public involvement in Chinese criminal justice inspire a follow-up question: with the impacts of current policing and sentencing practices, is the society exclusive or inclusive? In the US, a variety of researchers have insisted that the US is increasingly becoming an exclusive society due to the punitive turn of criminal justice. Some even contend that the US fight against crime through prisons and jails is a new Jim Crow, or a coercive reallocation of labor.[35] Then how about China? Whether China is an exclusive or inclusive society depends on how to define "exclusive" and "inclusive." An exclusive society is much concerned with personal protection and the assessment and avoidance of risk.[36] It favors surveillance and imprisonment to facilitate public fear of punishments. On the contrary, the inclusive society emphasizes respect for human dignity, personal identity, a sense of public duty and social responsibility.[37] Instead of penalties and blame, it focuses on the obligations of the community to treat or support the underclass. Thus, inclusive and exclusive are distinct from each other in the way the society treats offenders and potential offenders, and the beliefs the citizens hold about disobedience.

In China, the expanding criminal law, growing police force and rising number of prisoners all suggest an exclusive society with increased repressive and segregation. The governance of the CCP is the top reason for the police state, but it is not the only reason for the exclusion. Rapid urbanization transforms China into a strangers' society.[38] The large territory, huge population, declining social trust and intense social polarization raise difficulties of social management. Hence authorities resort to coercion which costs less time and effort. This pragmatic solution is similar to UK policing, which has gone through a managerialism turn in the past decades, based on macro concerns of the system's effectiveness rather than the traditional moralized justice. The emergence of managerialism, deemed as the outcome of neoliberal policies in the West, also partly resulted from failures of rehabilitation. Rather than tracing the deep problems of individualized disordered behaviors, the state was inclined to pursue the operational efficiency of policing. It is problematic that concerns of social utility may override principles of responsibility.

Therefore, either for the repression of the society, or real policing requirements for social order, China is an exclusive state. Given the "continuing commitment to the primacy of state power,"[39] there are few chances of fundamental reorientation. In criminological literature, scholars who are concerned about Western social exclusion tend to suggest resorting to community-based correction to reduce the segregation. What they expect is a shift from criminalization of social policy to the socialization of criminal justice and crime-prevention policies. For instance, Gordon Hughes prefers an inclusive, civic and safe cities model in contrast to the models of fortress, privatized cities, and hierarchical, paternalistic cities.[40] While in China, though both the scope and degree of public participation has been intensified, Chinese society lacks spaces for the communities to self-censor. The CCP is unwilling to distribute power among the social groups. One obvious difference between the politicized Maoist period and the economically focused post-Mao leadership has been the current state's reluctance to endorse, much less encourage, popular protests.[41] Since it fears social protests, social empowerment remains slow. The state power remains strong and solid even though it has introduced "technologies of the self" with "scientific social engineering and socialist planning" combined with neoliberal strategies of "governing from a distance," which are much gentler.[42]

Therefore, surveillance from the government, distrust between members of the public and over-reliance on criminal penalties to punish and deter make the society even more exclusive. In the legislation, consultation may generate popular expectations for inclusion and responsiveness,[43] but for the society as a whole, the change will take a long time. We really should reconsider what is a good society, and how it will be achieved.

8.3 Conclusion

This book aims to explore the social, legal and political rationales of the preventive shift of Chinese criminal law. Using the eighth amendment of the Chinese criminal law as case studies, it examines the problem, policy and political streams of lawmaking. It argues that Chinese legislation has become more responsive and inclusive, which leads to the rapid growth of the legal system. Besides attention paid to public mood, the party-state has been promoting participation from the public. However, efficient debates are needed to maintain the proper boundary of criminal law, so that the legislation will not become a combined result of public mood and bureaucratic dominance. Otherwise, criminal lawmaking will turn into a too "bold" project in China.

The book relates changes of Chinese criminal law to the social and political context of China. In contrast to previous studies that examine these two topics separately, the book is the most up to date study to combine them. It is a study of not only the law but also Chinese society. Besides, the book also includes the experiences of Western countries in the realm of criminal justice as references. The characteristics of Chinese lawmaking are not only examined through its own practices but also those of the other countries. In this way, the book also makes contributions to international comparative studies of the law.

The research basically relies on second-hand documents as references, including journal articles, official reports, newspapers, websites, etc. The lack of first-hand data is the biggest limitation of the book. In China, it is hard to obtain first-hand information since empirical research is difficult to carry out. While doing interviews, besides the difficulties of getting access to the participants, the interviewees commonly have various concerns that prevent them from telling the truth.

8.4 Changes after the eighth amendment

After the enactment of the eighth amendment in 2011, China promulgated the ninth and the tenth amendments to the Chinese Criminal Law in 2015 and 2017. The 11th amendment has just been enacted at the end of 2020.[44] Until now, China has witnessed frequent revisions of criminal law with increased provisions. Compared with other basic laws of China, criminal law is revised more regularly. Compared with the previous seven amendments, that were mostly focused on specific offences, revisions after that cover not only the general part, including doctrines that apply to all crimes, but also the special part that classifies and defines particular elements of offences. In these amendments, except the 10th amendment which has one single provision that introduces the crime of insulting national songs and anthem, as a response to the enactment of National Anthem Law in 2017 to fill in the gap of criminal law, the preventive shift is evident in the 9th amendment and the 11th one.

In the ninth amendment, this shift can be identified in new terrorism-related offences. The amendment created five new offences in clauses under Article 120 of the Chinese Criminal Law, including preparation of acts of terrorism, instigation of acts of terrorism, obstruction of justice, the forcible use of terrorist or extremist clothing and logos and illegal possession of materials that advocate terrorism and extremism.[45] In these new offences, preparatory offences and inciting terrorist acts are substantive offenses defined as inchoate crime. As substantive offences, such acts have a higher tendency of being punished. Penalties for the offense are increased. The general inchoate liability will also apply to these offences, widening the preventive circle.

Besides offences of preparation of terrorism and solicitation, another prominent proactive change is the introduction of "pre-inchoate" offences in the ninth amendment, that is, offences of advocating terrorism and possessing materials that advocate terrorism. At present, these two offences are the most common terrorism-related offences in China. Although other countries have similar offences, Chinese practices are much more preventive. In the crime of advocating terrorism, the defendants will be convicted if they: (1) advocate terrorism through speeches or messages; or (2) make or distribute books, audio or other materials that are directly or indirectly related with terrorist activities. In China, a common conviction is forwarding images or videos into WeChat groups with the *mens rea* of recklessness of generating risks to the public. Some offenders simply shared one video with others; while some were even sentenced due to posting one joke in a WeChat group such as “let’s join jihad.”[46] The threats that such behaviors pose are minor, indirect and uncertain.

In the latter crime of possession, similar to the offence of advocating terrorism, people are convicted for downloading terrorism-related images or videos from foreign websites onto public or private computers. In existing cases, almost all the materials the defendants possess are digital images and videos, rather than particular materials, such as certain weapons, or instructions on how to make those arms. The harm is neither concrete nor huge. Constituting the offence also does not require the specific intent of carrying out terrorism or inducing others to join terrorist groups. Most defendants are not extremists, terrorists nor persons with the intent of participating in terrorism in the future. They download images or videos due to curiosity or personal entertainment. Criminal law is the most severe penalty in China. Considering acts of possessing other cyber materials, such as obscene images and videos, are not offences in China, possession crimes related to terrorism are exceptional. These “pre-inchoate” offences are preventive measures for the pursuit of public security.

Therefore, to fight terrorism, the Chinese criminal law also shows a clear preemptive trend. The post-crime orientation of criminal justice is increasingly overshadowed by the pre-crime logic of security. It is hard to assess how many risks those cyber acts will actually generate. The criteria of assessing the degree of risk are subjective, ambiguous and strict. What is evident is that internet censorship is intensified at the same time as the development of those preventive anti-terrorism methods.

Except for the 9th amendment, the 11th amendment brings about 6 major areas of updates with some 30 revised or newly added provisions. The doctrine of crime prevention has become increasingly central to Chinese criminal law. It introduces new endangerment crimes against public security, expands the boundary of the crime of manufacturing and selling fake or poor-quality medications, respecifies the elements of the crime of impairing infectious disease prevention and treatment, etc.[47] Within these changes, the preventive technique of lawmaking, as shown in the eighth amendment in 2011, is evident. For instance, similar to drunk driving, the amendment proposes to criminalize acts of interfering with bus drivers by snatching the steering wheel, which will endanger public safety. This came after the whole country was shocked by a tragic incident in which a bus plunged over 160 ft off a bridge into the Yangtze River during a fight between the passenger and the bus driver in the city of Chongqing in October 2018. This incident ended up with 13 deaths and 2 missing.[48] National awareness, government responses and academic discussions on the incident finally gave rise to revisions of criminal law. The same happened with acts of throwing objects out of high-rise buildings, another focus of the 11th amendment.

Therefore, Chinese lawmakers commonly argue that the laws repond to public demand. The preventive move enhances the trust between the government and the public through a top-down approach in both procedural and substantial aspects. Especially with the establishment of the national security state, the new institutional and regulatory mechanism will give rise to the increased expansion of criminal law for protection and governance. However, given that authoritarianism is more likely to lead to the expansion of the penal system, it is hoped that the party-state will give equal consideration to restraining the rapid development of criminal law to avoid sliding into a thoroughly surveillance society.

Notes

1 John W. Kingdon, *Agendas, Alternatives and Public Policies, Update Edition, with an Epilogue on Health Care*, 2nd ed. (New York: Pearson, 2010) 165.
2 John W. Kingdon, *Agendas, Alternatives and Public Policies, Update Edition, with an Epilogue on Health Care*, 2nd ed. (New York: Pearson, 2010) 186.
3 John W. Kingdon, *Agendas, Alternatives and Public Policies, Update Edition, with an Epilogue on Health Care*, 2nd ed. (New York: Pearson, 2010) 187.
4 Weiwei Zhang, *The China Wave: Rise of a Civilizational State* (Hackensack: World Scientific, 2012) 108.
5 Frank J. Remington, "Criminal Law Revision Codification vs. Piecemeal Amendment" (1953) 33 *Nebraska Law Review* 402. This approach will avoid over-disturbance to other criminal statutes.
6 Jan Michiel Otto et al., *Law-Making in People's Republic of China* (The Hague: Kluwer Law International, 2000), Introduction.
7 Neil Diamant, Stanley Lubman & Kevin O'Brien, *Engaging the Law in China: State, Society, and Possibilities for Justice* (Stanford, CA: Stanford University Press, 2005) 6.
8 Frank J. Remington & Victor G. Rosenblum, "The Criminal Law and the Legislative Process" (1960) 1960 *Current Problems in Criminal Law* 497.
9 Xu Zhang, "Social Development and Revisions of Criminal Law: Based on German Experience" (2003) 2 *Law and Social Development* 29–30.
10 The criminal code of Canada has also been revised numerous times. Besides these general changes, the law against terrorism emerges as a focus of numerous countries all over the world. Anti-terrorism legislation is "preemptive" in that it seeks to punish or apply coercive sanctions on the basis of what is anticipated might happen in the future. In Australia, since 2001 there have been more than 35 pieces of federal anti-terrorism legislation passed. The UK, US and Canada also passed a series of anti-terrorism laws in the 2000s. See Jude McCulloch, "Contemporary Comments: Australia's Anti-Terrorism Legislation and the Jack Thomas Case" (2006) 18 *Current Issues in Criminal Justice* 358. The quantity and pace of legislative change in this area have reduced the opportunity for informed public debate. Andrew Ashworth & Lucia Zedner, "Counterterrorism Laws and Security Measures", in Andrew Ashworth & Lucia Zedner, eds, *Preventive Justice* (Oxford: Oxford University Press, 2014) 171–195.
11 Ben Goold & Liora Lazarus, eds, *Security and Human Rights* (Oxford: Hart Publishing, 2007) 225.
12 Frank J. Remington, "Criminal Law Revision Codification vs. Piecemeal Amendment" (1953) 33 *Nebraska Law Review* 397.
13 See John W. Kingdon, *Agendas, Alternatives and Public Policies, Update Edition, with an Epilogue on Health Care*, 2nd ed. (New York: Pearson, 2010).
14 John Pratt, *Penal Populism* (New York: Routledge, 2007).

15 John W. Kingdon, *Agendas, Alternatives and Public Policies, Update Edition, with an Epilogue on Health Care*, 2nd ed. (New York: Pearson, 2010) 149.
16 See Vanessa Barker, *The Politics of Imprisonment: How the Democratic Process Shapes the Way America Punishes Offenders* (Oxford: Oxford University Press, 2009).
17 Vanessa Barker, *The Politics of Imprisonment: How the Democratic Process Shapes the Way America Punishes Offenders* (Oxford: Oxford University Press, 2009) 172.
18 Michael Cavadino & James Dignan, *Penal Systems: A Comparative Approach* (London: Sage Publications, 2006) 342.
19 "Three Represents" is a guiding socio-political theory credited to Jiang Zemin, which was ratified by the Communist Party of China at the Sixteenth Party Congress in 2002. Jiang Zemin first introduced his theory on February 25, 2000. The official statement of the ideology stipulates that the Communist Party of China should be representative of advanced social productive forces, advanced culture and the interests of the overwhelming majority.
20 "Harmonious Society" is a key feature of Hu Jintao's signature ideology of the Scientific Development Concept developed in the mid-2000s, being re-introduced by the Hu–Wen administration during the 2005 National People's Congress. The philosophy is recognized as a response to the increasing social injustice and inequality emerging in Chinese society as a result of unchecked economic growth, which have led to social conflict.
21 Lucia Zedner, *Security (Key Ideas in Criminology)* (London: Routledge, 2009) 4.
22 David M. Lampton, "Xi Jinping and the National Security Commission: Policy Coordination and Political Power" (2015) 24 *Journal of Contemporary China* 769.
23 Lucia Zedner, *Security (Key Ideas in Criminology)* (London: Routledge, 2009) 10.
24 Xiaoyang Qiao, "To Enhance the Legislative Project" *The People's Congress of China* (25 December 2014).
25 Songshan Liu, "Reflections on the Chinese Legislative Plan" (2014) 12 *Political Science and Law* 86–96. The commission did not make the plans in 2011 and 2012, and the legality and necessity of making the plans are repeatedly criticized.
26 David Twain & Donald Rebovich, "An Evaluation of the Impact of Criminal Law Revision" (1984) 12 (4) *Journal of Criminal Justice* 404.
27 David Twain & Donald Rebovich, "An Evaluation of the Impact of Criminal Law Revision" (1984) 12 (4) *Journal of Criminal Justice* 404.
28 Penny Green, "Criminal Justice and Democratizations in Turkey: The Paradox of Transition", in Penny Green & Andrew Rutherford, eds, *Criminal Policy in Transition* (Oxford: Hart Publishing, 2000) 195.
29 Penny Green, "Criminal Justice and Democratizations in Turkey: The Paradox of Transition", in Penny Green & Andrew Rutherford, eds, *Criminal Policy in Transition* (Oxford: Hart Publishing, 2000) 196.
30 Vanessa Barker, *The Politics of Imprisonment: How the Democratic Process Shapes the Way America Punishes Offenders* (Oxford: Oxford University Press, 2009).
31 Rene van Swaaningen, "Policy and Practice in Modern Britain: Influences, Outcomes and Civil Society", in Penny Green & Andrew Rutherford, eds, *Criminal Policy in Transition* (Oxford: Hart Publishing, 2000) 82.
32 Penny Green & Andrew Rutherford, eds, *Criminal Policy in Transition* (Oxford: Hart Publishing, 2000) 12.
33 Neil Diamant, Stanley Lubman & Kevin O'Brien, *Engaging the Law in China: State, Society, and Possibilities for Justice* (Stanford, CA: Stanford University Press, 2005) 6.
34 Expert intellectuals deliberated on the course of China's healthcare reform in conferences sponsored by state ministries. See Yoel Kornreich, Ilan Vertinsky & Pitman Potter, "Consultation and Deliberation in China: The Making of China's Health-Care Reform" (2012) 68 *The China Journal* 201.

35 Katherine Beckett & Bruce Western, "Crime Control, American Style: From Social Welfare to Social Control", in Penny Green & Andrew Rutherford, eds, *Criminal Policy in Transition* (Oxford: Hart Publishing, 2000) 31.
36 Rene van Swaaningen, "Policy and Practice in Modern Britain: Influences, Outcomes and Civil Society", in Penny Green & Andrew Rutherford, eds, *Criminal Policy in Transition* (Oxford: Hart Publishing, 2000) 80.
37 Rene van Swaaningen, "Policy and Practice in Modern Britain: Influences, Outcomes and Civil Society", in Penny Green & Andrew Rutherford, eds, *Criminal Policy in Transition* (Oxford: Hart Publishing, 2000) 80.
38 Anxieties due to risks, such as fear of minor crimes of theft, robbery and fraud, deteriorate social cohesion.
39 Pitman Potter, "The Chinese Legal System: Continuing Commitment to the Primacy of State Power" (1999) 159 *The China Quarterly* 673.
40 Gordon Hughes, *Understanding Crime Prevention: Social Control, Risk and Late Modernity* (Berkshire: Open University Press, 1998) 133–152.
41 Ching Kwan Lee, "State & Social Protest" (2014) 143 (2) *Daedalus* 128.
42 Guobin Yang, "Internet Activism & the Party-State in China" (2014) 143 (2) *Daedalus* 110.
43 See Yoel Kornreich, Ilan Vertinsky & Pitman Potter, "Consultation and Deliberation in China: The Making of China's Health-Care Reform" (2012) 68 *The China Journal* 176.
44 Wang Bixue, "Criminal Law to Be Revised on Six Aspects: Throwing Objects from High-Rise Buildings Maybe Criminalized", *People's Daily* (29 June, 2020) A02.
45 *Criminal Law*, RS 2015, s120.
46 A number of cases of advocating terrorism have been decided in the capital city, Beijing.
47 An Explanation on the 11th Draft Amendment to the PRC's Criminal Law by the Legislative Affairs Commission of the Standing Committee of the National People's Congress, online: pkulaw.cn <https://www.pkulaw.com/protocol/51e78abb3a002802aa4c64e7a954f2edbdfb.html>.
48 "Police: Fight between Driver, Passenger Causes Chongqing Bus Tragedy", online: CGTN <https://news.cgtn.com/news/3d3d514f31676a4d30457a6333566d54/share_p.html>.

Bibliography

Legislation

Criminal Law, RS 2011, c1, s3-5.
Criminal Law, RS 2011, c2, s133 (2).
Criminal Law, RS 2011, c3, s141.
Criminal Law, RS 2011, c6, s338.
Criminal Procedure Law, RS 2012, c7, s73.
Criminal Procedure Law, RS 2012, c7, s83.
Criminal Procedure Law, RS 2012, c9, s148.
The Road Traffic Safety Law, RS 2011, c9, s91.
Public Security Administration Punishments Law, c3.

Secondary Material

Books

Anyangwe, Carlson, *Criminal Law in Cameroon: Specific Offences* (Bamenda: CMR: Langaa RPCIG, 2011).

Ashworth, Andrew, *Principles of Criminal Law* (Oxford: Oxford University Press, 2009) 456.

Ashworth, Andrew & Lucia Zedner, *Preventive Justice* (Oxford: Oxford University Press, 2014).

Auerswald, David P. & Colton C. Campbell, eds, *Congress and the Politics of National Security* (Cambridge: Cambridge University Press, 2011) 86.

Barker, Vanessa, *The Politics of Imprisonment: How the Democratic Process Shapes the Way America Punishes Offenders* (Oxford: Oxford University Press, 2009).

Barton, Adrian & Nick Johns, *The Policy-Making Process in the Criminal Justice System* (London, UK: Routledge, 2013) 1.

Bell, Emma, *Criminal Justice and Neoliberalism* (Basingstoke: Palgrave Macmillan, 2011).

Berg, Bruce L., *Qualitative Research Methods for the Social Sciences* (New York: Pearson, 2008) 325.

Callaghan, Karen & Frauke Schnell, *Framing American Politics* (Pittsburgh, PA: University of Pittsburgh Press, 2005).

Cavadino, Michael & James Dignan, *Penal Systems: A Comparative Approach* (London: Sage Publications, 2006) 339.

Chu, Huaizhi, *Outline of Criminal Sciences Integration* (Beijing: Peking University Press, 2007).

Clarke, Donald C., ed, *China's Legal System: New Developments, New Challenges* (Cambridge: Cambridge University Press, 2008) 12.

Davis, Deborah S., ed, *The Consumer Revolution in Urban China* (Berkeley and Los Angeles, CA: University of California Press, 2000).

Duff, Antony et al., *The Boundaries of the Criminal Law* (Oxford: Oxford University Press, 2010).

Duff, Antony & Stuart Green, *Philosophical Foundations of Criminal Law* (Oxford: Oxford University Press, 2013).

Ericson, Richard V. & Aaron Doyle, eds, *Risk and Morality* (Toronto, ON: University of Toronto Press, 2003).

Ericson, Richard V. & Kevin D. Haggerty, *Policing the Risk Society* (Toronto, ON: University of Toronto Press, Scholarly Publishing Division, 1997) 52.

Eriksson, Johan & Erik Noreen, *Setting the Agenda of Threats: An Explanatory Model* (Uppsala, Sweden: Dept. of Peace and Conflict Research, Uppsala University Dept., 2002).

Foucault, Michel, *Discipline and Punishment* (New York: Vintage Books, 1995).

Garland, David, *Punishment and Modern Society: A Study in Social Theory* (Chicago, IL: The University of Chicago Press, 1993).

———. *The Culture of Control* (Chicago, IL: University of Chicago Press, 2001).

Goold, Ben & Liora Lazarus, eds, *Security and Human Rights* (Oxford: Hart Publishing, 2007).

Green, Penny & Andrew Rutherford, eds, *Criminal Policy in Transition* (Oxford: Hart Publishing, 2000) 12.

Hall, Daniel E., *Criminal Law and Procedure*, 7th ed. (New York: Delmar Cengage Learning, 2014) 666.

Harrison, Karen, *Dangerousness, Risk and the Governance of Serious Sexual and Violent Offenders* (London: Routledge, 2011).

Hirschel, David, William Wakefield & Scott Sasse, *Criminal Justice in England and the United States* (Sudbury, MA: Jones & Bartlett Learning, 2007).

Hughes, Gordon, *Understanding Crime Prevention* (Buckingham: Open University Press, 1998).

Husak, Douglas, *Overcriminalization* (Oxford: Oxford University Press, 2008).

Johnston, Les & Clifford Shearing, *Governing Security: Explorations in Policing and Justice* (London, UK: Routledge, 2003).

Jones, Trevor & Tim Newburn, *Policy Transfer and Criminal Justice: Exploring US Influence over British Crime Control Policy* (Berkshire: Open University Press, 2007).

Liu, Jianhong, Lening Zhang & Steven F. Messnereds, eds, *Crime and Social Control in a Changing China* (Westport, CT: Greenwood Press, 2001) 1–10.

Lubman, B. Stanley, *Bird in a Cage: Legal Reform in Post-Mao China* (Stanford, CA: Stanford University Press, 2002).

Lupton, Deborah, *Risk Key Ideas* (London, UK: Routledge, 1999) 30.

Matthews, Roger & Jock Young, eds, *New Politics of Crime and Punishment* (Devon, UK: Willan Publishing, 2011).

McConville, Michael et al., *Criminal Justice in China: An Empirical Enquiry* (Cheltenham: Edward Elgar, 2011).

O'Malley, P., *Crime and the Risk Society* (Aldershot: Ashgate, 1998).

———. *Crime and Risk* (Los Angeles, CA: Sage Publications, 2010).

Peerenboom, Randall, *China's Long March toward Rule of Law* (Cambridge: Cambridge University Press, 2002) 130.

Potter, Pitman, *China's Legal System* (Cambridge: Polity Press, 2013).

Pratt, John, *Penal Populism* (New York: Routledge, 2007).

Sabatier, A. Paul & Weible Christopher M., eds, *Theories of the Policy Process*, 3rd ed. (Boulder, CO: Westview Press, 2014) 30.

Sheppard, Michael, *Appraising and Using Social Research in the Human Services: An Introduction for Social Work and Health Professionals* (London: Jessica Kingsley Publishers, 2004) 28.

Shute, Stephen & A. P. Simester, *Criminal Law Theory: Doctrines of the General Part* (Oxford: Oxford University Press, 2002) 83.

Simon, Jonathan, *Governing Through Crime: How the War on Crime Transformed American Democracy and Created a Climate of Fear* (New York: Oxford University Press, 2007).

Smith, Philip, *Punishment and Culture* (Chicago, IL: The University of Chicago Press, 2008).

Sullivan, G. R. & Ian Dennis, eds, *Seeking Security: Pre-Empting the Commission of Criminal Harms* (Oxford: Hart Publishing, 2012).

Tang, Wenfang, *Public Opinion and Political Change in China* (Stanford, CA: Stanford University Press, 2005).

Trevaskes, Susan, *Policing Serious Crime in China: From 'Strike hard' to 'Kill fewer'* (Oxon: Routledge, 2010).

Whitman, James Q., *Harsh Justice: Criminal Punishment and the Widening Divide between America and Europe* (Oxford: Oxford University Press, 2003).

Woodman, Gordon & Diethelm Klippel, eds, *Risk and the Law* (New York: Routledge-Cavendish, 2008) 80.

Wong Kam, C., "Legalism and Constitutionalism in the People's Republic of China" (2006) 1 (2) *International Journal of Criminal Justice Sciences* 1–26.

Wong Kam, C., *Chinese Policing: History and Reform (New Perspectives in Criminology and Criminal Justice)* (New York: Peter Lang Publishing, 2009).

Yin, Robert K., *Case Study Research: Design and Methods* (Los Angeles, CA: Sage Publications, 2013) 20.

Zedner, Lucia, *Security* (London, UK: Routledge, 2009).

Articles

Alford, Willam P. & Yuanyuan Shen, "Limits of the Law in Addressing China's Environmental Dilemma" (1997) 16 *Stan Environmental Law Journal* 127.

Ashworth, Andrew & Lucia Zedner, "Defending the Criminal Law: Reflections on the Changing Character of Crime, Procedure, and Sanctions" (2008) 2 *Criminal Law and Philosophy* 21–51.

Ashworth, Andrew & Lucia Zedner, "Preventive Orders: A Problem of Under-Criminalization?", in R. A. Duff, ed, *The Boundaries of the Criminal Law* (Oxford: Oxford University Press, 2010) 62.

Ashworth, Andrew & Lucia Zedner, "Just Prevention: Prevention Rationales and the Limits of the Criminal Law", in R. A. Duff & S. Green, eds, *Philosophical Foundations of Criminal Law* (Oxford: Oxford University Press, 2011) 302.

———. "Prevention and Criminalization: Justifications and Limits" (2012) 15 *New Criminal Law Review* 546.

Asp, Petter, "Preventionism and Criminalization of Nonconsummate Offences", in Andrew Ashworth et al., eds, *Prevention and the Limits of the Criminal Law* (Oxford: Oxford University Press, 2013) 23–46.

Baker, Stewart A. & John Kavanagh, eds, *Patriot Debates: Experts Debate the USA Patriot Act* (Chicago, IL: American Bar Association, 2005).

Bakken, Borge, "China, a Punitive Society?" (2011) 6 *Asian Criminology* 42.

———. "Punishment in China", in Liqun Cao, Ivan Y. Sun & Bill Hebenton, eds, *The Routledge Handbook of Chinese Criminology* (New York: Routledge, 2013) 45.

Balla, Steven J., "Health System Reform and Political Participation on the Chinese Internet" (2014) 7 *China Information* 219.

Baxter, P & Susan Jack, "Qualitative Case Study Methodology: Study Design and Implementation for Novice Researchers" (2008) 13 (4) *The Qualitative Report* 544.

Beckett, Katherine & Bruce Western, "Crime Control, American Style: From Social Welfare to Social Control", in Penny Green & Andrew Rutherford, eds, *Criminal Policy in Transition* (Oxford: Hart Publishing, 2000) 31.

Beland, Daniel, "Gender, Ideational Analysis and Social Policy" (2009) 16 (4) *Social Politics* 558–581.

Belkin, Ira, "China's Criminal Justice System" (2000) 6 (2) *Washington Journal of Modern China* 61.

Bennett, Andrew, "Process Tracing and Causal Inference", in Henry Brady & David Collier, eds, *Rethinking Social Inquiry: Diverse Tools, Shared Standards*, 2nd ed. (Plymouth: Rowman and Littlefield, 2010) 1.

Boscarino, Jessica E., "Surfing for Problems: Advocacy Group Strategy in US Forestry Policy" (2009) 37 (3) *Policy Studies Journal* 415–434.

Bourdieu, Pierre, "The Force of Law: Toward a Sociology of the Juridical Field" (1987) 38 *Hastings Law Journal* 805–853.

Bourgon, Jerome, "Chinese Executions: Visualizing Their Differences with European Supplies" (2003) 2 (1) *European Journal of East Asian Studies* 153–184.

Bracey, Dorothy H., "Policing the People's Republic", in Ronald J. Troyer, John P. Clark & Dean G. Rojek, eds, *Social Control in the People's Republic of China* (New York: Praeger, 1989) 133.

Brodsgaard, Kjeld Erik & Zheng Yongnian, "Whither the Chinese Communist Party", in Kjeld Erik Brodsgaard & Zheng Yongnian, eds, *The Chinese Communist Party in Reform* (Oxon: Routledge, 2006) 4.

Cannon, Kathleen A., "Water as a Source of Conflict and Instability in China" (2006) 30 (2) *Strategic Analysis* 317–318.

Chen, Xiaoming, "Community and Policing Strategies: A Chinese Approach to Crime Control" (2002) 12 *Policing and Society* 10.

Chen, Xingliang, "Criminal Law in the Risk Society and Risk of Criminal Law" (2011) 4 *Studies in Law and Business* 11.

———. "Critical Doctrinal Analysis of Risk Society Theory" (2014) 1 *Peking University Law Review* 103–127.

Cheng, Yan, "The Target of Criminal Law in the Risk Society" (2012) 29 *Criminal Law Review* 283–300.

Cobb, Roger, Jennie-Keith Ross & Marc Howard Ross, "Agenda Building as a Comparative Political Process" (1976) 70 *The American Political Science Review* 127.

Cochran, Patricia, *Common Sense and Legal Judgement: Community Knowledge, Political Power and Rhetorical Practice* (Montreal; Kingston; London; Chicago: McGill-Queen's University Press; 2, 2017) 53.

Cohen, D. Michael, James G. March & Johan P. Olsen, "A Garbage Can Model of Organizational Choice" (1972) 17 (1) *Administrative Science Quarterly* 1–15.

Collier, D. Michael, "Understanding Process Tracing" (2011) 44 (4) *Political Science and Politics* 824.

Dai, Liping, "Tackling Diffuse Water Pollution from Agriculture in China: Drawing Inspiration from the European Union" (2014) 10 (2) *Utrecht Law Review* 139.

Deng, Zhenglai, "Civil Society and Reconstruction of the State System of Knowledge Administration" (2000) 3 *Open Times* 15.

Diamant Neil, J., Stanely B. Lubman & Kevin J. O'Brien, eds, "Law and Society in the People's Republic of China", in Neil J. Diamant et al., *Engaging the Law in China: State, Society and Possibilities for Justice* (Stanford, CA: Stanford University Press, 2005) 16–17.

Dicks, Anthony, "The Chinese Legal System: Reforms in the Balance" (1989) 119 *The China Quarterly* 571.

Du, Jinfeng, "Police-Public Relations--A Chinese View" (1997) 30 (1) *Australian and New Zealand Journal of Criminology* 87. About the strong enforcement of approach against drunk driving, see Ying Li et al., "The Drink Driving Situation in China" (2012) 13 (2) *Traffic Injury Prevention* 105.

Du, Wenmin et al., "Drug Safety Surveillance in China and Other Countries: A Review and Comparison" (2008) 11 *Value in Health* (Supplement 1) 131.

Duckett, Jane & Ana Inés Langer, "Populism versus Neoliberalism: Diversity and Ideology in the Chinese Media's Narratives of Health Care Reform" (2013) 6 *Modern China* 653–680.

Duff, Antony & David Garland, "Introduction: Thinking about Punishment" in R. A. Duff and David Garland, eds, *A Reader on Punishment* (Oxford: Oxford University Press, 1995) 43.

Dutton, Michael, "Toward a Government of the Contract: Policing in the Era of Reform", in Borge Bakken, ed, *Crime, Punishment and Policing in China* (New York: Rowman and Littlefield, 2005) 190.

Garland, David, "'Governmentality' and Problem of Crime: Foucault, Criminology and Sociology" (1997) 1 (2) *Theoretical Criminology* 173–208.

Green, Penny, "Criminal Justice and Democratizations in Turkey: The Paradox of Transition", in Penny Green & Andrew Rutherford, eds, *Criminal Policy in Transition* (Oxford: Hart Publishing, 2000) 195.

Economy, Elizabeth, "Environmental Governance in China: State Control to Crisis Management" (2014) 143 (2) *Daedalus* 184.

Epstein, Edward J., "Law and Legitimation in Post-Mao China", in Pitman B. Potter, ed, *Domestic Law Reforms in Post-Mao China* (New York: M.E. Sharpe, 1994) 24.

Feeley, M. & J. Simon, "Actuarial Justice: The Emerging New Criminal Law", in David Nelken, ed, *The Futures of Criminology* (London: Sage, 1994) 353–381.

Feng, Xiaotian & Xiao, Yuan, "Popular Culture and Values of the Chinese Youth, Thirty Years after the Economic Reform", in Kam-yee Law & Yushuo Zheng, eds, *Changed and Unchanged: Thirty Years of Reform in China* (Hong Kong: City University of Hong Kong Press, 2009) 281.

Fishkin, James S. et al., "Deliberative Democracy in an Unlikely Place: Deliberative Polling in China" (2010) 40 (02) *British Journal of Political Science* 447.

Garland, David, "The Rise of Risk", in Richard V. Ericson & Aaron Doyle, eds, *Risk and Morality* (Toronto, ON: University of Toronto Press, 2003) 48–86.

Haggerty, Kevin D., "From Risk to Precaution, The Rationalities of Personal Crime Prevention", in Richard V. Ericson & Aaron Doyle, eds, *Risk and Morality* (Toronto, ON: University of Toronto Press, 2003) 193.

Hallsworth, Simon, "Rethinking the Punitive Turn Economies of Excess and the Criminology of the Other" (2000) 2(2) *Punishment and Society* 145–160.

Hamann, Trent H., "Neoliberalism, Governmentality, and Ethics" (2009) 6 *Foucault Studies* 38.

Hao, Yanbing, "Values and Role of Criminal Law in the Risk Society" (2009) 07 *Chinese Criminal Justice* 15–23.

Harcourt, Bernard E., "The Collapse of the Harm Principle" (1999) 90 *Journal of Criminal Law & Criminology* 109.

———. "The Shaping of Chance: Actuarial Models and Criminal Profiling at the Turn of the Twenty-First Century" (2003) 70 *University of Chicago Law Review* 105–128.

———. *Against Prediction: Profiling, Policing, and Punishing in an Actuarial Age* (Chicago, IL: University of Chicago Press, 2006).

———. "Neoliberal Penalty: A Brief Genealogy" (2010) 14 (1) *Theoretical Criminology* 75.

He, Baogang & Mark E. Warren, "Authoritarian Deliberation: The Deliberate Turn in Chinese Political Development" (2011) 9 (2) *Perspectives on Politics* 275.

He, Lei, "Prison Population and Chinese Criminal Law Reforms" (2013) 8 *Chinese Criminal Law Science* 104–108.

Herweg, Nicole, "Straightening the Three Streams: Theorizing Extensions of the Multiple Streams Framework" (2015) 54 (3) *European Journal of Political Research* 436.

Herweg, Nicole, Christian Huß & Reimut Zohlnhofer, "Straightening the Three Streams: Theorizing Extensions of the Multiple Streams Framework" (2015) 54 (3) *European Journal of Political Research* 435–449.

Huang, Philip C., "Introduction to 'Constitutionalism, Reform, and the Nature of the Chinese State: Dialogues among Western and Chinese Scholars, III'" (2010) 36 (1) *Modern China* 10.

Huang, Xiaoxi, "Cooperation on the Fights against Drug Safety", *China Police Daily* (12 December 2009) 01.

Indermaur, David, "A Matter of Judgment: The Effect of Information and Deliberation on Public Attitudes to Punishment" (2012) 14 *Punishment & Society* 149.

Jia, Ling & Qimei Bi, "On Criminalizing Drunk Driving" (2010) 09 *Law Science Magazine* 86–89.

Jiang, Mengya & Shimei Gai, "Analysis on the Chinese Judicial Interpretation" (2004) 4 *Journal of Nanjing Party Institute of CCP* 45–50.

Jiang, Yihua, "The Pursuit of Modernity: Reconstruction of Thoughts in Contemporary China", in Qing Liu & Xiaochun Guan, eds, *Liberalism and Thoughts on the Chinese Modernity: Essays in the Conference of "Transforms of the Chinese Modern Thoughts"* (Hong Kong: The Chinese University Press, 2003) 120.

Jin, Zegang & Yi Yan, "Why Identical Cases Have Different Verdicts: Reflections on the Water Pollution Case of Yancheng and the Chemical Major Pollution Case of Yixin in Corporation" (2011) 2 *Journal of Shanghai Jiaotong University* 31–32.

Jones, Trevor & Tim Newburn, "Comparative Criminal Justice Policy-Making in the United States and The United Kingdom: The Case of Private Prisons" (2005) 45 *British Journal of Criminology* 58–80.

Kang, Liu, "Searching for a New Cultural Identity: China's Soft Power and Media Culture Today" (2012) 21 (78) *Journal of Contemporary China* 921.

Kemshall, Hazel & Mike Maguire, "Public Protection, Partnership and Risk Penalty: The Multi-Agency Risk Management of Sexual and Violent Offenders" (2001) 3 *Punishment & Society* 237–264.

Kingdon, John W., *Agendas, Alternatives and Public Policies, Update Edition, with an Epilogue on Health Care*, 2nd ed. (New York: Pearson, 2010) 162.

Kornreich, Yoel, Ilan Vertinsky & Pitman Potter, "Consultation and Deliberation in China: The Making of China's Health-Care Reform" (2012) 68 *The China Journal* 201.

Kugler, Matthew B. et al., "Differences in Punitiveness across Three Cultures: A Test of American Exceptionalism in Justice Attitudes" (2013) 103 (4) *Journal of Criminal Law & Criminology* 1071–1114.

Lagerkvist, Johan, "The Rise of Online Public Opinion in the People's Republic of China" (2005) 3 *China: An International Journal* 123.

Lam, Wai Fung & Kwan Nok Chan, "How Authoritarianism Intensifies Punctuated Equilibrium: The Dynamics of Policy Attention in Hong Kong" (2014) 28 (4) *Governance* 549–570.

Lampton, David M., "How China is Ruled: Why it is Getting Harder for Beijing to Govern", in Gideon Rose, ed, *Tiananmen and After* (Foreign Affairs, 2014) 119.

Lao, Dongyan, "Public Policy and Criminal Law in a Risk Society" (2007) 3 *Social Sciences in China* 126–127.

———. "Risk Society Theory and Shifting Criminal Law Theory" (2014) 1 *Peking University Law Review* 70–102.

Lee, Ching Kwan, "State & Social Protest" (2014) 143 (2) *Daedalus*128.

Lepp, Alan W., "Note, The Death Penalty in Late Imperial, Modern, and Post-Tiananmen China" (1990) 11 *Michigan Journal of International Law* 987–1038.

Lewis-Beck, Michael S., Wenfang Tang & Nicholas F. Martini, "A Chinese Popularity Function: Sources of Government Support" (2013) 67 (1) *Political Research Quarterly* 16.

Li, Hong, "Reflections on Criminal Law in the Risk Society" (2001) 3 *People's Procuratorial Semimonthly* 16–20.

Li, Liying, "The Death Penalty for Economic Crimes in Reformed China", in Xiaobing Li & Qiang Fang, eds, *Modern Chinese Legal Reform: New Perspectives* (Lexington, KY: University Press of Kentucky, 2013) 171–188.

Li, Ziping, "Legitimacy of Judicial Interpretation of Chinese Criminal Law" (2009) 5 *Legal Forum* 74–79.

Liebman, Benjamin L., "Watch Dog or Demagogue? The Media in the Chinese Legal System" (2005) 105 (1) *Columbia Law Review* 154.

———. "China's Courts: Restrained Reforms" (2007) 21 *Colum J Asian Law* 86.

———. "Assessing China's Legal Reforms" (2009) 23 *Colum J Asian Law* 27.

———. "A Return to Populist Legality? Historical Legacies and Legal Reform", in Elizabeth Perry & Sebastian Heilmann, eds, *Mao's Invisible Hand* (Cambridge: Harvard University Asia Center Press, 2011) 166.

———. "Legal Reform: China's Law-Stability Paradox" (2014) 143 (2) *The Journal of the American Academy of Arts & Sciences* 98.

———. "Leniency in Chinese Criminal Law? Everyday Justice in Henan" (2015) 33 (1) *Berkeley Journal of International Law* 153–222.

Liu, Mingxiang, "The Risk of Criminal Law of Risk Control and Its Regulation" (2011) 4 *Studies in Law and Business* 16–19.

Liu, Sida & Terence C. Halliday, "Political Liberalism and Political Embedded ness: Understanding Politics in the Work of Chinese Criminal Defense Lawyers" (2011) 45 (4) *Law & Society Review* 832.

Liu, Songshan, "Reflections on the Chinese Legislative Plan" (2014) 12 *Political Science and Law* 86–96.

Liu, Wei, "Trend of the Amendment of Criminal Law and Its Principles" (2011) 5 *Political Science and Law* 95–101.

Long, Min, "Balances of Social Order and Freedom: Conflicts of Values of Criminal Law in the Risk Society" (2010) 9 *Journal of Gansu Institute of Political Science and Law* 145–149.

Lu, Jianping, "On Strengthening Criminal Law Protection for the People's Livelihood" (2010) 12 *Law Science Magazine* 10–13.

Lubman, B. Stanley, "Introduction: The Future of Chinese Law" (1995) 1 *The China Quarterly* 1.

Ma, Kechang, "Position of Criminal Policy of Combining Justice with Mercy" (2007) 4 *China Legal Science* 117–122.

Mackenzie, Geraldine, "Sentencing and Public Confidence: Results from a National Australian Survey on Public Opinions towards Sentencing" (2012) 45 *Australian and New Zealand Journal of Criminology* 57.

Malley, P., "Risk and Responsibility", in Andrew Barry et al., *Foucault and Political Reason: Liberalism, Neo-Liberalism, and Rationalities of Government* (Chicago, IL: University of Chicago Press, 1996) 203.

———. "Governing Risk", in A Sarat, ed, *The Blackwell Companion to Law and Society* (Oxford: Blackwell Publishing, 2005) 292–308.

———. "Risk and Restorative Justice: Governing Through the Democratic Minimization of Harms", in Ivo Aertson, TomDaems & Luc Robert, *The Institutionalization of Restorative Justice* (Portland, OR: Willan Publishing, 2006).

———. "Reinventing Prevention: Why Did 'Crime Prevention' Develop So Late?" (2007) 47 (3) *British Journal of Criminology* 375.

———. "Neoliberalism and Risk in Criminology", in T. Anthony & C. Cunneen, eds, *The Critical Criminology Companion* (New South Wales: Federation Press, 2008).

———. "Governmentality and Risk", in J. Zinn, ed, *Social Theories of Risk and Uncertainties* (Oxford: Oxford University Press, 2008) 52–75.

McCarthy, Michael T. "USA Patriot Act" (2002) 39 *Harvard Journal on Legislation* 435.

Mclendon, Michael, "Setting the Governmental Agenda for State Decentralization of Higher Education" (2003) 74 (5) *Journal of Higher Education* 479–515.

Melossi, Dario, "The Cultural Embeddedness of Social Control: Reflections on the Comparison of Italian and North-American Cultures Concerning Punishment", in Tim Newburn & Richard Sparks, eds, *Criminal Justice and Political Cultures* (Cullompton: Willan, 2001) 407.

Minzner, Carl, "China's Turn against Law" (2011) 59 *American Journal of Comparative Law* 935.

Mo, Liangyuan, "Use of Law in Hot Discussed Cases: Based on 7 Cases of Drunk Driving" (2012) 8 *Legal Science Monthly* 133–134.

Monahan, John, "A Jurisprudence of Risk Assessment: Forecasting Harm among Prisoners, Predators and Patients" (2006) 92 (3) *Virginia Law Review* 391–435.

Munro, R, "Judicial Psychiatry in China and Its Political Abuses" (2000) 14 (1) *Columbia Journal of Asian Law* 1–128.

Nan, Lianwei, "Critical Analysis and Reflections on the Risk Society Theory" (2012) 4 *Chinese Journal of Law* 138–153.

Nathan, Andrew J., "China's Changing of the Guard, Authoritarian Resilience" (2003) 14 (1) *Journal of Democracy* 6.

Nelken, David, "Comparative Criminal Justice, Beyond Ethnocentricism and Relativism" (2009) 6 (4) *European Journal of Criminology* 299.

Nelson, Rebecca, "Water Pollution in China: How Can Business Influence for Good?" (2008) 7 *Asian Business & Management* 489.

Norrie, Alan, "Citizenship, Authoritarianism and the Changing Shape of the Criminal Law", in Bernadette McSherry, Alan Norrie & Simon Bronitt, eds, *The Re-direction of Criminalization and the Futures of Criminal Law* (Oxford: Bloomsbury Publishing, 2008) 15.

———. "The Problem of Mistaken Self-Defense: Citizenship, Chiasmus, and Legal Form" (2010) 13 (2) *New Criminal Law Review: An International and Interdisciplinary Journal* 357.

Otto, Jan Michiel & Yuwen Li, "Overview of Law-Making in China", in Jan Michael Otto et al., *Law-Making in People's Republic of China* (The Hague: Kluwer Law International, 2000).

Overton, Aaron B., "Federal Gang Laws: A New Tool against a Growing Threat or Overbroad and Dangerous" (2008) 9 *Rutgers Race & Law Review* 432.

Paler, Laura, "China's Legislation Law and the Making of a More Orderly and Representative Legislative System" (2005) 182 *The China Quarterly* 301–318.

Pang, Cuiming, "Self-censorship and the Rise of Cyber Collectives: An Anthropological Study of a Chinese Online Community" (2008) 3 *Intercultural Communication Studies* 60.

Perry, Elizabeth J., "Growing Pains: Challenges for a Rising China" (2014) 143 (2) *Daedalus* 5–13.

Potter, Pitman, "The Chinese Legal System: Continuing Commitment to the Primacy of State Power" (1999) 159 *The China Quarterly* 673.

Qian, Xiaoping, "Western Experience on Environmental Protection Legislation" (2014) 3 *Political Science and Law* 137.

Ramsay, Peter, "Preparation Offences, Security Interests, Political Freedom", in R.A. Duff et al., *The Structures of the Criminal Law* (Oxford: Oxford University Press, 2011) 227.

Remington, Frank J., "Criminal Law Revision Codification vs. Piecemeal Amendment" (1953) 33 Nebraska Law Review 402.

Remington, Frank J. & Victor G. Rosenblum, "The Criminal Law and the Legislative Process" (1960) 481 *Current Problems in Criminal Law* 496.

Roberson, Paul, "Hybrid Principles for the Distribution of Criminal Sanctions" (1987) 82 *Northwestern University Law Review* 19–24.

Roberts, J. V., "Public Opinion and Mandatory Sentencing: A Review of International Findings" (2003) 4 *Criminal Justice and Behavior* 502.

———. "New Media Influences on Public View of Sentencing" (1990) 14 *Law and Human Behavior* 453.

Rooij, Benjamin van, "The People vs. Pollution: Understanding Citizen Action Against Pollution in China" (2010) 19 (63) *Journal of Contemporary China* 55.

Rose, Nikolas, "Government and Control" (2000) 40 *British Journal of Criminology* 321–339.

Rosenzweig, Joshua, "Disappearing Justice: Public Opinion, Secret Arrest and Criminal Procedure Reform in China" (2013) 70 *The China Journal* 73–97.

Rowlands, Ian H., "The Development of Renewable Electricity Policy in the Province of Ontario: The Influence of Ideas and Timing" (2007) 24 (3) *Review of Policy Research* 185–207.

Scanlon, Zoe, "Punishing Proximity: Sentencing Preparatory Terrorism in Australia and the United Kingdom" (2014) 25 (3) *Current Issues in Criminal Justice* 763–783.

Simester, A. P. & Andrew Von Hirsch, "Remote Harms and Non-constitutive Crimes" (2009) 28 (1) *Criminal Justice Ethics* 90.

Simon, Jonathan, "Managing the Monstrous: Sex Offenders and the New Penology" (1998) 4 *Psychology, Public Policy and Law* 452.

Simon, M. V. & L. R. Alm, "Policy Windows and Two-Level Games: Explaining the Passage of Acid-Rain Legislation in the Clean Air Act of 1990" (1995) 13 (4) *Environment and Planning C: Government and Policy* 459–478.

Slobogin, Christopher, "A Jurisprudence of Dangerousness" (2003) 98 *Northwestern University Law Review* 1–62.

Spires, Anthony J., "Contingent Symbiosis and Civil Society in an Authoritarian State: Understanding the Survival of China's Grassroots NGOs" (2011) 117 (1) *American Journal of Sociology* 1–45.

Steiker, Carol S., "The Limits of the Preventive State" (1998) 3 *The Journal of Criminal Law and Criminology* 771–808.

———. "Capital Punishment and American Exceptionalism" (2002) 81 *Oregon Law Review* 97–130.

Stern, Rachel E., "The Political Logic of China's New Environment Courts" (2014) 72 *The China Journal* 58.

Stewart, Kathryn, David Silcock & Fred Wegman, "Reducing Drink Driving in Low- and Middle-Income Countries: Challenges and Opportunities" (2012) 13 (2) *Traffic Injury Prevention* 93–95.

Storch, Sabine & Georg Winkel, "Coupling Climate Change and Forest Policy: A Multiple Streams Analysis of Two German Case Studies" (2013) 36 *Forest Policy and Economics* 14–26.

Sun, Ivan Y. & Yuning Wu, "Chinese Policing in a Time of Transition, 1978–2008" (2010) 26 *Journal of Contemporary Criminal Justice* 25.

Swaaningen, Rene van, "Policy and Practice in Modern Britain: Influences, Outcomes and Civil Society", in Penny Green & Andrew Rutherford, eds, *Criminal Policy in Transition* (Oxford: Hart Publishing, 2000) 82.

Tai, Zixue, "Networked Resistance: Digital Populism, Online Activism, and Mass Dissent in China" (2015) 13 (2) *Popular Communication* 120–121.

Tang, Liyang, "China's Regional Inequity in Pharmacist's Drug Safety Practice" (2012) 11 *International Journal for Equity in Health* 38.

Tang, Yi-lang et al., "Alcohol and Alcohol-Related Harm in China: Policy Changes Needed" (2013) 91 Bulletin of the World Health Organization 270–276.

Tanner, Murray Scot, "Organizations and Politics in China's Post-Mao Law-Making System", in Pitman B. Potter, ed, *Domestic Law Reforms in Post-Mao China* (New York: M.E. Sharpe, 1994) 87.

———. "How a Bill Becomes a Law in China: Stages and Processes in Lawmaking" (1995) 141 *The China Quarterly* 39.

———. *The Politics of Lawmaking in Post-Mao China: Institutions, Processes, and Democratic Prospects* (Clarendon Press, 1998) 27.

Thornton, John L., "Long Time Coming, The Prospects for Democracy in China" (2008) 87 (1) *Foreign Affairs* 15.

Tian, Hongjie, "Position of Criminal Law in the Risk Society" (2011) 4 *Studies in Law and Business* 20.

Travis, R. & N. Zahariadis, "A Multiple Streams Model of US Foreign Aid Policy" (2002) 30 *Policy Studies Journal* 495–514.

Trevaskes, Susan, "Courts on the Campaign Path in China: Criminal Court Work in the 'Yanda 2001' Anti-Crime Campaign" (2002) 42 *Asian Survey* 674.

———. "The Private/Public Security Nexus in China" (2007) 34 *Social Justice* 38.

———. "Political Ideology, the Party, and Politicking: Justice System Reform in China" (2011) 37 *Modern China* 333.

Truex, Rory, "Consultative Authoritarianism and Its Limits" (2014) 6 *Comparative Political Studies* 7.

Tulich, Tamara, "A View Inside the Preventive State: Reflections on a Decade of Anti-terror Law" (2012) 21 (2) *Griffith Law Review* 2.

Twain, David & Donald Rebovich, "An Evaluation of the Impact of Criminal Law Revision" (1984) 12 (4) *Journal of Criminal Justice* 404.

Wang, Alex L., "The Search for Sustainable Legitimacy: Environmental Law and Bureaucracy in China" (2013) 37 *Harvard Environmental Law Review* 365.

Wang, Cheng-Tong Lir, Sida Liu & Terence C. Halliday, "Advocates, Experts and Suspects: Three Images of Lawyers in Chinese Media Reports" (2014) 21 (2) *International Journal of The Legal Profession* 195.

Wang, Mark et al., "Rural Industries and Water Pollution in China" (2008) 86 *Journal of Environment Management* 651.

Wang, Yaozhong, "Legal Analysis of Impaired Driving" (2012) 5 *Science of Law* 124–125.

Wang, Yuhua & Carl F. Minzner, "Rise of the Security State" (2015) 222 *The China Quarterly* 339.

Wang, Zhaoxin et al., "The Underestimated Drink Driving Situation and the Effects of Zero Tolerance Laws in China" (2015) 16 (5) *Traffic Injury Prevention* 430.

Wright, Teresa, "State-Society Relations in Reform-Era China: A Unique Case of Post-socialist State-Led Late Development?" (2008) 40 (3) *Comparative Politics* 369.

Xia, Yong, "Responses of Criminal Law to Risks to People's Livelihood" (2001) 04 *Studies in Law and Business* 6–10.

———. "Internet Activism & the Party-State in China" (2014) 143 (2) *Daedalus* 110.

Yang, Guobin, "Brokering Environment and Health in China: Issue Entrepreneurs of the Public Sphere Brokering News" (2010) 19 (63) *Journal of Contemporary China* 117.

Yang, Mingyu, "Surpassed Fragmented Authoritarianism? Reviews of *The Chinese Model of Consensus Decision Making: A Case Study of Healthcare Reform*" (2014) 7 *Journal of Shandong Academy of Justice* 4.

Yang, Zhenjie, "'Fragmented Authoritarianism' – The Facilitator Behind the Chinese Reform Miracle: A Case Study in Central China" (2013) 6 (1) *China Journal of Social Work* 12.

Yang, Zhiqiong, "Drunk Driving in the US" (2011) 2 *Law Science Magazine* 35–44.

Yin, Robert K., "A (Very) Brief Refresher on The Case Study Method", in Robert K. Yin, ed, *Applications of Case Study Research* (Los Angeles, CA: Sage Publications, 2008) 10.

Yuan, Chunxiang, "Analysis of Cases of Environmental Pollution from 2002–2011: Based on Data from Courts Nationwide" (2012) 12 *Legal Information* 19–23.

Yung, Corey Rayburn, "Sex Offender Exceptionalism and Preventive Detention" (2011) 101 (3) *The Journal of Criminal Law and Criminology* 971.

Zahariadis, Nikolaos, "Selling British Rail: An Idea Whose Time Has Come?" (1996) 29 (4) *Comparative Political Studies* 400–422.

Zedner, Lucia, "Dangers of Dystopias in Penal Theory" (2002) 22 *Oxford Journal of Legal Studies* 341–366.

———. "Against Prediction: Profiling, Policing, and Punishing in an Actuarial Age" (2008) 11 *New Criminal Law Review* 359–362.

———. "Fixing the Future: The Pre-emptive Turn in Criminal Justice", in Bronnit, S, McSherry, B & Norrie, A., eds, *Regulating Deviance: The Redirection of Criminalization and the Futures of Criminal Law* (Oxford: Hart Publishing, 2009) 53.

———. "Pre-crime and Pre-punishment: A Health Warning" (2010) 81 *Criminal Justice Matters* 25.

———. "Ambiguity and Mutiple Streams", in Paul A. Sabatier & Christopher M. Weible, eds, *Theories of the Policy Process*, 3rd ed. (Boulder, CO: Westview Press, 2014) 26.

Zhang, Jianwei, "Scope and Boundary of Judicial Interpretation of Chinese Criminal Procedure Law" (2013) 7 *Tsinghua Law Review* 24–35.

Zhang, Juan & Pal Nylri, "'Walled' Activism: Transnational Social Movements and the Politics of Chinese Cyber-Public Space" (2014) 36 (1) *International Development Planning Review* 111–132.

Zhao, Bingzhi & Bin Yuan, "Discussion on Main Issues of Drunk Driving" (2011) 3 *Criminal Law Review* 159.

Zhao, Jianmin & Rongwei Lai, "Principle of the CCP's Leadership in NPC" (2000) 2 *Mainland China Studies* 3–10.

Zhao, Linda Shuo, "Anomie Theory and Crime in a Transitional China (1978–)" (2008) 18 *International Criminal Justice Review* 151.

Zhang, Mingkai, "Crime with Risks" (1998) 1 *Tsinghua Law Review* 118–142.

———. "Criminal Law in the Cyber Age: On the Principle of Necessity" (2014) 9 *People's Procuratorate Semi-Monthly* 9–12.

Zhang, Taisu, "The Pragmatic Court: Reinterpreting the Supreme People's Court of China" (2011) 25 *Columbia Journal of Asian Law* 4.

Zhang, Weiwei, *The China Wave: Rise of a Civilizational State* (Hackensack: World Scientific, 2012) 108.

Zhang, Xiaohu, "Chinese Crime Rates in the Era of Transformation" (2002) 1 *Journal of Ningxia University* 62–66.

Zhang, Xu, "Social Development and Revisions of Criminal Law: Based on German Experience" (2003) 2 *Law and Social Development* 29–30.

Zhong, Lena Y. & Peter N. Grabosky, "The Pluralization of Policing and the Rise of Private Policing in China" (2009) 52 (5) *Criminal Law and Social Change* 448.

Zhou, Yuqiong & Patricia Moy, "Parsing Framing Processes: The Interplay between Online Public Opinion and Media Coverage" (2007) 57 *Journal of Communication* 79.

Zhu, Huaxin, Xuegang Shan & Jiangchun Hu, "2008 Report on Cyber Opinions", online: Cyberspace Administration of China < http://www.cac.gov.cn/2014-08/01/c_1111903561.htm> (2009).

Zhu, Huaxin, Xuegang Shan & Jiangchun Hu, "2009 Report on Cyber Opinions", online: Cyberspace Administration of China < http://www.cac.gov.cn/2014-08/01/c_1111902745.htm> 2010).

Zohlnhofer, Zeimut & Friedbert Rub, "Forum Section: Theoretically Refining the Multiple Streams Framework" (2015) 54 *European Journal of Political Research* 412.

Zou, Keyuan, "The Party and The Law", in Kjeld Erik Brodsgaard & Yongnian Zheng, eds, *The Chinese Communist Party in Reform* (London: Routledge, 2006) 78.

Website Resources

Chao, Loretta, "China Drunk-Driver Case Hits a Nerve: Driver in Fatal Crash Faces Mild Charges, Sparking Abuse-of-Power Allegations", online: The Wall Street Journal <http://www.wsj.com/articles/SB10001424052748704062604576105873345920788> (Last viewed 20 October 2015).

Duihua Human Rights Journal, "China's New Criminal Procedure Law: 'Disappearance Clauses' Revised", online: Duihua <http://www.duihuahrjournal.org/2012/03/chinas-new-criminal-procedure-law.html> (Last viewed 25 October 2015).

Feng, Jia, "The Case of Yancheng Water Pollution: Problems in Judicature", online: Brill <http://referenceworks.brillonline.com/entries/chinese-research-perspectives-online/the-case-of-yancheng-water-pollution-problems-in-judicature-C9789004183025_015> (Last viewed 16 October 2015).

Haitao, Cheng, "Rising Crime Rates in Parallel with High Sense of Security", online: Sina <http://news.sina.com.cn/c/2006-01-20/17218925755.shtml> (Last viewed 10 August 2014).

Horsley, Jamie P., "Public Participation in the People's Republic: Developing a More Participatory Governance Model in China", online: Yale Law School <http://www.law.yale.edu/documents/pdf/Intellectual_Life/CL-PP-PP_in_the__PRC_FINAL_91609.pdf> (Last viewed 5 August 2015).

Hualing, Fu, "The Varieties of Law in China", online: Human Rights in China <http://www.hrichina.org/en/crf/article/5422> (Last viewed 20 October 2015).

Huaxin, Zhu, "2008 Analysis Report of Public Opinions on the Internet", online: People <http://media.people.com.cn/GB/22114/52789/115416/6852601.html> (Last viewed 23 October 2015).

Jianqiang, Liu, "China's Environment Ministry an 'Utter Disappointment'", online: Chinadialogue <https://www.chinadialogue.net/article/show/single/en/57

88-China-s-environment-ministry-an-utter-disappointment-> (Last viewed 16 October 2015).

Jie, Feng, "Inside Story of the Judicial Interpretation of the Offense of Drunk Driving: The Era of Harsher Penalties?" *Southern Weekly* (4 July 2013) online: Southern Weekly <http://www.infzm.com/content/92067> (Last viewed 13 August 2015).

Langfitt, Frank, "For Complainers, A Stint in China's "Black Jails", online: NPR <http://www.npr.org/2012/11/01/163949720/for-complainers-a-stint-in-chinas-black-jails> (Last viewed 26 October 2015).

Loke-Khoon, Tan, "Counterfeiting in the Pharmaceutical Industry: A Look at the Bitter Pill in China", online: Baker & McKenzie <http://www.bakermckenzie.com/de-DE/RRChinaCounterfeitingPharmaceuticalBitterPill/> (Last viewed 9 December 2014).

Ma, Jie, "Controlling Pollution: Coming of Harsher Penalties?", *Southern Weekly* (4 July 2013) online: Southern Weekly <http://www.infzm.com/content/92067> (Last viewed 13 August 2015).

Maosheng, Li, "Lectures on General Principles of Criminal Law", online: NTU College of Law <http://www.law.ntu.edu.tw/main.php?mod=document&func=show:document&show:edu=main&site_id=0&show:folder=24> (Last viewed 20 August 2013).

Shishi, Li, "Explanation of the First Draft of the Eighth Amendment of Criminal Law", online: <http://www.npc.gov.cn/huiyi/lfzt/xfxza8/2011-05/10/content_1666058.htm> (Last viewed 22 December 2014).

Webb, Stephen A., "Risk", online: (2006) 4 (2) *Social Work and Society International Online Journal* <http://www.socwork.net/sws/article/view/166/555> (Last viewed 17 February 2014).

Weifang, He, "The Chinese Reliance of the Websites", online: <http://past.nbweekly.com/Print/Article/1884_0.shtml> (Last viewed 5 September 2014).

Xia, Hua, "China Focus: China Mulls New Amendment to Criminal Law", online: Xinhua <http://www.xinhuanet.com/english/2020-06/29/c_139173585.htm> (Last viewed 13 August 2020).

"China: Secret 'Black Jails' Hide Severe Rights Abuses", online: Human Rights Watch <https://www.hrw.org/news/2009/11/11/china-secret-black-jails-hide-severe-rights-abuses> (Last viewed 1 July 2015).

"CNNIC Released the 33rd Statistical Report on Internet Development in China", online: CNNIC <http://www1.cnnic.cn/AU/MediaC/rdxw/hotnews/201401/t20140117_43849.htm> (Last viewed 10 September 2014).

"Crime and Corruption Top Problems in Emerging and Developing Countries", online: Pew Research Center <https://www.pewresearch.org/global/2014/11/06/crime-and-corruption-top-problems-in-emerging-and-developing-countries/> (Last viewed 14 August 2020).

"Debates with Those Who Claim for Harsh Penalties on Li Qiming", online: Tianya <http://bbs.tianya.cn/post-free-2026026-1.shtml> (Last viewed 19 October 2015).

"Drunk Diver: Killing 9 in the Downtown of Nanjing", online: Sohu <http://news.sohu.com/s2009/nanjingcrash/> (Last viewed 8 December 8 2014).

"Is it Fair for Sun Weiming to Receive Life Imprisonment?", online: Tianya <http://bbs.tianya.cn/post-free-1682626-1.shtml> (Last viewed 19 October 2015).

"Livelihood Survey in Two Sessions 2011", online: China Economic Net<http://www.ce.cn/xwzx/gnsz/zg/201103/01/t20110301_22257907.shtml> (Last viewed 10 August 2020).

"New Judicial Interpretations of Offences of Environmental Pollution Promulgated", online: Xinhua <http://news.xinhuanet.com/legal/2013-06/18/c_124871016.htm> (Last viewed 24 August 2013).

"Police: Fight between Driver, Passenger Causes Chongqing Bus Tragedy", online: CGTN <https://news.cgtn.com/news/3d3d514f31676a4d30457a6333566d54/share_p.html> (Last viewed 12 August 2020).

"Speeding in Hangzhou: Causing One Death", online: Sina <http://news.sina.com.cn/z/fjzbc/> (Last viewed 8 December 2014).

"Survey Topics on China", online: Pew Research Center <http://www.pewglobal.org/topics/china/> (Last viewed 27 October 2015).

"The 33rd Statistical Report on Internet Development in China", online: CNNIC < http://www1.cnnic.cn/AU/MediaC/rdxw/hotnews/201401/t20140117_43849.htm> (Last viewed 10 September 2014).

"The 45th China Statistical Report on Internet Development in China", online: CNNIC < http://www.cnnic.cn/hlwfzyj/hlwxzbg/hlwtjbg/202004/t20200428_70974.htm> (Last viewed 10 August 2020).

"The Case Study as a Research Method: Uses and Users of Information -- LIS 391D.1 -- Spring 1997", online: The University of Texas at Austin School of Information <https://www.ischool.utexas.edu/~ssoy/usesusers/l391d1b.htm> (Last viewed 8 September 2015).

"The Chinese Celebrate Their Roaring Economy, as They Struggle with Its Costs", online: Pew Research Center < http://www.pewglobal.org> (Last viewed 28 October 2015).

"The No.000027 Bill to the Third Session of 11th National Committee of CPPCC", online: CPPCC <http://www.cppcc.gov.cn/2011/09/19/ARTI1316434127187911.shtml> (Last viewed 28 October 2015).

"Water of Yancheng City in Jiangsu Province Seriously Polluted: Leaving the Whole City Out of Water", online: Sina <http://news.sina.com.cn/z/jsyczlswr/index.shtml> (Last viewed 14 August 2015).

"Zhang Ming Bao Sentenced to Life Imprisonment, While Family of the Victim asked for Capital Punishment", online: Tianya <http://bbs.tianya.cn/post-free-1769848-1.shtml> (Last viewed 19 October 2015).

Others

Changyu, Li, "Partner of Grandall Law Firm Shi Jie: A Protector as Well as a Builder", *People's Daily* (22 November 2014) A03.

Chaoxin, Chu, "Fake Medications that Being Lost Control", *Southern Weekly* (25 November 2011).

Guangquan, Zhu, "Necessity of Creating the Offence of Impaired Driving in Our Criminal Law", *Social Sciences in China* (18 August 2009) A7.

Jones, Michael D et al., "A River Runs Through It: A Multiple Streams Meta-Review" (Paper delivered at the workshop on "Ambiguity and Public Policy", 14–15 November 2014), [unpublished].

"Zero-Tolerance on Drunk Driving: Comments of Officials from the Bureau of Road Traffic Safety of the Ministry of Public Security on the Amendment to Road Traffic Safety Law", *Guang Ming Daily* (28 April 2011).

Keqin, Wang, "Shanxi Vaccine Scandal", *China Economic Times* (17 March 2010).

Mingyan, Wei, "China Going to Establish Police Specialized on Food & Drug Control", *The Beijing News* (29 March 2014) A36.

Qiao, Xiaoyang, "To Enhance the Legislative Project", *The People's Congress of China* (25 December 2014).

Yin, Lu, "Reporting Public Opinion Polls in China" (Paper delivered at the 65th Annual Conference of World Association of Public Opinion Research of Hong Kong, 15 June 2012) [unpublished].

Zhiming, Gao, "History of the Concepts of Legally Protected Interests: Based on German Theories", (Master book, Taiwan National University Law Faculty 2001)" [unpublished].

Index

Andrew Ashworth 8, 25
authoritarian 1, 4, 8, 11, 39, 83, 94, 96–98, 109, 111, 119, 125–127, 129, 134, 138, 141–143

case study 1–2, 4, 10–13, 15, 24, 28, 46, 51–52, 59–60, 80, 144
CCP 1, 16, 47, 50, 53–54, 69, 72, 79–80, 86, 91–100, 102–104, 106, 108–109, 111, 119, 124–127, 135, 137–144
Chinese dream 94, 139
Chinese scholars 4–6, 36–37, 108
civil society 84
combining leniency with severity 94–95
consultative authoritarian 96
counterfeit medications 61
crime prevention 2–4, 6, 8, 10–11, 15, 24, 26–27, 36–39, 102, 119, 121–122, 129, 146
crime rate 35, 38, 68, 70–71, 73, 87, 124, 128, 137, 142
criminal policy 1, 5, 52, 94, 124, 128, 136, 141
cyber populism 104

David Garland 9
Dongyan Lao 5, 7, 36
drunk driving 1, 12, 25, 28–30, 33, 46–48, 54, 59–60, 65, 67, 81–82, 86–87, 96, 99, 101–103, 107, 111, 125, 146

eighth amendment 1–3, 6, 12, 15, 24–25, 27–32, 36, 46, 49–50, 60, 65, 67, 82–83, 87, 93, 96, 99, 101–103, 106, 134–135, 139–141, 144–146
environmental crime 32
exclusive 121, 134, 143–144

fake medicine scandal 61
fear of crime 59, 69–70, 79, 94, 103, 119, 127
focusing events 16, 49, 52–54, 59–60, 62, 64–65, 73, 85, 96, 103, 105, 107–108, 110–111, 125

garbage can model 13, 51–52
global context 12, 14

harmonious society 94, 139
high-profile cases 60, 109
human rights 35–36, 39, 72, 107, 122, 124
hypothesis 15, 121

inchoate crime 2, 25–26, 33, 36, 120, 134, 145
inclusive 1, 53, 63, 109, 121, 134, 137, 139, 143–144
internet 29, 35, 47, 59–61, 63–66, 70, 72–74, 79, 84, 103–108, 146

John Kingdon 15, 46, 50, 54
judicial review 136, 141–142
just desserts 24–25, 34, 84, 86

legal experts 106, 108
legislation 3, 14–16, 35–36, 38, 46–47, 50–51, 53–54, 59, 63, 72, 82–83, 86, 91–93, 95–101, 103, 106–109, 111, 124, 126, 128, 134, 137, 139–141, 144
legislative history 46, 125
legitimacy 1, 8, 59, 63, 66, 68, 72, 84, 94, 100, 103, 108, 111, 125–127, 129, 138–139, 141
Lucia Zedner 8, 25, 140

managerialism 127, 129, 143
manufacturing and selling fake medications 1, 12, 25, 30, 48, 111

mass line 72, 74, 102, 124
media 16, 35, 46–47, 51, 53, 60–66, 68–71, 73, 91, 95–97, 103–106, 108–109, 111, 125–126, 136–138, 142
Ministry of Health 48, 102
Ministry of Public Security 13, 16, 25, 47–48, 50, 70, 81, 85, 96, 99–102, 111, 126
Ministry of State Security 25, 39, 96
MSA 13–16, 46, 52–54, 79, 83–84, 134
Multiple Streams Approach 13, 46

neoliberal 10, 14, 37–38, 121–122, 124, 129, 143–144
netizen 47, 62–65, 69, 74
NGO 16, 79, 81–82, 84–85, 135
NPC 16, 47, 51, 54, 80–82, 91, 93–99, 102–103, 106, 109–110, 138, 140, 142

party-state 39, 59, 61, 63, 66, 73–74, 79, 91–92, 94, 99, 103, 105, 109, 111, 119, 125, 127, 129, 139, 143–144
penal populism 9, 16, 66, 72, 137–138
penal welfarism 123
police 7, 9, 25, 27, 39, 47–49, 60–61, 70–73, 87, 92, 99–104, 119, 125–129, 138–139, 142–143
policing 7, 9, 14, 24–26, 36, 47, 53, 61, 70, 72–73, 79, 94, 101–102, 104, 121, 123–125, 128–129, 138, 143
policy entrepreneurs 52, 54, 79–81, 83–85, 102, 135
policy stream 14, 16, 52, 54, 79–87, 134, 136
policy window 13, 52–53, 134–146
Political Consultative Conference 1, 54, 64, 81–82, 85, 96
political risk 27, 39, 108–109
political stream 13–15, 52–54, 80, 91–94, 96–111, 134, 136–139, 144
prevention 2–4, 6–11, 15, 24–27, 32, 34–39, 49, 61, 84, 86–87, 102, 119–122, 128–129, 135, 144, 146
preventive justice 2, 6–8, 11, 14, 24, 27, 120
preventive orders 8, 26–27, 122, 142
problem stream 16, 52–53, 59–68, 70–74, 79, 83, 134, 136–138
proposal 14–16, 46, 49–50, 52–54, 61, 79–85, 91, 96, 101, 106–108, 111, 134–138
public emotion 59
public opinion 1, 11, 15–16, 52–53, 63–64, 67–68, 71, 73, 80, 92, 96–97, 103–105, 108, 110, 137
public security 2–3, 5, 11, 13, 15–16, 25, 27–35, 39, 47–48, 50, 70, 72–73, 81, 85, 96, 98–104, 108, 111, 120, 122, 126–127, 135, 139–141, 146
punitive turn 14, 111, 141, 143

risk 1–11, 14–16, 24–27, 29–39, 59, 71–72, 82, 86, 92, 94, 97, 108–109, 111, 119–123, 128, 136, 138, 143, 146
risk society 4–8, 10, 24, 36–37, 119, 121–122
rule of law 7, 11, 37, 50, 92, 94–95, 97, 100, 102, 104, 106–111, 122, 124–125, 136

safety 1–3, 7, 15, 29–30, 34–37, 47–49, 59, 61–62, 66–67, 69–73, 79, 81, 84–85, 93, 102, 105, 138, 146
security 2–3, 5, 7, 11, 13, 15–16, 24–25, 27–39, 47–48, 50, 54, 59, 62, 66–70, 72–73, 79, 81, 84–85, 94, 96, 98–105, 108, 111, 119–122, 124–129, 135–136, 138–141, 146
sense of security 16, 59, 67–70, 72–73, 79, 104, 138
social stability 16, 94, 98, 100, 103, 138–140
strike hard 70, 94–95, 124
Supreme People's Court 16, 32, 34, 98–99, 101
Supreme People's Procuratorate 31, 48, 50, 98–99, 101
surveillance 24–26, 39, 70, 120, 122–123, 125, 128, 140, 143–144
survey 12, 59–60, 62, 64, 67–70, 72–73, 92, 96, 103–104, 124

terrorism 4, 6, 8–9, 25–27, 37, 53, 83, 120, 123, 128, 135, 145–146
three-stream framework 46
trust 16, 38–39, 54, 59, 62, 72–74, 108, 137–138, 143, 146
Two Sessions 1, 72, 81, 83, 96, 135

welfare state 38, 141
western criminal justice 3–4, 14, 111, 119, 121, 123, 128
western scholarship 4, 10, 16, 25

Xingliang Chen 6–7, 37